BSD UNIX
TOOLBOX

D0867845

BSD UNIX®
TOOLBOX

1000+ Commands for FreeBSD®, OpenBSD, and NetBSD® Power Users

Christopher Negus
François Caen

WILEY

Wiley Publishing, Inc.

BSD UNIX® Toolbox:
1000+ Commands for FreeBSD®, OpenBSD, and NetBSD® Power Users

Published by
Wiley Publishing, Inc.
10475 Crosspoint Boulevard
Indianapolis, IN 46256
www.wiley.com

Copyright © 2008 by Wiley Publishing, Inc., Indianapolis, Indiana
Published simultaneously in Canada
ISBN: 978-0-470-37603-4

Manufactured in the United States of America
10 9 8 7 6 5 4 3 2 1

Library of Congress Cataloging-in-Publication Data is available from the publisher.

As always, I dedicate my work on this book to my wife, Sheree.

— Christopher Negus

To my wife, Tonya, for supporting me in all my endeavors.

— François Caen

About the Authors

Christopher Negus is the author of the best-selling *Fedora* and *Red Hat Linux Bibles*, *Linux Toys, Linux Troubleshooting Bible,* and *Linux Bible 2008 Edition.* He is a member of the Madison Linux Users Group. Before becoming a full-time writer, Chris served for eight years on development teams for the UNIX operating system at AT&T, where UNIX was created and developed. He also worked with Novell on Linux development and Caldera Linux.

François Caen, through his company Turbosphere LLC, hosts and manages business application infrastructures, with 95 percent running on Linux systems. As an open source advocate, he has lectured on OSS network management and Internet services and served as president of the Tacoma Linux Users Group. François is a Red Hat Certified Engineer (RHCE). In his spare time, he enjoys managing enterprise Cisco networks.

About the Technical Editor

Thomas Blader first began dabbling in Linus/UNIX in 1993 with Yggdrasil Linux and BSD. Since 1997, he has worked for the same company as a Solaris/Linux administrator. He has recently become involved with network security. He also does UNIX-related consulting and software development as well as book writing and editing.

Credits

Acquisitions Editor
Jenny Watson

Development Editor
William Bridges

Technical Editor
Thomas Blader

Production Editor
Daniel Scribner

Copy Editor
Michael Koch

Editorial Manager
Mary Beth Wakefield

Production Manager
Tim Tate

**Vice President and
Executive Group Publisher**
Richard Swadley

Vice President and Executive Publisher
Joseph B. Wikert

Project Coordinator, Cover
Lynsey Osborn

Compositor
Laurie Stewart,
Happenstance Type-O-Rama

Proofreader
David Parise,
Word One

Indexer
Melanie Belkin

Contents at a Glance

Contents

Contents

Contents

Contents

Acknowledgments

I would like to acknowledge the FreeBSD, OpenBSD, and NetBSD development communities, who have continued the noble tradition begun by the Berkeley Software Distribution decades ago. Their efforts have led to some of the most secure and stable computer operating systems in or out of the free and open source software world.

Special thanks to François Caen for giving up most of his free time over the past year as we developed and wrote the books in our Toolbox series. Thomas Blader did his usual excellent job tech editing this book. At Wiley, I'd like to thank Jenny Watson for sticking with us through the development of the book. Special thanks to Bill Bridges, who kept us on track during a challenging development schedule.

— *Christopher Negus*

I would like to thank Chris Negus for giving me the opportunity to co-author this book with him. We had wanted to write together for the last couple of years, and this Toolbox series was the perfect fit for our collaboration.

I couldn't have worked on this book without the unrelenting support from my wife, Tonya. Thank you for emptying the dishwasher all those times even though we both know it's my job.

Thanks to Thomas Blader for his detailed tech editing. Having done some tech editing in the past, I know what a tough job it can be. Thanks to Sara Shlaer and Jenny Watson at Wiley for being the most patient cat-herders out there. Special thanks to Wayne Tucker and Jesse Keating for all the knowledge they've shared with me during and before this project.

— *François Caen*

Introduction

BSD UNIX Toolbox provides you with more than 1,000 specific command lines to help you become a BSD power user. Whether you are a systems administrator or desktop user, the book will show you commands to create file systems, troubleshoot networks, lock down security, and dig out almost anything you care to know about your BSD system.

This book's focus for your BSD command line journey is FreeBSD, one of the most popular BSD derivatives in the world. Tapping into the skills needed to run those systems can help you to work with your own BSD systems and to learn what you need as a BSD professional.

Who Should Read This Book

This book is for anyone who wants to access the power of a BSD system as a systems administrator or user. You may be a free and open source software (FOSS) enthusiast, a BSD professional, or possibly a computer professional who is increasingly finding the Windows systems in your data center supplanted by BSD and Linux boxes.

The bottom line is that you want to find quick and efficient ways of getting FreeBSD, NetBSD, and OpenBSD systems working at peak performance. Those systems may be a few desktop systems at work, a file and print server at your school, or a home web server that you're doing just for fun.

In the best case, you should already have some experience with BSD, Linux or other UNIX-like systems. However, if you are a computer professional with skills managing other types of operating systems, such as Windows, you should be able to easily adapt your knowledge to be able to use the specific commands we cover in the book.

What This Book Covers

This is not a beginner's BSD UNIX book. Before you jump in, it would be best if you have a basic working knowledge of what BSD and other UNIX systems are, how the shell works, and what processes, file systems, and network interfaces are. The book will then supplement that knowledge with information you need to do the following activities:

❏ **Get software** — FreeBSD offers both binary software packages and source packages in the ports database that can be used to download, build, and install software from source code. With tools such as pkg_info, pkg_add, and pkg_delete, you'll learn the best ways to find, download, install, and otherwise manage software from the command line.

❑ **Access applications** — Find what's available from the FreeBSD distribution, then select and install the ones you want using the sysinstall utility.

❑ **Use the shell** — Find neat techniques and tips for using the shell.

❑ **Play with multimedia** — Play and work with multimedia content from your computer. You can also modify audio and image files, and then convert the content of those files to different formats.

❑ **Work with files** — Use, manipulate, convert, and secure a wide range of file types in BSD systems.

❑ **Administer file systems** — Access, format, partition, and monitor your file storage hardware (hard disks, CD/DVD drives, floppy disks, USB flash drives, and so on). Then create, format, and check the file systems that exist on those hardware devices.

❑ **Back up and restore data** — Use simple commands to gather, archive, and compress your files into efficient backup archives. Then store those archives locally or on remote computers.

❑ **Work with processes** — List running processes in a variety of ways, such as by CPU use, processor use, or process ID. Then change running processes to have them run in the background or foreground. Send signals to processes to have them re-read configuration files, stop and resume processing, or stop completely (abort).

❑ **Manage the system** — Run commands to check system resources, such as memory usage, boot loaders, and kernel modules.

❑ **Monitor networks** — Bring wired, wireless, and dial-up network connections up and down. Check routing, DNS, and host information. Keep an eye on network traffic.

❑ **Get network resources** — Connect to BSD and Windows remote file systems using FTP, NFS, and Samba facilities. Use shell-based commands to browse the Web.

❑ **Do remote administration** — Access and administer other computers using remote login (ssh, telnet, and so on), and screen. Learn about remote administration interfaces, such as SWAT and CUPS.

❑ **Lock down security** — Set up firewalls and system logging to secure your BSD systems.

❑ **Get reference information** — Use the appendixes at the end of this book to get more information about the shell (such as metacharacters and shell variables) and personal configuration files.

Hopefully, if we have done it right, it will be easier to use this book than to Google for the command lines or GUI tools you need.

After you have mastered many of the features described in this book, you'll have gained the following advantages:

❑ **Hundreds of commands** — By compressing a lot of information into a small space, you will have access to hundreds of useful commands, in over 1,000 command lines, in a handy form to carry with you.

❑ **Critical BSD information** — This book lists connections to the most critical information on the Web for succeeding with BSD systems in general and FreeBSD in particular.

❑ **Transferable knowledge** — Most of the same commands and options you use in BSD systems will work exactly the same way on other UNIX-like systems. Different UNIX systems, on the other hand, offer different graphical administration tools. And even within a particular distribution, graphical tools change more often than commands do.

❑ **Quick problem solving** — By the time others have started up a desktop and launched a graphical administration tool, you will have already run a half dozen commands and solved the problem.

❑ **Enduring value** — Many of the commands described in this book were used in early UNIX systems. So you are gaining tools that reflect the experience of thousands of computer experts for more than 30 years.

Because the full documentation for commands used in BSD systems consists of thousands of man pages, info text, and help messages, you will surely want to reach beyond the pages of this book from time to time. Luckily, FreeBSD and other UNIX systems include helpful information installed on the system itself. Chapter 1 contains descriptions of how to access that information that is probably already installed, or can be easily installed, on your BSD system.

How This Book Is Structured

This book is neither a pure reference book (with alphabetically listed components) nor a guide (with step-by-step procedures for doing tasks). Instead, the book is organized by topics and aimed at including as many useful commands and options as we could fit in.

Chapter 1 starts by giving you a basic understanding of what BSD is and how it relates to the operating systems that are derived from BSD, such as FreeBSD, NetBSD, and OpenBSD. Then it describes some of the vast resources available to support your experience with this book (such as man pages, info material, and help text). Chapter 2 provides a quick overview of installation and then describes useful commands such as pkg_info and pkg_add for getting and managing your BSD software.

Chapters 3, 4, 5, and 6 describe commands that a regular user may find useful on BSD systems. Chapter 3 describes tools for using the shell, Chapter 4 covers commands for working with files, and Chapter 5 describes how to manipulate text. Chapter 6 tells how to work with music and image files.

Starting with Chapter 7, we get into topics relating to system administration. Creating and checking file systems is covered in Chapter 7, while commands for doing data backups are described in Chapter 8. Chapter 9 describes how to manipulate running processes, and Chapter 10 describes administrative tools for managing basic components, such as hardware modules, CPU use, and memory use.

Chapter 11 begins the chapters devoted to managing network resources by describing how to set up and work with wired, wireless, and dial-up network interfaces. Chapter 12 covers text-based commands for web browsing, file transfer, file sharing, chats, and e-mail. Tools for doing remote system administration are included in Chapter 13.

Chapter 14 covers how to lock down security using features such as firewalls and logging. After that there are three appendices that provide reference information for text editing, shell features (metacharacters and variables), and personal configuration files.

What You Need to Use This Book

Although we hope you enjoy the beauty of our prose, this is not meant to be a book you curl up with in front of a nice fire with a glass of wine. We expect you will be sitting in front of a computer screen trying to connect to a network, fix a file system, or add a user. The wine is optional.

In other words, the book is meant to be a companion as you work on a FreeBSD, NetBSD, or OpenBSD operating system. All those systems are available for the x86 and x86_64 computer architectures. Some specific versions of those systems are also available for IBM PowerPC, SPARC, Intel ia64 (Itanium), and Alpha. If you don't already have one of those systems installed, refer to Chapter 2 for information on getting and installing those systems.

All the commands in this book have been tested against FreeBSD on x86 or x86_64 architecture. However, because many of these commands have been around for a long time (some dating back over 30 years to the original UNIX days), most will work exactly as described here on NetBSD, OpenBSD, and other derivative systems, regardless of CPU architecture.

Many of the commands described in this book will work on other UNIX and Linux systems as well. Because this book focuses on FreeBSD and other BSD-based distributions, descriptions will differ from other UNIX-like systems most prominently in the areas of packaging, installation, and GUI administration tools.

Conventions

To help you get the most from the text and keep track of what's happening, we've used a number of conventions throughout the book. In particular, we have created styles for showing commands that allow us to fit as many command lines as possible in the book.

With command examples, computer output (shell prompts and messages) is shown in regular monospace font, computer input (the stuff you type) is shown in bold monospace font, and a short description (if included) appears in italics. Here is an example:

```
$ ls *jpg          List all JPEG files in the current directory
hat.jpg
dog.jpg
...
```

To save space, output is sometimes truncated (or skipped altogether). Three dots (...) are sometimes used to indicate that additional output was cut. If a command is particularly long, backslashes will appear at the end of each line to indicate that input is continuing to the next line. Here is an example:

```
# oggenc NewSong.wav -o NewSong.ogg \
    -a Bernstein -G Classical          \
    -d 06/15/1972 -t "Simple Song"  \
    -l "Bernsteins Mass"               \
    -c info="From Kennedy Center"
```

In the example just shown, you can type the backslashes to have all that information included in the single command. Or, you can simply put all the information on a single line (excluding the backslashes). Note that command prompts are shown in one of two ways:

```
$               Indicates a regular user prompt
#               Indicates the root prompt
```

As noted, when a dollar sign prompt ($) appears, any user can run the command. With a pound sign prompt (#), you probably need to be the root user for the command to work.

Notes and warnings appear as follows:

NOTE *Warnings and notes are offset and placed in italic like this.*

As for styles in the text:

- ❑ We *highlight* new terms and important words with italics when we introduce them.
- ❑ We show keyboard strokes like this: Ctrl+A. If the command requires you to type an uppercase letter, the combination will show this: Ctrl+Shift+A.
- ❑ We show file names, URLs, and code within the text like so: `persistence.properties`.

One final technique we use is to highlight text that describes what an upcoming command is meant to do. For example, we may say something like, "use the following command to **display the contents of a file**." We've styled descriptions in this way to provide quick visual cues to the readers, so you can easily scan the page for that command you just knew had to be there.

1

Starting with BSD Systems

Whether you use BSD systems every day or just tweak one once in a while, a book that presents efficient ways to use, check, fix, secure, and enhance your system can be an invaluable resource.

BSD UNIX Toolbox is that resource.

BSD UNIX Toolbox is aimed primarily at BSD power users and systems administrators. To give you what you need, we tell you how to quickly locate and get software, monitor the health and security of your systems, and access network resources. In short, we cut to the most efficient ways of using BSD systems.

IN THIS CHAPTER

Find BSD resources

Learn quick and powerful commands

Have a handy reference to many useful utilities

Work as BSD gurus do

Our goal with *BSD UNIX Toolbox* is to pack a lot of useful information for using BSD systems into a small package that you can carry around with you. To that end, we describe:

❑ **Commands** — Tons of command line examples to use BSD systems in helpful and clever ways

❑ **GUI Tools** — Quick pointers to graphical administration tools to configure your system

❑ **Software packages** — Short procedures to find and download tons of applications

❑ **Online resources** — Listings of the best locations to find BSD forums, mailing lists, IRC channels, and other online resources

❑ **Local documentation** — Tools for gathering more information from man pages, doc directories, help commands, and other resources on your BSD system

Because you're not a beginner with BSD systems, you won't see a lot of screenshots of windows, icons, and menus. What you will see, however, is the quickest path to getting the information you need to use your BSD system to its fullest extent.

If this sounds useful to you, please read on.

About FreeBSD, NetBSD, and OpenBSD

In the early 1970s, AT&T released the UNIX source code to several colleges and universities, allowing them to begin changing, adapting, and improving that code as they pleased. That decision has led to the development of every major free and open source software operating system today, not least of which are the systems based on the Berkeley Software Distribution (BSD).

The twisty history of BSD is easy to Google for, if you care to learn the details. For our purposes, let's just say that:

❑ BSD began as a set of software add-ons to AT&T's Sixth Edition UNIX.

❑ Over the years, BSD developers split off on their own development path, rewriting software with the intention of replacing all AT&T copyrighted code.

❑ In the early 1990s, AT&T's UNIX System Laboratories sued BSD developers (Berkeley Software Design, Inc.) for copyright infringement.

❑ Although the lawsuit was eventually settled (with only a few files needing to be changed from the BSD code), the Linux operating system was able to become a leader of open source software development while questions surrounding free BSD were being threshed out.

❑ In 1995, the final version of BSD from Berkeley was released under the name 4.4BSD-Lite, release 2. Today's BSD operating systems, including FreeBSD, NetBSD, and OpenBSD, are all based to some extent on 4.4BSD-Lite.

Operating systems derived from BSD have a well-earned reputation for stability and security. BSD was developed at a time when computing resources (disk space, network bandwidth, and memory) were meager by today's standards. So BSD systems were operated by efficient commands, instead of the bloated applications and dumbed-down graphical interfaces often seen today.

Because of the nature of BSD systems, people running those systems required a high level of expertise. Even when simplified graphical user interfaces based on the X Window System began to appear, to effectively operate a BSD system you still needed to know about such things as kernels, device drivers, modules, and daemons. Because security came before ease-of-use, a BSD expert needed to know how to deal with the fact that many features they may have wanted were not installed, or were turned off, by default.

If you are someone who has used Linux before, transitioning to a BSD system shouldn't be too hard. However, BSD systems tend to behave a bit more like older UNIX systems than they do like Linux. Many interfaces are text-based, offering lots of power if you know what you are doing. Despite that fact, however, all the major desktop components that, for example, you get with the GNOME desktop environment are available with BSD systems. So you don't have to live on the command line.

Here is a list of popular BSD-based operating systems that are still being developed today:

❑ **FreeBSD** (www.freebsd.org) is the most popular of the BSD operating system distributions. It can be operated as a server, workstation, or desktop system, but has also been used in network appliances and special-purpose embedded systems. It has a reputation for maximum performance.

❑ **NetBSD** (www.netbsd.org) has a reputation for being very portable, with versions of NetBSD running as an embedded system on a variety of hardware. NetBSD can run on anything from 32-bit and 64-bit PCs to personal digital assistants (PDAs) to VAX minicomputers.

❑ **OpenBSD** (www.netbsd.org) is a popular system for network servers, although it can operate as a workstation or network appliance as well. The goal of OpenBSD is to attain maximum security. Unlike FreeBSD and NetBSD, which are covered under the BSD license, OpenBSD is covered primarily under the more-permissive Internet Systems Consortium (ISC) license.

❑ **DragonFly BSD** (www.dragonflybsd.org) was originally based on FreeBSD. Its goal was to develop technologies different from FreeBSD in such areas as symmetric multiprocessing and concurrency. So the focus has been on expanding features in the kernel.

Other free (as in no cost, as well as freedom to do what you like with the code) operating systems based on BSD include Darwin (on which Mac OS X is based) and desktop-oriented systems such as PC-BSD and DesktopBSD. FreeSBIE is a live CD BSD system. Proprietary operating systems that have been derived from BSD include:

❑ **Mac OS X** (www.apple.com/macosx) is produced by Apple, Inc. and focuses on adding an easy-to-use graphical interface to sell with its line of computers. There is also a Mac OS X Server product available. Although Mac OS X was originally based on Darwin, it is considered a closed-source operating system with open source components.

❑ **SunOS** (www.sun.com) was developed by Sun Microsystems and was very popular as a professional workstation system. Sun stopped development of SunOS in favor of Solaris. However, because Solaris represented a merging of SunOS and UNIX System V, many BSD features made their way into Solaris.

There is a larger list of BSD distributions that you can find at the DistroWatch site (`http://distrowatch.com/search.php?category=BSD`). Besides offering descriptions of those BSD distributions, you can also find links to where you can purchase or download the software.

Finding BSD Resources

Although there is still a BSD web site (`www.bsd.org`), it largely acts as a pointer to BSD resources related to particular BSD distributions. The following sections contain useful links related to the FreeBSD, NetBSD, and OpenBSD sites.

FreeBSD Resources

Here are links to useful resources from the FreeBSD site (`www.freebsd.org`):

❏ **Support for FreeBSD** (`freebsd.org/support.html`) — You can find connections to both community and commercial support for FreeBSD.

❏ **Getting FreeBSD software** (`freebsd.org/where.html`) — Links to information for downloading or purchasing FreeBSD installation CDs or DVDs are listed on this site. This includes links to software for different architectures (i386, amd64, powerpc, and so on).

❏ **FreeBSD features list** (`freebsd.org/about.html`) — Describes the key features of FreeBSD.

❏ **News on FreeBSD** (`freebsd.org/news/`) — This is a gathering point for news about FreeBSD. There are links to news flashes, press releases, articles, and development status. You can also find links here to development sites and forums related to FreeBSD and BSD in general.

❏ **FreeBSD projects** (`freebsd.org/projects/`) — Provides information about FreeBSD development projects. Besides basic development projects for FreeBSD, you can also find links to special projects (such as Google Summer of Code) and FreeBSD initiatives associated with established open source projects (such as Java, GNOME, KDE, and OpenOffice.org).

NetBSD Resources

Here are links to useful resources from the NetBSD site (`www.netbsd.org`):

❏ **NetBSD support** (`netbsd.org/support`) — Provides information about community and professional support, supported hardware, bug submissions, and security.

❏ **Getting NetBSD software** (`netbsd.org/releases`) — Links to information for downloading NetBSD CDs or DVDs are listed on this site. There are bittorrent, FTP, and HTTP methods for downloading software.

❏ **About NetBSD** (`netbsd.org/about`) — Describes the key features of NetBSD.

❑ **NetBSD news** (`netbsd.org/changes/`) — Contains the latest news about NetBSD. This includes ongoing lists of development changes to NetBSD.

❑ **Software packages** (`netbsd.org/docs/software/packages.html`) — Find information about the NetBSD Packages Colledction (pkgsrc). This includes information on available packages, documentation, and supported platforms.

OpenBSD Resources

Here are links to useful resources from the OpenBSD site (`www.openbsd.org`):

❑ **OpenBSD support** (`openbsd.org/support.html`) — Provides information on commercial support and consulting available for OpenBSD around the world.

❑ **Getting OpenBSD software** (`openbsd.org/ftp.html`) — Links to information for downloading OpenBSD CDs or DVDs are listed on this site. Software mirrors are available via FTP, HTTP, ASF, and RSYNC.

❑ **Goals of OpenBSD project** (`openbsd.org/goals.html`) — Describes the goals of the OpenBSD project.

❑ **OpenBSD News** (`openbsd.org/press.html/`) — Contains links to press coverage of OpenBSD.

❑ **Frequently asked questions** (`cvs.openbsd.org/faq`) — Contains the Frequently Asked Questions (FAQ) list for OpenBSD.

BSD Community Connections

If you want to communicate with the FreeBSD, OpenBSD, or NetBSD communities, Table 1-1 shows a quick list of links to the most useful communications venues related to those projects.

Table 1-1: Online Resources to Connect to BSD Communities

BSD Activities	Internet Sites

Mailing lists	`lists.freebsd.org/mailman/listinfo`
	`www.openbsd.org/mail.html`
	`www.netbsd.org/mailinglists`

IRC chats	`www.netbsd.org/community/#chat` `www.freebsd.org/community/irc.html`

Forums	`www.bsdforums.org`
	`www.bsdnexus.com`
	`www.freebsdwiki.net`

Blogs	`planet.freebsdish.org`

Continued

5

Table 1-1: Online Resources to Connect to BSD Communities (*continued*)

BSD Activities	Internet Sites
Community Wikis	wiki.netbsd.se
Usenet Newsgroups	News:comp.unix.bsd.freebsd.misc News:comp.unix.bsd.freebsd.announce News:comp.unix.bsd.netbsd.announce News:comp.unix.bsd.netbsd.misc News:comp.unix.bsd.misc
Documentation	www.freebsd.org/docs.html www.openbsd.org/cgi-bin/man.cgi netbsd.org/docs
News	news.vejas.lt

Focusing on BSD Commands

These days, many important tasks in BSD can be done from both graphical interfaces and from commands. However, the command line has always been, and still remains, the interface of choice for BSD power users.

Graphical user interfaces (GUIs) are meant to be intuitive. With some computer experience, you can probably figure out, for example, how to add a user, change the time and date, and configure a sound card from a GUI. For these cases, we'll mention which graphical tool you could use for the job. For the following cases, however, you will probably need to rely on the command line:

❏ **Almost any time something goes wrong** — Ask a question at an online forum to solve some BSD problem you are having and the help you get will almost always come in the form of commands to run. Also, command line tools typically offer much more feedback if there is a problem configuring a device or accessing files and directories.

❏ **Remote systems administration** — If you are administering a remote server, you may not have graphical tools available. Although remote GUI access (using X applications or VNC) and web-based administration tools may be available, they usually run more slowly than what you can do from the command line.

❏ **Features not supported by GUI** — GUI administration tools tend to present the most basic ways of performing a task. More complex operations often require options that are only available from the command line.

❑ **GUI is broken or not installed** — If no graphical interface is available, or if the installed GUI isn't working properly, you may be forced to work from the command line. Broken GUIs can happen for lots of reasons, such as when you use a third-party, binary-only driver from NVIDIA or ATI and a kernel upgrade makes the driver incompatible. Also, many BSD servers don't even have GUIs installed.

The bottom line is that to unlock the full power of your BSD system, you must be able to use shell commands. Thousands of commands are available for BSD to monitor and manage every aspect of your BSD system.

But whether you are a BSD guru or novice, one challenge looms large. How do you remember the most critical commands and options you need, when a command shell might only show you this:

$

BSD UNIX Toolbox is not just another command reference or rehash of man pages. Instead, this book presents commands in BSD systems by the way you use them. In other words, instead of listing commands alphabetically, we group together commands for working with file systems, connecting to networks, and managing processes in their own sections, so you can access commands by what you want to do, not only by how they're named.

Likewise, we won't just give you a listing of every option available for every command. Instead, we'll show you working examples of the most important and useful options to use with each command. From there, we'll tell you quick ways to find more options, if you need them, from man pages, the info facility, and help options.

Finding Commands

All the commands described in this book may not be installed when you go to run them. You might type a command and see a message similar to:

```
mycommand: command not found
```

This might happen for the following reasons:

❑ You mistyped the command name.

❑ The command is not in your PATH.

❑ You may need to be the root user for the command to be in your PATH.

❑ The command is not installed on your computer.

Table 1-2 shows some commands you can run to look for a command you want to use.

Table 1-2: Finding Commands

Command and Sample Output	Description
$ **type mount** mount is /sbin/mount	Show the first mount command in PATH.
$ **whereis mount** mount: /sbin/mount /usr/share/man/man8/mount.8.gz	Show binary and man page for mount.
$ **locate xrdb.1.gz** /usr/local/man/man1/xrdb.1.gz	Find xrdb.1.gz anywhere in file system.
$ **which umount** /sbin/umount	Find umount command anywhere in your PATH or aliases.
$ **pkg_info -W convert** /usr/local/bin/convert was installed by package ImageMagick-6.3.6.9	Find which package the convert command is from.

If you suspect that the command you want is not installed, you can search the ports database for the package that it is in. If you find the right package (for example, bzflag) and it isn't installed, install it from the Internet as root by typing the following:

```
# find /usr/ports | grep ImageMagick
/usr/ports/gtraphics/ImageMagick
...
# pkg_add -r ImageMagick
```

The command just shown grabs the ImageMagick binary package (in tar bzip2 format) from a BSD software repository and installs it from the local system. Refer to Chapter 2 for information on other methods of installing software, such as using the ports system.

Command Reference Information in BSD

Original BSD, Linux and UNIX documentation was all done on manual pages, generally referred to as *man pages*. A slightly more sophisticated documentation effort came a bit later with the *info* facility. Within each command itself, help messages are almost always available.

This reference information is component oriented — in other words, there are separate man pages for nearly every command, file format, system call, device, and other component of a BSD system. Documentation more closely aligned to whole software packages is typically stored in a subdirectory of the /usr/local/share/doc directory.

All three reference features — man pages, info documents, and help messages — are available in BSD systems.

Using help Messages

The -h or --help options are often used to display help messages for a command. The following example illustrates how to display help for the ogg123 command:

```
$ ogg123 --help | less
ogg123 from vorbis-tools 1.1.1
 by the Xiph.org Foundation (http://www.xiph.org/)

Usage: ogg123 [<options>] <input file> ...

  -h, --help     this help
  -V, --version  display Ogg123 version
  -d, --device=d uses 'd' as an output device
      Possible devices are ('*'=live, '@'=file):
        oss* null* wav@ raw@ au@
  -f, --file=filename  Set the output filename for a previously
      specified file device (with -d).

...
```

The preceding output shows how the ogg123 command line is used and lists available options. Piping the output to the less command lets you page through it.

Using man Pages

Suppose you want to find man pages for commands related to a certain word. Use the apropos command to search the man page database. This shows man pages that have crontab in the man page NAME line:

```
$ apropos crontab
crontab(1)    -  maintain crontab files for individual users (V3)
crontab(5)    -  tables for driving cron
```

The apropos output here shows each man page NAME line that contains crontab. The number shows the man page section in which the man page appears. (We discuss sections shortly.)

The whatis command is a way to show NAME lines alone for commands that contain the word you enter:

```
$ whatis cat
cat        (1)  - concatenate files and print on the standard output
```

The easiest way to display the man page for a term is with the man command and the command name. For example:

```
$ man find
FIND(1)       FreeBSD General Commands Manual             FIND(1)
NAME
       find -- walk a file hierarchy
```

```
SYNOPSIS
        find [-H | -L | -P] [-EXdsx] [-f pathname] [pathname ...] expression
  ...
```

The preceding command displays the first man page found for the find command. As you saw in the earlier example, some terms have multiple man pages. For example, there is a man page for the crontab command and one for the crontab files. Man pages are organized into sections, as shown in Table 1-3.

Table 1-3: man Page Sections

Section	Description
1	General user commands
2	System calls
3	Programming routines / library functions
4	Devices
5	Configuration files and file formats
6	Games
7	Miscellaneous
8	Administrative commands and daemons
9	Kernel Interface

The following code shows some other examples of useful options with the man command.

```
$ man -a mount          Shows all man pages related to component
$ man 5 crontab         Shows section 5 man page for component
$ man mount -P more     Use more, not less to page through
$ man -f mount          Same as the whatis command
$ man -k mount          Same as the apropos command
```

Man pages are also available on the Internet. Here are some nice sites for finding BSD man pages:

```
http://www.freebsd.org/cgi/man.cgi
http://www.openbsd.org/cgi-bin/man.cgi
http://netbsd.gw.com/cgi-bin/man-cgi?++NetBSD-current
```

Using info Documents

In some cases, developers have put more complete descriptions of commands, file formats, devices, or other BSD components in the info database. You can enter the info database by simply typing the `info` command or by opening a particular component:

```
$ info ls
```

The previous command shows information on the `ls` command. Use up, down, left, and right arrows and Page Up and Page Down to move around the screen. Home and End keys go to the beginning and end of a node, respectively. When you are displaying info screen, you can get around using the keystrokes shown in Table 1-4.

Table 1-4: Moving Through the Info Screen

Keystroke	Movement
?	Display the basic commands to use in info windows.
L	Go back to the previous node you were viewing.
n, p, u	Go to the node that is next, previous, or up.
Tab	Go to the next hyperlink that is in this node.
Enter	Go to the hyperlink that is under the cursor.
R	Follow a cross-reference.
Q	Quit and exit from info.

Software packages that have particularly extensive text available in the info database include gimp, festival, libc, automake, zsh, sed, tar, and bash. Files used by the info database are stored in the `/usr/share/info` directory.

Summary

Although you certainly can read this book from cover to cover if you like, the book is designed to be a reference to hundreds of features in BSD systems that are most useful to power users and systems administrators. Because information is organized by topic, instead of alphabetically, you don't have to know the commands in advance to find what you need to get the job done.

Most of the features described in this book will work equally well in FreeBSD, NetBSD, OpenBSD, and other BSD systems. In fact, many of the commands described here are in such widespread use that you could use them exactly as described here on most Linux and UNIX systems as well.

The next chapter describes how to get and install BSD software.

2

Installing FreeBSD and Adding Software

In the tradition of the first UNIX systems, FreeBSD offers a text-based installation facility that includes a utility called *sysinstall*. The installer is aimed at professionals, who are more interested in power and flexibility than fancy graphical screens and hand-holding. After initialization you can run sysinstall again, to add more software packages and configure some network settings.

IN THIS CHAPTER

Installing FreeBSD

Getting software packages with pkg_add

Using ports to get and install software

Despite its simplicity, the installer offers many of the same powerful features that you can find in more refined Linux and UNIX installers. It can configure your hard disks and install from different local media (CD, DVD, or hard disk) or remote servers (FTP, HTTP or NFS servers). It also leads you through the initial configuration of users, mice, network services, and other important start-up features.

After installation, FreeBSD offers tools such as pkg_info, pkg_add, pkg_delete, and pkg_check to add and otherwise work with software packages in FreeBSD. You can also run the sysinstall utility again to install more packages after your initial FreeBSD install. To install packages from source code, FreeBSD offers the ports collection, along with tools such as portsnap and portupgrade.

This chapter highlights critical issues you need to know during the initial FreeBSD installation. It also provides detailed examples of commands just mentioned for managing software after installation.

Before Installing FreeBSD

You can get FreeBSD installation software from the *Getting FreeBSD* web page at www.freebsd.org/where.html. From that page, you can find where to purchase FreeBSD CDs or DVDs. For example, you can purchase a four-CD set or single DVD from the FreeBSD Mall (www.freebsdmall.com), with or without the FreeBSD handbook.

You can also learn where to download free ISO images for supported FreeBSD architectures from the *Getting FreeBSD* page. Supported architectures include: Intel i386, Alpha/AXP, AMD 64-bit (Athalon64, Athlon64-FX or Opteron), ia64, PowerPC, and Sparc64. For example, available downloads of several FreeBSD releases can be obtained from: `ftp.freebsd.org/pub/FreeBSD/ISO-IMAGES-i386`

From the `http://FreeBSD.org/docs.html` page, you can access FreeBSD documentation that can help you if you hit any snags during installation. For example, select the FAQ for installation tips, supported hardware, bootloaders, and other topics you need to get started.

To simply erase everything on your computer's hard disk to install FreeBSD, you don't have to prepare your hard disks in advance. If you want to keep any data from your hard disk, back up that data before proceeding. To keep existing data on your hard disk and add FreeBSD, you may need to resize existing disk partitions and repartition your disk. Refer to Chapter 7 for information on disk resizing and partitioning commands.

> **NOTE** *If you are booting multiple operating systems from the same computer, the order in which those systems are installed is important. If you want Windows on the machine, install it first, because it will overwrite your boot manager and make FreeBSD temporarily unbootable. Linux system installers usually ask whether or not you want to install a boot loader, and may even let you configure that boot loader to boot FreeBSD as well. If the boot manager is erased, access the FreeBSD file system and run* bootinst.exe boot.bin *from the* tools *directory on the CD to reinstall the FreeBSD boot manager.*

Installing FreeBSD

The FreeBSD installation procedure described in this section uses the three-CD FreeBSD installation set. The computer described has an *x86* architecture and an available Ethernet connection to the Internet (to add software that is not on the CDs). This procedure was tested on FreeBSD 7 and 6.3.

Booting the Install Disc

Insert the first install CD into your drive and reboot. When the following FreeBSD boot screen appears, follow the procedure below to **install FreeBSD on your computer:**

```
        Welcome to FreeBSD!

1. Boot FreeBSD [default]
2. Boot FreeBSD with ACPI disabled
3. Boot FreeBSD in Safe Mode
4. Boot FreeBSD in single user mode
5. Boot FreeBSD with verbose logging
6. Escape to loader prompt
7. Reboot
      Select option, [Enter] for default
      or [Space] to pause timer
```

Press the spacebar (to pause the timer) or let the default install begin (by pressing Enter or letting the timer time out). If you want to view or change boot settings, type **6**. When you see the OK prompt, type **?** to view available commands. Here are some **commands you can run from the boot prompt**:

`boot`	Starts install process
`show`	List available boot variables
`set` *xx*=??	Set boot variables (for example, **set acpi_load=NO** to turn off ACPI during the install)
`unset` *xx*	Unset a selected boot variable
`lsdev`	List potential boot device names
`lsmod`	List modules that are loaded
`ls`	List files
`load`	Load a selected kernel or module
`smap`	View BIOS SMAP
`more`	Page through a file (for example, **more README.txt**)

To disable or enable features in the kernel, add them to the `kernel_options=` variable. When you are ready to continue on to the install process, type **boot**.

Starting the Install Process

FreeBSD offers a text-/menu-based install procedure. Throughout the install procedure, use these keys: Space (select or toggle item) or Enter (to finish with an item). Also, use Up Arrow (previous item), Down Arrow (next item), Right Arrow (next item or group), or Left Arrow (previous item or group). To scroll text, select Page Up (scroll text boxes up one page), Page Down (scroll text boxes down one page), or F1 (display help text).

1. **Select Country.** The default country is the United States. The `sysinstall` Main Menu appears, displaying a list of install types and other options.

2. **Select Install Type.** To install, select Standard (recommended), Express (quick install for experts), or Custom (custom install for experts). This procedure describes the Standard install. If you are presented with a screen to partition your hard disk(s), proceed to the next step.

3. **Disk Partitioning.** The installer provides you with a screen-oriented FDISK to partition your hard drive. (See Chapter 7 for more details on partitioning with FDISK.) Here are your options:

```
A = Entire Disk   G= set Drive Geometry  C= Create Slice  F = 'DD' Mode
D = Delete Slice  Z= Toggle Size Units   S= Set Bootable  | = Wizard m.
T = Change Type   U = Undo All Changes   Q= Finish
```

Assuming you want to use the whole hard disk to install FreeBSD, use arrow keys to highlight any old slice and type **D** to delete it. Then you can select one of the following ways of partitioning the disk:

❑ A: Use the entire hard disk for FreeBSD. This selection leaves space at the beginning of the slice so you can add a boot manager in the future. If you want to be able to install and boot multiple operating systems from the local

15

computer, adding a boot manager (such as LILO or GRUB) will let you do that. Use this on multi-boot and home PCs.

❑ F: To dedicate the computer completely to FreeBSD, select F and select No when asked if you want to keep the disk able to be compatible with other operating systems. This approach assigns the entire disk to FreeBSD (starting at absolute sector 0), so there is no space for a boot manager. The FreeBSD disk label is used as the disk's boot manager. Use this only on dedicated FreeBSD systems, in particular Internet servers.

❑ C: Highlight any unused space and type **C** to create a new slice. You can create several slices in this way.

In most cases where you are using FreeBSD for the whole disk, select A (to have the most flexibility going forward). Then select Q to continue.

NOTE *If you are used to partitioning hard disks in Linux, the term slice may be new to you. In FreeBSD, you can assign part or all of a hard disk to a slice, then divide that slice into smaller areas (multiple file systems and swap areas) within that slice. You can do this using the Label Editor.*

4. **Select Boot Manager**. Select BootMgr (FreeBSD Boot Manager), Standard (install standard MBR without a boot manager), or None (to not change the MBR).

5. **Create BSD Partitions**: Within the BSD slice you created with FDISK, you can use the FreeBSD Disklabel Editor to partition the parts of your FreeBSD system. If you are dedicating the whole disk to FreeBSD, you can select A (auto defaults) to have the editor divide up your disk automatically. Or you can create individual partitions by selecting C (Create). Here is the list of options:

```
C = Create       D = Delete    M = Mount pt.
N = Newfs Opts   Q = Finish    S = Toggle SoftUpdates  Z = Custom Newfs
T = Toggle Newfs U = Undo      A = Auto Defaults       R = Delete+Merge
```

Here are some tips for partitioning your disk:

❑ The UFS2 file system is the default for FreeBSD 5.1 and later.

❑ Root file system must be less than 1.5TB.

❑ Set Soft Updates policy to cause metadata and data blocks to be written asynchronously to disk (with extra state information).

Here's what was automatically assigned for the 40GB hard disk dedicated to FreeBSD:

```
Part        Mount        Size Newfs     Part
----        -----        ---- -----     ----
ad0s1a      /            512MB UFS2      Y
ad0s1b      swap         476MB SWAP
ad0s1c      /var        1262MB UFS2+S   Y
ad0s1d      /tmp         512MB UFS2+S   Y
ad0s1e      /usr       36325MB UFS2+S   Y
```

When you are done, type **Q** to finish.

6. **Choose distributions**. FreeBSD calls pre-set groups of software *distributions*. You can choose the distributions that are most useful to you as the basis for the system you are installing (such as X-User for a desktop system or Minimal for a minimal installation). Or, you can choose Custom to select the exact software you want.

7. **FreeBSD Ports Collection**. You are asked if you want to install the FreeBSD ports collection (except not with a minimal install). If you have the required 400MB of space available, say yes. It will help you add software in the future.

8. **Choose install media**. Options include CD/DVD, FTP server, FTP Passive (server though a firewall), HTTP (FTP via an HTTP proxy), DOS partition, NFS (network file system), File System (local hard disk partition), Floppy (set of floppies), and Tape (SCSI or QIC).

9. **Confirm to start installing**. This is the last chance to exit before your hard disk contents are overwritten.

10. **Configuration questions**. When the FreeBSD system is installed, you are asked a set of questions about how you want your system configured. Here is a quick list of those questions and the default answers:

```
Configure Ethernet or SLIP/PPP network devices? Yes
```

If you answered yes, you can configure an Ethernet card, parallel Port IP, SLIP, or PPP connection. You can set your IP addresses manually or use DHCP. You can also configure IPv6 networking, if appropriate for your network.

```
Machine a network gateway? No
```

With at least two network interfaces, you can have your computer act as a network gateway. For example, your FreeBSD system could provide other computers on your LAN with Internet access.

```
Configure inetd and network services it provides? No
```

The inetd daemon provides access to a variety of services, particularly legacy UNIX services including finger and telnet. More modern equivalent services are now used more often.

```
Would you like to enable SSH login? No
```

The SSH daemon is the most common method for providing secure remote login and remote execution service to your computer. Most will choose Yes to enable this service if they plan to remotely administer their system.

```
Anonymous FTP access? No
```

Enabling anonymous FTP access allows users who don't have a valid login to your machine to access files from your machine that are configured in public FTP directories.

```
Do you want to configure this machine as an NFS Server? No
```

17

Enabling the system as an NFS server allows you to share local directories, so other computers on your network can mount them.

NFS Client? **Yes**

Enabling the system as an NFS client lets you mount shared directories from other computers on your network.

Customize system console settings? **No**

You can change system console settings, such as fonts, keymaps, and terminal type.

Set timezone? **Yes**

Set the timezone for the machine.

Linux binary compatibility? **Yes**

Allows you to run Linux software on FreeBSD by installing the components that Linux applications need to run.

PS/2, serial or bus mouse? **No**

Select Yes if your computer has a mouse and you want to enable it. You can then choose to test and run the mouse daemon, to make sure it is working.

Browse software collection now? **Yes**

Use arrow keys to highlight a package you want to install and press Enter. When you see the list of applications associated with each package, highlight each package you want (arrow keys) and press the space bar to mark each application for installation. Review the applications you have chosen and select OK.

Add initial user accounts? **Yes**

Add a regular user account for every day use of the system. You can also add new groups to the system.

Add root user password

Assign a password to the root user.

Visit configuration menu for last options? **No**

This takes you to the FreeBSD Configuration Menu where you can change settings (packages, partitioning, time zone, mouse, and so on) chosen during installation.

Return to sysinstall screen (exit when done) **No**

If you want to return to the sysinstall main menu, you can do so at this point. You can also run the sysinstall command at any time after you reboot the system, to make further changes to your configuration.

```
Reboot? Yes
```

Remove the installation media and reboot the system to run the newly installed system from hard disk.

When the system reboots, you can log in using the user name and password you set during installation.

Adding, Deleting, and Managing Software

After installing FreeBSD, you can install additional software using either *Ports* or *Packages*. The FreeBSD ports collection approach lets you install software from source code. The Packages approach lets you install applications that are pre-built into binaries. Experts tend to use the ports system to get the latest software. New users might be more comfortable with Packages provided that bugs have been worked out in the build process.

For installing binaries, the sysinstall utility lets you select where to install from (CD, DVD, FTP, and so on), then choose which packages to install. If a package is already on your computer, you can use commands such as pkg_add, pkg_delete, and pkg_info to work with that package. For building packages using the ports system, you use the make command.

Finding Software

At any time, you can find out what software is available with FreeBSD using the FreeBSD Ports Search page (www.freebsd.org/ports). If you know a component (command, system call, file format, and so on), but don't know what package it is in, you can search man pages from the FreeBSD site (www.freebsd.org/cgi/man.cgi). You can also use pkg_info to get information about software that is already installed.

To **search the FreeBSD Ports system** for a particular software package, go to the search page www.freebsd.org/ports. Type the term(s) to search for, the description area to search, and the particular category of software. You will see a listing of results by category and package name. The following searches everything for md5sum:

```
Search for:   md5sum      All          All Sections        Submit
Category security
cfv-1.18.1
    Utility to both test and create .sfv, csv and md5sum files
    Long description : Sources : Changes : Download
    Maintained by: ports@FreeBSD.org
    Requires: py25-fchksum-1.7.1, python25-2.5.1 1
```

19

To **read about available commands**, file formats and other things before you install them, use the FreeBSD Hypertext Man Pages page (www.freebsd.org/cgi/man.cgi). Search by man page name or keyword. This example searches for the pkg_info man page:

```
Man Page or Keyword Search:    pkg_info        | Submit |   | Reset |
?  Man    | All Sections |     | FreeBSD Ports |
o  Apropos Keyword Search (all sections) | html | Output format
home | help


PKG_INFO(1)      FreeBSD General Commands Manual    PKG_INFO(1)


NAME
     pkg_info -- a utility for displaying information on software packages
```

You can **check whether a package is already installed** and **list information about installed packages** using the pkg_info command. (Depending on your shell, you may need to wrap wildcard characters in quotes, as in: pkginfo "cdrtools*".) Here are examples:

```
# pkg_info | less                   Show name/index line for all packages
# pkg_info -I gnome* | less          Show name/index line for matching packages
# pkg_info cdrtools* | less          Show info for installed package cdrtools
# pkg_info -d cdrtools* | less       Show long description of package
# pkg_info -c cdrtools* | less       Show comment line of package
# pkg_info -f cdrtools* | less       Show list of files in package
# pkg_info -L cdrtools* | less       Show list of full paths to files in package
# pkg_info -i gnome-games* | less    Show install script for package (if any)
# pkg_info -k kdebase* | less        Show de-install script for package (if any)
```

You can **find out about package dependencies** using the pkg_info command. Here are examples:

```
# pkg_info -R cdrtools* | less       Show packages required by installed package
# pkg_info -r cdrtools* | less       Show packages requested package depends on
```

Before you install the packages that interest you, there are other ways to get information about packages and categories as well. If you installed the ports database, you could simply **search the /usr/ports directory**, since packages are organized by directories named after each category and package name. For example:

```
# find /usr/ports -type d | grep quake | less    Show ports with quake in the name
```

If you want to **search your entire system for any sign of a particular package, command or file**, you can use the locate command to search the entire file system. That is, provided that you configured the locate database to include the entire contents of your file system. Chapter 4 contains information on how to create a locate database.

Perhaps the most obvious way to browse through available groups and packages is to view the packages in the sysinstall utility, as described in the next section.

Installing Software Packages (binary)

You can install precompiled, binary packages that are that are ready to run using
either a menu interface (sysinstall) or a command-line interface (pkg_add). Both
sysinstall and pkg_add will try to get and install the packages you request, along
with any dependent packages your selected packages need to run.

After you have installed FreeBSD, you can run the sysinstall utility again to add more software
packages. As root user, type /usr/sbin/sysinstall to display the sysinstall
Main Menu. Then select Configure ⇨ Packages, and choose the medium you want to
install from (CD/DVD, FTP, HTTP, and so on). You may have to select the location
and network interface to reach your chosen online software site as well. Figure 2-1
shows an example of the Package Selection screen of the sysinstall utility.

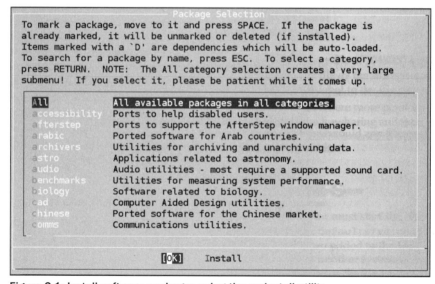

Figure 2-1: Install software packages using the sysinstall utility.

Use keystrokes described during installation to move among the categories and packages to select what you want to install. If any of the packages you select are dependent
on other packages that are not already installed, those dependent packages will be
marked with a D and automatically installed with your selections. After you have made
your selections, tab to the OK button, then select Install to begin installing the packages.

If you prefer the command line to a menu interface, you can use the pkg_add command to
add packages to your BSD system. The packages you request can be either in a local directory or in a BSD software repository. Here are examples:

```
# pkg_add bsdtris-1.1_7.tbz      Install bsdtris from local directory
```

```
# pkg_add -r freebsd-games        Download/install freebsd-games from network
# pkg_add -r -K xmines            Download/install xmines, save pkg to local dir
# pkg_add -v lsof-4.79D.tbz       Install lsof in verbose mode
Requested space: 455200 bytes, free space: 1155635200 bytes
    in /var/tmp/instmp.09jSIz
extract: Package name is lsof-4.79D
extract: CWD to /usr/local
extract /usr/local/sbin/lsof
   . . .
```

To **verify the contents of a package** before installing it, you can use the -M (Master) option to pkg_add. With -M, instead of installing a package, the contents of the package are copied to a subdirectory of /var/tmp, where you can inspect them before installing. For example, with memdump-1.01.tbz in the local directory, type this:

```
# pkg_add -M memdump-1.01.tbz     Put package contents in /var/tmp to check
```

With the package extracted to the /var/tmp directory, you can now examine the contents of the package. Look for directories with names such as instmp.??????, where each ? is replaced by a letter or number. The -M option can be used in conjunction with the -S (Slave) mode.

Removing Software Packages (binary)

To remove previously installed software packages, you can use the pkg_delete command. Here are some examples of pkg_delete for **deleting a package**:

```
# pkg_delete -n dbus-0.93_3       Check what would happen before deleting package
pkg_delete: package 'dbus-0.93_3' is required by these other packages
and may not be deinstalled:
dbus-glib-0.71
avahi-0.6.14
policykit-0.1.20060514_2
hal-0.5.8.20060917_2
  . . .
pkg_delete: 1 package deletion(s) failed
```

The -n option to pkg_delete shows you what would happen when you run the pkg_delete live, without actually running it. Running pkg_delete -n before actually deleting the package is a good idea. This will tell you dependencies on the package, if there are any, but not actually delete the package. If there are no dependencies, it will show you the exact files that would be deleted, so you can see if there's anything you would miss.

Here are some other useful options for deleting packages with pkg_delete:

```
# pkg_delete xmines*       Delete package, using wildcard
# pkg_delete -i akode*     Delete set of packages, confirming each
delete akode-2.0.1,1? y
  ...
# pkg_delete -v xmines*    Delete with verbose output
pkg_delete: no such package 'xmines*' installed
pkg_delete: 1 package deletion(s) failed
```

Think hard before you use any of the following options with pkg_delete. The first example below **forces the named package to be deleted,** even if other packages are depend-ent on it. In the second example, all installed packages are deleted, which I presume brings the system down to just the base system (I'm not going to try this myself, but mention it because the option is there):

```
# pkg_delete -f metacity*  Forcibly remove package (no dependency checks)
# pkg_delete -a            Danger, Danger! This will remove all installed packages
```

Another option that's a bit dangerous, but potentially useful is the -r option. Use this option if you want to **remove a package, plus all packages that depend on it.** Before you use this option, it is probably a good idea to do some non-destructive trials. For example:

```
# pkg_delete -n -r gstreamer* | less Non-destructive results of recursive delete
# pkg_delete -r gstreamer*    Danger! Recursively delete package and dependencies
```

Installing Software Using Ports (source code)

The BSD ports collection contains sets of make files, patches, and descriptive informa-tion needed to get, compile and install thousands of applications that have been *ported* to FreeBSD. When you install the ports collection, it is stored in the /usr/ports direc-tory. From there, you can run a few simple commands to build selected applications from source code and install them on your system.

In general, installing packages from the ports collection is generally preferred by more expert users. That's because building from source code offers opportunities for checking the code, modifying it to work efficiently for your uses, and incorporating the latest patches.

When you first installed FreeBSD, you were given the opportunity to install the ports collection. If you chose not to do that at the time, you can install the ports collection later, as described in the following section.

Getting the Ports Collection

There are several ways to get the ports collection for your FreeBSD system after the system is installed. Choices include `sysinstall`, `portsnap`, or `cvsup`. Of the three, the `sysinstall` method is probably the most intuitive, but each is pretty easy to use. This first procedure either **installs or updates your ports collection using portsnap**:

1. Create the ports directory (if it doesn't already exist):

```
# mkdir /usr/ports
```

2. If it is not already installed, install `portsnap`:

```
# pkg_add -r portsnap
```

3. Download ports collection to `/var/db/portsnap`:

```
# portsnap fetch
```

4. Do one of the following to either install a new `/usr/ports` or update an existing `/usr/ports` collection, respectively:

```
# portsnap extract          Install a new ports collection
```

or

```
# portsnap update           Update an existing ports collection
```

To **use sysinstall to install the ports collection**, run the `sysinstall` command as root user. Then select Configure ➪ Distributions ➪ ports. With ports selected, select OK. When prompted, select the location of the ports collection (CD, DVD, FTP site, etc.) and the ports collection will be extracted to the `/usr/ports` directory structure.

To **use cvsup to install the ports collection**, do the following:

1. Create the ports directory:

```
# mkdir /usr/ports
```

2. Install `cvsup`:

```
# pkg_add -r cvsup-without-gui
```

3. Run the `cvsup` command, replacing `cvsup.FreeBSD.org` with a FreeBSD mirror site nearer to your location and optionally copying and modifying the ports-supfile:

```
# cvsup -L 2 -h cvsup.FreeBSD.org /usr/share/examples/cvsup/ports-supfile
```

Regardless of which of the three procedures you used to get your FreeBSD ports collection, the next section provides instructions for using the ports collection to install applications on your FreeBSD system.

Getting and Installing Applications with Ports

Applications in the ports collection are available via *port skeletons*. A port skeleton is represented by a directory in the /usr/ports directory structure that contains components needed to get the source code, compile it, and install the components.

Basically, the skeleton contains all the information needed to build an application from source code, without containing the source code itself. The source code itself is contained in a tarball referred to as a *distfile*. During the build process you get the distfile from a FreeBSD mirror site on the Internet or from a local disk.

Here's how to **see the port skeleton for the ftpcopy application**:

```
# cd /usr/ports/ftp/ftpcopy        Change to the ftpcopy directory in ports
# ls -CF                           Lists the contents of the ftpcopy directory
Makefile     distinfo    files/   pkg-descr     pkg-plist
```

The Makefile file is used by the make command to describe how the application is to be compiled. The distinfo file contains the md5 and sha256 checksums needed to check the download files used to build the port. The files directory contains any patch files to the application, such as those needed to get the application to run in FreeBSD or to fix a security problem.

The pkg-descr file contains a description of the package and usually a web site for the project that created the software. The pkg-plist file identifies the files installed from the application and the locations in the local file system where to install them. Besides the executable commands (for example, ftpcp, ftpcopy, and ftpls), the file might also contain libraries, images, or documentation (such as ChangeLog, README or other documents).

Doing a Quick Build

For the most basic type of application installation with ports, all you need to do is run a few make commands. Continuing with the example of the ftpcopy application, here's how you can **install an application using a ports collection**:

```
# cd /usr/ports/ftp/ftpcopy        Change to the ftpcopy directory in ports
# make build                       Download and build ftpcopy application
=> ftpcopy-0.6.7.tar.gz doesn't seem to exist in /usr/ports/distfiles/.
=> Attempting to fetch from http://www.ohse.de/uwe/ftpcopy/.
===>  Extracting for ftpcopy-0.6.7
=> MD5 Checksum OK for ftpcopy-0.6.7.tar.gz.
=> SHA256 Checksum OK for ftpcopy-0.6.7.tar.gz.
===>   ftpcopy-0.6.7 depends on file: /usr/local/bin/perl5.8.8 - found
===>   Patching for ftpcopy-0.6.7
===>   ftpcopy-0.6.7 depends on file: /usr/local/bin/perl5.8.8 - found
```

```
===>  Applying FreeBSD patches for ftpcopy-0.6.7
===>   ftpcopy-0.6.7 depends on file: /usr/local/bin/perl5.8.8 - found
===>  Configuring for ftpcopy-0.6.7
===>  Building for ftpcopy-0.6.7
       . . .
```

 # make install   *Install ftpcopy binaries and documents*

```
===>  Installing for ftpcopy-0.6.7
===>   Generating temporary packing list
===>  Checking if ftp/ftpcopy already installed
cd /usr/ports/ftp/ftpcopy/work/web/ftpcopy-0.6.7/compile && install  -s -o root
-g wheel -m 555 ftpcopy ftpls /usr/local/bin && install  -o root -g wheel -m
444 ftpcopy.1 ftpcp.1 ftpls.1 /usr/local/man/man1 && install  -o root -g wheel
-m 555 ftpcp /usr/local/bin
/bin/mkdir -p /usr/local/share/doc/ftpcopy && cd
/usr/ports/ftp/ftpcopy/work/web/ftpcopy-0.6.7/compile && install  -o root -g
wheel -m 444 ChangeLog NEWS  README THANKS ftpcopy.html ftpls.html
/usr/local/share/doc/ftpcopy
===>   Compressing manual pages for ftpcopy-0.6.7
===>   Registering installation for ftpcopy-0.6.7
```

 # make clean   *Clean up files left behind from build*

```
===>  Cleaning for perl-5.8.8
===>  Cleaning for ftpcopy-0.6.7
```

 # pkg_info ftpcopy*   *Check that ftpcopy package was installed*

```
ftpcopy-0.6.7     Command line ftp tools for listing and mirroring
```

 # pkg_info -L ftpcopy*   *List files from ftpcopy package*

```
Information for ftpcopy-0.6.7:
Files:
/usr/local/man/man1/ftpcopy.1.gz
/usr/local/man/man1/ftpcp.1.gz
/usr/local/man/man1/ftpls.1.gz
/usr/local/bin/ftpcp
/usr/local/bin/ftpcopy
/usr/local/bin/ftpls
/usr/local/share/doc/ftpcopy/ChangeLog
/usr/local/share/doc/ftpcopy/NEWS
   . . .
```

After changing to the directory representing the application you want to install, you run three make commands. The make build command downloads the software package (source code distfile), runs checksums to check its validity, applies patches, fulfills dependencies, and builds the binaries (commands).

The make install command puts the application's files where they need to go in the file system, compresses man pages, and registers the package as installed. The make clean command cleans up temporary files left behind.

After a package is installed, you can use the pkg_info command to verify that the package is installed. Then run pkg_info again with -L to list the contents of the package.

Using Other make Options

There are other options you can run with the make commands that let you do portions of what was done in the previous procedure separately. Remember that all these commands should be run from the directory associated with the port. To run checksums on the application's distfile, type the following:

```
# make checksum              Run checksums on the application's distfile
=> MD5 Checksum OK for ftpcopy-0.6.7.tar.gz.
=> SHA256 Checksum OK for ftpcopy-0.6.7.tar.gz.
```

To do the build up to the configure portion, run the following:

```
# make configure            To the make up to the configuration
```

To remove the package, type the following:

```
# make deinstall            Remove the package
```

If you have made changes to the source code, documents or other components of the package, you might want to repackage those changes into a new distfile. The following result is that the package is installed and a new distfile tarball is created:

```
# make package                 Create a new distfile tarball of application
===>  Installing for ftpcopy-0.6.7
...
Creating package /usr/ports/ftp/ftpcopy/ftpcopy-0.6.7.tbz
Registering depends:.
Creating bzip'd tar ball in '/usr/ports/ftp/ftpcopy/ftpcopy-0.6.7.tbz'
```

To just download the application's distfile to the /usr/ports/distfiles directory, type the following:

```
# make fetch                 Download the distfile but don't install it
=> ftpcopy-0.6.7.tar.gz doesn't seem to exist in /usr/ports/distfiles/.
=> Attempting to fetch from http://www.ohse.de/uwe/ftpcopy/.
ftpcopy-0.6.7.tar.gz              100% of   131 kB   44kBps
```

To download the selected distfile, plus any dependent distfiles, as follows:

```
# make fetch-recursive       Download the distfile, plus dependencies
```

While we are on the subject of using make to make cool stuff, here is something useful if you are interested in README files. By running the following commands, in the /usr/ports directory, you can create a README.html file for every package and consolidate those files in a /usr/ports/README.html file. Here's an example:

```
# cd /usr/ports
# make readmes              Create lots of README.html files in /usr/ports
```

Checking Packages and Ports

FreeBSD comes with a lot of tools for making sure that the software you install is both safe and up-to-date. There are also tools for comparing installed packages to see if they match what is in the latest ports and to update your ports collection to the latest versions. This section contains examples of commands for checking your installed packages.

Checking Installed Packages Against Ports

You can use the `pkg_version` command to find out if one or more installed packages is up-to-date with the latest version available from the ports collection. For example, to check if packages with a given string in their name is up-to-date, try using the `-s` option as follows:

```
# pkg_version -v          Check if all packages are up-to-date (verbose)
# pkg_version -v -s ftp    Check if ftp packages are up-to-date with ports
ftpcopy-0.6.7                        = up-to-date with port
lftp-3.5.4_1                         = up-to-date with port
```

The ports collection index file is stored in /usr/ports/INDEX-6, by default. When you run the `pkg_version` command, packages are checked against that file. To check against a different INDEX file, for example one from an earlier or later release, add the name of that INDEX file (either locally or on the Internet) to the end of the command line as follows:

```
# pkg_version /tmp/INDEX          Check packages against local INDEX file
```

Upgrading Ports

To keep your ports collection up-to-date, you can use the `portupgrade` command. Once `portupgrade` is installed, you can use it to either update ports individual packages or update the entire ports collection. Here's an example of updating an individual package in the ports collection:

```
# pkg_add -r portupgrade
# portupgrade -R konqueror     Update Konqueror software, if it's installed
[Rebuilding the pkgdb <format:bdb_btree> in /usr/ports ...
      15918 port entries found.....................................
```

Another tool for upgrading installed ports is `portmanager`. After installing `portmanager`, you can upgrade port skeletons for whatever ports you choose. Here are some examples:

```
# cd /usr/ports/ports-mgmt/portmanager

# make install clean          Compile and install portmanager.
# portmanager -u              Upgrade all ports
# portmanager math/gnumeric   Upgrade selected ports
```

Auditing Installed Packages

The portaudit command (pkg_add -r portaudit) lets you check your installed packages for known security vulnerabilities. Regardless of whether or not your FreeBSD system is using the latest ports collection, you can use portaudit to check your installed packages against a database of security advisories.

The portaudit database is kept in the /usr/local/etc/periodic/security directory. The portaudit package contains a script in that directory for updating the security advisories as they become available. Those advisories are updated by the FreeBSD security team, as well as by those who commit ports to the ports collection.

You can run portaudit to get the latest ports security database:

```
# portaudit -Fda          Download the ports security database
auditfile.tbz                        100% of    47 kB    26 kBps
New database installed.
```

Next you can check all installed packages against the ports security database by typing the following:

```
# portaudit -a           Check all installed packages against security database
Affected package: libxine-1.1.2_2
Type of problem: libxine -- buffer overflow vulnerability.
Reference:
<http://www.FreeBSD.org/ports/portaudit/6ecd0b42-ce77-11dc-89b1-000e35248ad7.htm
l>

Affected package: xorg-server-6.9.0_5
Type of problem: xorg -- multiple vulnerabilities.
Reference:
<http://www.FreeBSD.org/ports/portaudit/fe2b6597-c9a4-11dc-8da8-0008a18a9961.htm
l>
    . . .
44 problem(s) in your installed packages found.
You are advised to update or deinstall the affected pacakge(s) immediately.
```

Instead of waiting for packages to be installed, you can check a single package for vulnerabilities before it is installed using the -f option:

```
# portaudit -f /usr/ports/distfiles/ftpcopy*   Check a package for
vulnerabilities
0 problem(s) found.
```

In the information produced by portaudit, security vulnerabilities are accompanied by links to descriptions of the vulnerabilities found. Then you can decide whether or not you want to update, patch, or remove the vulnerable software package.

Cleaning Up the Ports Collection

After each time you install a package from the ports system, it is usually best to run the make clean command to get rid of the temporary files created during the builds. If you forget to do that some time, a lot of unneeded files can fill your disk space. You can clean out groups of unneeded files in your ports collection at once using the portsclean command (portsclean is in the portupgrade package: pkg_add -r portupgrade).

Although work files are cleaned out when you run the make clean command, the distfiles (source code tarballs) that are downloaded to /usr/ports/distfiles are not cleaned out. Depending on how many ports you install, this directory can grow quite large. You can use the -D option to portsclean to **remove ports that not are referenced by any ports any longer:**

```
# portsclean -D          Remove unreferenced distfiles
Detecting unreferenced distfiles...
```

Likewise, you can have portsclean check all distfiles and **remove any distfiles that are not referenced by a port that is installed** currently:

```
# portsclean -DD          Remove unreferenced distfiles of uninstalled ports
Detecting unreferenced distfiles...
[Updating the pkgdb <format:bdb_btree> in /var/db/pkg ...
   - 440 packages found (-0 +2) .. done]
Delete /usr/ports/distfiles/LPRng-3.8.28.tgz
```

You **clean out all your ports work files at once** using the -C option:

```
# portsclean -C          Remove ports work files
Cleaning out /usr/ports/*/*/work...
Delete /usr/ports/ftp/ftpcopy/work
Delete /usr/ports/net/samba-nmblookup/work
  ...
```

Packages that are not referenced by other packages (called leaf packages) can be cut interactively using the pkg_cutleaves command (as root user, type this: pkg_add -r pkg_cutleaves). To **list unreferenced packages,** type the following:

```
# pkg_cutleaves -lc          List unreferenced packages
3dm-2.04.00.018,1 - 3ware RAID controller monitoring daemon and web server
  ...
```

You can **cut unreferenced packages as follows:**

```
# pkg_cutleaves          Step through unreferenced packages list (keep or delete)
package 1 of 147
3dm-2.04.00.018,1 - 3ware RAID controller monitoring daemon and web server
3dm-2.04.00.018,1 - [keep]/(d)elete/(f)lush marked pkgs/(a)bort? d
3dm-2.04.00.018,1 - 3ware RAID controller monitoring daemon and web server
```

```
Package 2 of 147:
44bsd-more-20000521 - The pager installed with FreeBSD before less(1) was
imported
44bsd-more-20000521 - [keep]/(d)elete/(f)lush marked pkgs/(a)bort? f

Deleting 3dm-2.04.00.018,1 (package 1 of 1).
Go on with new leaf packages ((y)es/[no])? no
** Deinstalled packages:
3dm-2.04.00.018,1
** Number of deinstalled packages: 1
```

As each unreferenced package is displayed, you can **mark it to keep** (press Enter) **or delete**
(d). After you have marked some packages, you can **flush them by typing f**. You can quit at
any time by **typing a to abort**.

Summary

Despite not having a graphical installer, FreeBSD offers some sophisticated tools for
installing and working with software packages. Initial installation is done using the
sysinstall utility. After the system is installed, you have the choice of installing
additional software packages from binary packages or source code.

For working with binary packages, you can use pkg_add, pkg_delete, and pkg_info.
For building packages from source code, you can use the make command, with a variety
of options.

There are many tools available to manage your computer's ports collection. You can use
portupgrade to update some or all of the ports in the collection. If you have security
concerns about your computer, the portaudit command can download a database
of security issues. Then it can scan all of your installed packages and report on poten-
tial security holes contained in the software.

Because files can build up over time in temporary directories when you install a
lot of applications from ports, you can use commands such as portsclean and
pkg_cutleaves to clean up unneeded files. With portsclean you can clean out
work directories of files left behind. With pkg_cutleaves, you can remove packages
that are not referenced by any other package.

3

Using the Shell

The use of a shell command interpreter (usually just called a shell) dates back to the early days of the first UNIX systems. Besides their obvious use of running commands, shells have many built-in features such as environment variables, aliases, and a variety of functions for programming.

There are several different shells to choose from on BSD systems. By default, the root user is assigned to use the C shell (csh) and a regular user is assigned the Bourne shell (sh). With Linux systems, most users use what is called the Bourne Again Shell (bash). There are other shells available as well (such as zsh, ksh, or tcsh).

This chapter offers information that will help you use BSD shells, in general, and the bash shell, in particular.

Terminal Windows and Shell Access

The most common way to access a shell from a BSD graphical interface is using a Terminal window. From a graphical interface, you can often access virtual terminals to get to a shell. With no graphical interface, and a text-based login, you are typically dropped directly to a shell after login.

Using Terminal Windows

To open a Terminal window from GNOME, select Accessories ➪ Terminal. This opens a gnome-terminal window, displaying a bash shell prompt. From an XFce desktop, select the Terminal icon from the XFce panel. From KDE, select the Terminal Program icon to start a konsole terminal window. Figure 3-1 shows an example of a gnome-terminal window.

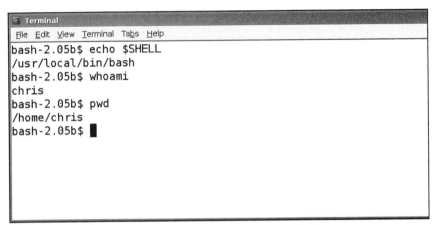

Figure 3-1: Type shell commands into a gnome-terminal window.

Commands shown in Figure 3-1 illustrate that the *current shell* is the bash shell (/usr/local/bin/bash); the *current user* is the desktop user who launched the window (chris), and the *current directory* is that user's home directory (/home/chris). The user name (chris) and hostname (localhost) appear in the title bar.

The gnome-terminal window not only lets you access a shell, it also has controls for managing your shells. For example, click File ⇨ Open Tab to open another shell on a different tab, click File ⇨ Open Terminal to open a new Terminal window, or select Terminal ⇨ Set Title to set a new title in the title bar.

You can also use control key sequences to work with a Terminal window. Open a shell on a new tab by typing Shift+Ctrl+t, open a new Terminal window with Shift+Ctrl+n, close a tab with Shift+Ctrl+w, and close a Terminal window with Shift+Ctrl+q. Highlight text and copy it with Shift+Ctrl+c, then paste it in the same or different window with Shift+Ctrl+v or by clicking the center button on your mouse.

Other key sequences for controlling Terminal windows include pressing F11 to show the window in *full screen mode*. Type Ctrl+Shift++ to zoom in (make text larger) or Ctrl+- (that's Ctrl and a minus sign) to zoom out (make text smaller). Switch among tabs using Ctrl+PageUp and Ctrl+PageDown (previous and next tab), or use Alt+1, Alt+2, Alt+3 and so on to go to tab one, two, or three (and so on). Type Ctrl+D to exit the shell, which closes the current tab or entire Terminal window (if it's the last tab).

The gnome-terminal window also supports profiles (select Edit ⇨ Current Profile). Some profile settings are cosmetic (*allow bold text, cursor blinks, terminal bell, colors, images*, and *transparency*). Other settings are functional. For example, by default, the terminal saves 500 scrollback lines (318 kilobytes). Some people like to be able to scroll back further and are willing to give up more memory to allow that.

If you launch gnome-terminal manually, you can add options. Here are some examples:

```
# gnome-terminal -x alsamixer          Start terminal with alsamixer displayed
# gnome-terminal --tab --tab --tab     Start a terminal with three open tabs
# gnome-terminal --geometry 80x20      Start terminal 80 characters by 20 lines
# gnome-terminal --zoom=2              Start terminal with larger font
```

Besides gnome-terminal, you can use many other Terminal windows. Here are some examples: xterm (basic terminal emulator that comes with X), aterm (terminal emulator modeled after Afterstep XVT VT102 emulator), and konsole (terminal emulator delivered with the KDE desktop). The Enlightenment desktop project offers the eterm terminal (which includes features such as message logs on the screen background). Each of the Terminal window commands just named can be obtained by installing the software package of the same name, except for konsole, which is in the kdebase package.

Using Virtual Terminals

When FreeBSD boots in multi-user mode, eight virtual consoles (represented by a console message window and virtual terminals ttyv0 through ttyv7) are created with text-based logins. If an X Window System desktop is running, X is probably running in virtual console 8. Virtual console 1 is where console messages are displayed. If X isn't running, chances are you're looking at virtual console 2.

From X, you can **switch to another virtual console** with Ctrl+Alt+F1, Ctrl+Alt+F2, and so on up to F8. From a text virtual console, you can switch using Alt+F1, Alt+F2 and so on. Press Alt+F9 to return to the X GUI. Each console allows you to log in using different user accounts. Switching to look at another console doesn't affect running processes in any of them. When you switch to virtual terminal one through six, you see a login prompt similar to the following:

```
FreeBSD/i386 (localhost) (ttyv1)
login:
```

Separate getty processes manage each virtual terminal. If you are in a Terminal window, type this command to see what getty processes look like before you log in to any virtual terminals:

```
# ps awx | grep -v grep | grep getty
  780 v1    Is+    0:00.01 /usr/libexec/getty Pc ttyv1
  781 v2    Is+    0:00.01 /usr/libexec/getty Pc ttyv2
  782 v3    Is+    0:00.01 /usr/libexec/getty Pc ttyv3
  783 v4    Is+    0:00.01 /usr/libexec/getty Pc ttyv4
  784 v5    Is+    0:00.01 /usr/libexec/getty Pc ttyv5
  785 v6    Is+    0:00.01 /usr/libexec/getty Pc ttyv6
  786 v7    Is+    0:00.01 /usr/libexec/getty Pc ttyv7
```

After you log in on the first console, getty handles your login, and then fires up an
sh shell:

```
# ps awx | grep -v grep | grep v0
  780  v0    Is    0:00.04 login [pam] (login)
 2300  v0    S     0:00.02 -sh (sh)
```

Virtual consoles are configured in the /etc/ttys file. You can have fewer or more
virtual terminals by adding or deleting getty lines from that file. (Look for the Virtual
terminals section.) Type the following to see which ttys are configured:

```
# grep ttyv /etc/ttys
ttyv0   "/usr/libexec/getty Pc"           cons25   on   secure
...
```

Using the Shell

After you open a shell (whether from a text-based login or Terminal window), the shell
environment is set up based on the user who started the shell. Each user's default shell
is assigned based on the user's entry in the /etc/passwd file. By default, the root
user's password is set to csh (/bin/csh) and regular users are set to sh (/bin/sh). To
use the bash shell, you can set the user's shell to /usr/local/bin/bash. Examples in
this section use the bash shell.

Bash shell settings for all users' shells are located in /etc/profile. User-specific shell
settings are determined by commands executed from several dot files in the user's home
directory (if they exist): .bash_profile, .bash_login, and .profile. When a shell is
closed, any commands in the user's ~/.bash_logout file are executed. Changing settings in these files permanently changes the user's shell settings but does not affect shells
that are already running. (Other shells use different configuration files.)

There are a variety of ways in which you can list and change your shell environment.
One of the biggest ways is to change which user you are; in particular, to become the
super user (see the section "Acquiring Super User Power" later in this chapter).

Using Bash History

The Bourne Again Shell (bash) is used by many UNIX-like systems. Built into bash,
as with other shells, is a history feature that lets you review, change, and reuse commands that you have run in the past.

When bash starts, it reads the ~/.bash_history file and loads it into memory. This file
is set by the value of $HISTFILE. During a bash session, commands are added to history

in memory. When bash exits, history in memory is written back to the .bash_history file. The **number of commands held in history during a bash session** is set by $HISTSIZE, while the **number commands actually stored in the history file** is set by $HISTFILESIZE:

```
$ echo $HISTFILE $HISTSIZE $HISTFILESIZE
/home/fcaen/.bash_history 500 500
```

To **list the entire history**, type **history**. To **list a previous number of history commands**, follow history with a number. This lists the previous five commands in your history:

```
$ history 5
975   mkdir extras
976   mv *doc extras/
977   ls -CF
978   vi house.txt
979   history
```

To **move among the commands** in your history, use the up arrow and down arrow. When a command is displayed, you can use the keyboard to **edit the current command** like any other command: left arrow, right arrow, Delete, Backspace, and so on. Here are some other ways to recall and run commands from your bash history:

```
$ !!                        Run the previous command
$ !997                      Run command number 997 from history
ls -CF
$ !997 *doc                 Append *doc to command 997 from history
ls -CF *doc
$ !?CF?                     Run previous command line containing the CF string
ls -CF *doc
$ !ls                       Run the previous ls command
ls -CF *doc
$ !ls:s/CF/l                Run previous ls command, replacing CF with l
ls -l *doc
```

Another way to **edit the command history** is using the fc command. With fc, you open the chosen command from history using the vi editor. The edited command runs when you exit the editor. Change to a different editor by setting the FCEDIT variable (for example, FCEDIT=gedit) or on the fc command line. For example:

```
$ fc 978                          Edit command number 978, then run it
$ fc                              Edit the previous command, then run it
$ fc -e /usr/local/bin/nano 989   Use nano to edit command 989
```

(Use pkg_add -r to install the text editor you want, such as nano, if it is not already installed. Chapter 5 describes several text editors and the packages they are in.)

Use Ctrl+r to **search for a string in history**. For example, typing Ctrl+r followed by the string ss resulted in the following:

```
# <Ctrl+r>
(reverse-i-search)`ss': sudo /usr/bin/less /var/log/messages
```

Press Ctrl+r repeatedly to **search backward through your history list** for other occurrences of the ss string.

> **NOTE** *By default, bash command history editing uses emacs-style commands. If you prefer the vi editor, you can use vi-style editing of your history by using the* set *command to set your editor to vi. To do that, type the following:* set -o vi.

Using Command Line Completion

You can use the Tab key to complete different types of information on the command line. Here are some examples where you type a partial name, followed by the Tab key, to have bash try to complete the information you want on your command line:

```
$ tracer<Tab>              Command completion: Completes to traceroute command
$ cd /home/ch<Tab>         File completion: Completes to /home/chris directory
$ cd ~jo<Tab>              User homedir completion: Completes to /home/john
$ echo $PA<Tab>            Env variable completion: Completes to $PATH
$ ping @<Tab>              Host completion: Show hosts from /etc/hosts
@davinci.example.com  @ritchie.example.com  @thompson.example.com
@localhost            @zooey
```

Redirecting stdin and stdout

Typing a command in a shell makes it run interactively. The resulting process has two output streams: stdout for normal command output and stderr for error output. In the following example, when /tmpp isn't found, an error message goes to stderr but output from listing /tmp (which is found) goes to stdout:

```
$ ls /tmp /tmpp
ls: /tmpp: No such file or directory
/tmp/:
gconfd-fcaen  keyring-b41WuB  keyring-ItEWbz  mapping-fcaen  orbit-fcaen
```

By default, all output is directed to the screen. Use the greater-than sign (>) to **direct output to a file**. More specifically, you can direct the standard output stream (using >) or standard error stream (using 2>) to a file. Here are examples:

```
$ ls /tmp /tmmp > output.txt
ls: /tmpp: No such file or directory
```

```
$ ls /tmp /tmmp 2> errors.txt
/tmp/:
gconfd-fcaen  keyring-b41WuB  keyring-ItEWbz  mapping-fcaen  orbit-fcaen
```

```
$ ls /tmp /tmmp 2> errors.txt > output.txt

$ ls /tmp /tmmp > everything.txt 2>&1
```

In the first example, stdout is redirected to the file output.txt, while stderr is still directed to the screen. In the second example, stderr (stream 2) is directed to errors.txt while stdout goes to the screen. In the third example, the first two examples are combined. The last example directs both streams to the everything.txt file. **To append to a file** instead of overwriting it, use two greater-than signs:

```
$ ls /tmp >> output.txt
```

If you don't ever want to see an output stream, you can simply **direct the output stream to a special bit bucket file** (/dev/null):

```
# ls /tmp 2> /dev/null
```

> **TIP**   *Another time you may want to redirect stderr is when you run jobs with crontab. You could redirect stderr to a mail message that goes to the crontab's owner. That way, any error messages can be sent to the person running the job.*

Just as you can direct standard output from a command, you can also **direct standard input to a command.** For example, the following command e-mails the /etc/hosts file to the user named chris on the local system:

```
$ mail chris < /etc/hosts
```

Using pipes, you can **redirect output from one process to another process** rather than just files. Here is an example where the output of the ls command is piped to the sort command to have the output sorted:

```
# ls /tmp | sort
```

In the next example, a **pipe and redirection are combined** (the stdout of the ls command is sorted and stderr is dumped to the bit bucket):

```
# ls /tmp/ /tmmp 2> /dev/null | sort
```

Pipes can be used for tons of things:

```
# pkg_info | grep -i gnome | wc -l
# ps auwx | grep firefox
# ps auwx | less
# whereis -m pkg_add | awk '{print $2}'
```

The first command line in the preceding code lists all installed packages, grabs those packages that have gnome in them (regardless of case), and does a count of how many lines are left (effectively counting packages with gnome in the name). The second command line displays Firefox processes taken from the long process list (assuming the Firefox web browser is running). The third command line lets you page through the process list. The last line displays the word *pkg_add:* followed by the path to the pkg_add man page, and then displays only the path to the man page (the second element on the line).

Using backticks, you can execute one section of a command line first and feed the output of that command to the rest of the command line. Here are examples:

```
# pkg_info -W `which mkisofs`
/usr/local/bin/mkisofs was installed by package cdrtools-2.01_6
# ls -l `which traceroute`
-r-sr-xr-x  1 root  wheel  19836 Jan 15 18:33 /usr/sbin/traceroute
```

The first command line in the preceding example finds the full path of the mkisofs command and finds the package that contains that command. The second command line finds the full path to traceroute and does a long list (ls -l) of that command.

A more advanced and powerful way to take the output of one command and pass it as a parameter to another is with the xargs command. For example, after installing the cdrtools package, I ran the following command:

```
# find /usr/local/bin | grep iso | xargs ls
/usr/local/bin/growisofs          /usr/local/bin/isodump
/usr/local/bin/iso-info           /usr/local/bin/isoinfo
/usr/local/bin/iso-read           /usr/local/bin/isovfy
/usr/local/bin/isodebug           /usr/local/bin/mkisofs
```

To display the command xargs is going to run, use the -t option as follows:

```
# cd /usr/local/bin
# echo iso* | xargs -t ls
ls iso-info iso-read isodebug isodump isoinfo isovfy
iso-info        isodebug        isoinfo
iso-read        isodump         isovfy
```

In the above example, the entire output of echo is passed to pkg_info. Using the -t option to xargs, a verbose output of the command line appears before the command is executed. Now have xargs pass each output string from ls as input to individual pkg_add commands. Use the -I option to define {} as the placeholder for the string:

```
# ls /usr/local/bin/mk* | xargs -t -I {} pkg_info -W {}
pkg_info -W /usr/local/bin/mkbundle
/usr/local/bin/mkbundle was installed by package mono-1.2.5.1
pkg_info -W /usr/local/bin/mkisofs
/usr/local/bin/mkisofs was installed by package cdrtools-2.01_6
```

As you can see from the output, separate pkg_info commands are run for each option passed by ls.

Using aliases

Use the `alias` command to **set and list aliases.** Some aliases are already set in each user's `~/.cshrc` file, if a user uses the `csh` shell. Here's how to **list the aliases that are currently set for that shell:**

```
# alias
h           (history 25)
j           (jobs -l)
la          (ls -a)
lf          (ls -FA)
ll          (ls -lA)
```

Aliases can also be set simply as a way of adding options to the default behavior of a command (such as `alias mv mv -i`, so that the user is always prompted before moving a file). To **define other aliases for the csh shell,** use the alias command, followed by the alias name and command to run. For example:

```
$ alias fi "find . | grep $*"
```

Using the alias just shown, typing `fi string` causes the current directory and its subdirectories to be searched for any file names containing the string you entered. You can **define your own aliases for the current bash session** as follows:

```
# alias la='ls -la'
```

Add that line to your `~/.bashrc` file for the definition to occur for each new `bash` session. **Remove an alias from the current bash session** using the `unalias` command, as follows:

```
# unalias la          Unalias the previously aliased la command
# unalias -a          Unalias all aliased commands
```

Tailing Files

To watch the contents of a plain text file grow over time, you can use the `tail` command. For example, you can watch as messages are added to the `/var/log/cron` file as follows:

```
# tail -f /var/log/cron
```

Press Ctrl+C to exit the `tail` command.

Acquiring Super-User Power

When you open a shell, you are able to run commands and access files and directories based on your user/group ID and the permissions set for those components. Many system features are restricted to the *root user*, also referred to as the *super user*.

Because BSD distributions have a reputation for extraordinary security, access to the root user account is discouraged except in very specific situations. By default, root access is only allowed from terminals listed in /etc/ttys as secure. That includes only virtual terminals accessible from the console.

So if you need to use the root account, the only way to do that, as FreeBSD is delivered, is to log in directly as root from the computer's console terminal. To be able to become root user, while logged in as another user, you need to change some security settings and use either the su or sudoers command as described below.

Using the su Command

Non-root users are prevented from becoming root users based on settings in the /etc/pam.d/su file. Those settings only allow the root user or members of the wheel group access to the root user account via the su command. If you change the /etc/pam.d/su file to allow a user to use the su command, you can run the su (super user) command to **become the root user**. However, simply using su, as in the following code, doesn't give you a login shell with the root user's environment:

```
$ su
Password:*****
# echo $MAIL
/var/mail/fcaen
```

After running su, the user still has fcaen's MAIL folder. To **enable the root user's environment,** use the su command with the dash option (-), as follows:

```
# exit
$ su -
Password: *****
# echo $MAIL
/var/mail/root
```

In most cases, use su -, unless you have a very specific reason not to. If no user is specified, su defaults to the root user. However, su can also be used **to become other users:**

```
$ su - cnegus
```

The su command can also be used to **execute a single command as a particular user** provided that the user has been given permission to use su at all:

```
$ su -c whoami
Password: ******
root
# su -c 'less /var/log/messages'
```

Although in the second example you are logged in as a regular user, when you run whoami with su -c, it shows that you are the root user. In the directly preceding example, the quotes are required around the less command line to identify

/var/log/messages as an option to less. As seen above, whoami can be useful to determine which user you're currently running a command as:

```
$ whoami
fcaen
```

Delegating Power with sudo

The sudo command allows very granular delegation of power to users other than the root user. The sudo facility is a great tool, when you have multiple users, for granting specific escalated privileges and logging everything the users do with those privileges. Unless otherwise specified, sudo runs as root. To use the sudo command, you must install the sudo package.

The sudo command is configured in /usr/local/etc/sudoers.

> **WARNING!** *Never edit this file with your normal text editor. Instead, always use the* visudo *command.*

If you look at the sudoers file that shipped with your distribution, you'll see different empty sections delimited by comments and one active statement:

```
root    ALL=(ALL) ALL
```

This means that the user root is allowed on any hosts to run any command as any user. Now add the following line setting the first field to a user account on your system:

```
fcaen ALL= /usr/bin/less /var/log/messages
```

Now fcaen (or whichever user you've added) can do the following:

```
$ sudo /usr/bin/less /var/log/messages
Password:
```

After fcaen types his own password, he can page through the /var/log/messages file. A timestamp is set at that time as well. For the next five minutes (by default), that user can type the command line above and have it work without being prompted for the password.

Every use of sudo gets logged in /var/log/messages:

```
Feb 24 21:58:57 localhost sudo: fcaen : user NOT in sudoers ; TTY=ttyv3 ;
PWD=/home/fcaen ; USER=root ; COMMAND=/usr/bin/less /var/log/messages
```

Next add this line to /etc/sudoers:

```
fcaen           server1=(chris)     /bin/ls /home/chris
```

Now fcaen can do the following:

```
$ sudo -u chris /bin/ls /home/chris
```

The `sudo` command just shown runs as chris and will work only on the host server1. In some organizations, the `sudoers` file is centrally managed and deployed to all the hosts, so it can be useful to specify `sudo` permissions on specific hosts.

Sudo also allows the definition of aliases, or predefined groups of users, commands, and hosts. Check the `sudoers` man page and the `/usr/local/etc/sudoers` file on your BSD system for examples of those features.

Using Environment Variables

Small chunks of information that are useful to your shell environment are stored in what are referred to as *environment variables*. By convention, environment variable names are all uppercase (although that convention is not enforced). If you use the `bash` shell, some environment variables might be set for you from various `bash` start scripts: `/etc/profile` and `~/.bash_profile` (if it exists).

To display all of the environment variables, in alphabetical order, that are already set for your shell, type the following:

```
$ set | less
BASH=/usr/local/bin/bash
BASH_VERSION='3.2.25(0)-release
BLOCKSIZE=K
COLUMNS=80
HISTSIZE=500
HOME=/home/fcaen
HOSTNAME=einstein
...
```

The output just shown contains only a few examples of the environment variables you will see. You can also set, or reset, any variables yourself. For example, to assign the value 123 to the variable ABC (then display the contents of ABC), type the following:

```
$ ABC=123
$ echo $ABC
123
```

The variable ABC exists only in the shell it was created in. If you launch a command from that shell (`ls`, `cat`, `firefox`, and so on), that new process will not see the variable. Start a new `bash` process and test this:

```
$ bash
$ echo $ABC

$
```

You can make variables part of the environment and inheritable by children processes by exporting them:

```
$ export ABC=123
$ c
$ echo $ABC
123
```

Also, you can concatenate a string to an existing variable:

```
# export PATH=$PATH:/home/fcaen
```

To list your bash's environment variables use:

```
# env
```

When you go to create your own environment variables, avoid using names that are already commonly used by the system for environment variables. See Appendix B for a list of shell environment variables.

Creating Simple Shell Scripts

Shell scripts are good for automating repetitive shell tasks. Bash and other shells include the basic constructs found in various programming languages, such as loops, tests, case statements, and so on. The main difference is that there is only one type of variable: strings.

Editing and Running a Script

Shell scripts are simple text files. You can create them using your favorite text editor (such as vi). To run, the shell script file must be executable. For example, if you created a shell script with a file name of myscript.sh, you could make it executable as follows:

```
$ chmod u+x myscript.sh
```

Or, instead of making it executable, you could precede the script with the bash command to run it (bash myscript.sh). Also, the first line of your bash scripts should always be the following:

```
#!/usr/local/bin/bash
```

As with any command, besides being executable the shell script you create must also either be in your PATH or be identified by its full or relative path when you run it. In other words, if you just try to run your script, you may get the following result:

```
$ myscript.sh
bash: myscript.sh: command not found
```

In this example, the directory containing `myscript.sh` is not included in your PATH. To correct this problem, you can edit your path, copy the script to a directory in your PATH, or enter the full or relative path to your script as shown here:

```
$ mkdir ~/bin ; cp myscript.sh ~/bin/ ; PATH=$PATH:~/bin
$ cp myscript.sh /usr/local/bin
$ ./myscript.sh
$ /tmp/myscript.sh
```

Avoid putting a dot (.) into the PATH to indicate that commands can be run from the current directory. This is a technique that could result in commands that have the same file name as important, well-known commands (such as `ls` or `cat`). The proper file could end up being overridden, if a command of the same name exists in the current directory.

Adding Content to Your Script

Although a shell script can be a simple sequence of commands, shell scripts can also be used as you would any programming language. For example, a script can produce different results based on giving it different input. This section describes how to use compound commands, such as `if`/`then` statements, `case` statements, and `for`/`while` loops in your shell scripts.

The following example code assigns the string `abc` to the variable `MYSTRING`. It then tests the input to see if it equals `abc` and acts based on the outcome of the test. The test is the section that takes place between the brackets ([ ]):

```
MYSTRING=abc
if [ $MYSTRING = abc ] ; then
echo "The variable is abc"
fi
```

To **negate the test**, use ! = instead of = as shown in the following:

```
if [ $MYSTRING != abc ] ; then
echo "$MYSTRING is not abc";
fi
```

The following are examples of **testing for numbers**:

```
MYNUMBER=1
if [ $MYNUMBER -eq 1 ] ; then echo "MYNUMBER equals 1"; fi
if [ $MYNUMBER -lt 2 ] ; then echo "MYNUMBER <2"; fi
if [ $MYNUMBER -le 1 ] ; then echo "MYNUMBER <=1"; fi
if [ $MYNUMBER -gt 0 ] ; then echo "MYNUMBER >0"; fi
if [ $MYNUMBER -ge 1 ] ; then echo "MYNUMBER >=1"; fi
```

Let's look at some **tests on file names**. In this example, you can check whether a file exists (-e), whether it's a regular file (-f), or whether it is a directory (-d). These checks are done with if/then statements. If there is no match, then the else statement is used to produce the result.

```
filename="$HOME"
if [ -e $filename ] ; then echo "$filename exists"; fi
if [ -f "$filename" ] ; then
    echo "$filename is a regular file"
elif [ -d "$filename" ] ; then
    echo "$filename is a directory"
else
    echo "I have no idea what $filename is"
fi
```

Table 3-1 shows examples of tests you can perform on files, strings, and variables.

Table 3-1: Operators for Test Expressions

Operator	Test being performed
-a *file*	Check that the file exists (same as −e).
−b *file*	Check whether file is a special block device.
−c *file*	Check whether file is a character special (such as serial device).
−d *file*	Check whether file is a directory.
−e *file*	Check whether file exists (same as −a).
−f *file*	Check whether file exists and is a regular file (for example, not a directory, socket, pipe, link, or device file).
−g *file*	Check whether file has the set-group-id bit set.
−h *file*	Check whether file is a symbolic link (same as −L).
−k *file*	Check whether file has the sticky bit set.
−L *file*	Check whether file is a symbolic link (same as −h).
−n *string*	Check whether the string length is greater than 0 bytes.
−O *file*	Check whether you own the file.
−p *file*	Check whether the file is a named pipe.
−r *file*	Check whether the file is readable by you.

Continued

47

Table 3-1: Operators for Test Expressions (*continued*)

Operator	Test being performed
-s *file*	Check whether the file exists and is it larger than 0 bytes.
-S *file*	Check whether the file exists and is a socket.
-t *fd*	Check whether the file descriptor is connected to a terminal.
-u *file*	Check whether the file has the set-user-id bit set.
-w *file*	Check whether the file is writable by you.
-x *file*	Check whether the file is executable by you.
-z *string*	Check whether the length of the string is 0 (zero) bytes.
expr1 -a *expr2*	Check whether both the first and the second expressions are true.
expr1 -o *expr2*	Check whether either of the two expressions is true.
file1 -nt *file2*	Check whether the first file is newer than the second file (using the modification timestamp).
file1 -ot *file2*	Check whether the first file is older than the second file (using the modification timestamp).
file1 -ef *file2*	Check whether the two files are associated by a link (a hard link or a symbolic link).
var1 = *var2*	Check whether the first variable is equal to the second variable.
var1 -eq *var2*	Check whether the first variable is equal to the second variable.
var1 -ge *var2*	Check whether the first variable is greater than or equal to the second variable.
var1 -gt *var2*	Check whether the first variable is greater than the second variable.
var1 -le *var2*	Check whether the first variable is less than or equal to the second.
var1 -lt *var2*	Check whether the first variable is less than the second variable.
var1 != *var2* *var1* -ne *var2*	Check whether the first variable is not equal to the second variable.

Another frequently used construct is the case command. Using the case statement, you can test for different cases and take an action based on the result. Similar to a switch statement in programming languages, case statements can take the place of several nested if statements.

```
case "$VAR" in
   string1)
      { action1 };;
   string2)
      { action2 };;
   *)
      { default action } ;;
esac
```

You can find examples of case usage in the system start-up scripts found in the /etc/rc.d/ directory. Each initscript takes actions based on what parameter was passed to it and the selection is done via a large case construct.

The bash shell also offers **standard loop constructs**, illustrated by a few examples that follow. In the first example, all the values of the NUMBER variable (0 through 9) appear on the for line:

```
for NUMBER in 0 1 2 3 4 5 6 7 8 9
do
   echo The number is $NUMBER
done
```

In the following examples, the output from the ls command (a list of files) provides the variables that the for statement acts on:

```
for FILE in `/bin/ls`; do echo $FILE; done
```

Instead of feeding the whole list of values to a for statement, you can increment a value and **continue through a while loop until a condition is met**. In the following example, VAR begins as 0 and the while loop continues to increment until the value of VAR becomes 3:

```
VAR=0
while [ $VAR -lt 3 ]; do
   echo $VAR
   VAR=$[$VAR+1]
Done
```

Another way to get the same result as the while statement just shown is to use the until statement, as shown in the following example:

```
VAR=0
until [ $VAR -eq 3 ]; do echo $VAR; VAR=$[$VAR+1]; done
```

If you are just starting with shell programming, refer to the Bash Guide for Beginners (`http://tldp.org/LDP/Bash-Beginners-Guide/html/index.html`). Use that guide, along with reference material such as the `bash` man page, to step through many examples of shell scripting techniques. If you use the C shell (`csh`) see Introduction to the C shell (`http://docs.freebsd.org/44doc/usd/04.csh/paper.html`) for further information.

Summary

Despite improvements in graphical user interfaces, the shell is still the most common method for power users to work with BSD systems. The `csh` and `sh` shells are used by default for the root user and regular users, respectively. These days, many people also use the Bourne Again Shell (`bash`) with BSD and other UNIX-like systems. It includes many helpful features for recalling commands (history), completing commands, assigning aliases, and redirecting output from and input to commands. You can make powerful commands of your own using simple shell scripting techniques.

4

Working with Files

Everything in a BSD file system can be viewed as a file. This includes data files, directories, devices, named pipes, links, and other types of files. Associated with each file is a set of information that determines who can access the file and how they can access it. This chapter covers many commands for exploring and working with files.

Understanding File Types

Directories and regular files are by far the file types you will use most often. However, there are several other types of files you will encounter as you use BSD. From the command line, there are many ways you can create, find, and list different types of files.

Files that provide access to the hardware components on your computer are referred to as *device files*. There are character and block devices. There are *hard links* and *soft links* you can use to make the same file accessible from different locations. Less often used directly by regular users are *named pipes* and *sockets*, which provide access points for processes to communicate with each other.

Using Regular Files

Regular files consist of data files (documents, music, images, archives, and so on) and commands (binaries and scripts). You can determine the type of a file using the `file` command. In the following example, you change to the directory containing bash shell documentation and use file to view some of the file types in that directory:

```
$ cd /usr/local/share/doc/libogg
$ file *
framing.html:     HTML document text
ogg:              directory
```

```
rfc3533.txt:      ASCII English text
stream.png:       PNG image data, 592 x 37, 8-bit colormap, non-interlaced
  ...
```

The `file` command that was run shows document and image files of different formats, related to libogg. It can look inside the files and determine that a file contains text with HTML markup (used in web pages), plain text, or an image. There is even a subdirectory shown (ogg).

Creating regular files can be done by any application that can save its data. If you just want to **create some blank files to start with**, there are many ways to do that. Here are two examples:

```
$ touch /tmp/newfile.txt          Create a blank file
$ cat /dev/null > /tmp/newfile2.txt   Create an empty file
```

Doing **a long list on a file is another way to determine its file type.** For example:

```
$ ls -l /tmp/newfile2.txt     List a file to see its type
-rw-rw-r--  1 chris chris 0 Sep 5 14:19 newfile2
```

A dash in the first character of the 10-character permission information (`-rw-rw-r--`) indicates that the item is a regular file. (Permissions are explained in the "Setting File and Directory Permissions" section later in this chapter.) Commands are also regular files, but are usually saved as executables. Here are some examples:

```
$ ls -l /usr/bin/apropos
-r-xr-xr-x  1 root wheel 2248 Jan 12 2007 /usr/bin/apropos
$ file /usr/bin/apropos
/usr/bin/apropos: Bourne shell script text executable
$ file /bin/ls
/bin/ls: ELF 32-bit LSB executable, Intel 80386, version 1 (FreeBSD), for
FreeBSD 6.3, dynamically linked (uses shared libs), stripped
```

You can see that the apropos command is executable by the x settings for owner, group, and others. By running `file` on apropos, you can see that it is a shell script. That's opposed to a binary executable, such as the ls command indicated above.

Using Directories

A *directory* is a container for files and subdirectories. Directories are set up in a hierarchy from the root (/) down to multiple subdirectories, each separated by a slash (/). Directories are called *folders* when you access them from graphical file managers.

To create new directories for storing your data, you can use the `mkdir` command. Here are examples of using `mkdir` to **create directories in different ways:**

```
$ mkdir /tmp/new            Create "new" directory in /tmp
$ mkdir -p /tmp/a/b/c/new   Create parent directories as needed for "new"
$ mkdir -m 700 /tmp/new2    Create new2 with drwx------ permissions
```

The first `mkdir` command simply adds the new directory to the existing /tmp directory. The second example creates directories as needed (subdirectories a, b, and c) to create the resulting new directory. The last command adds the -m option to set directory permissions as well.

You can **identify the file as a directory** because the first character in the 10-character permission string for a directory is a d:

```
$ file /tmp/new
/tmp/new: directory
$ ls -ld /tmp/new
drwxr-xr-x  2 chris chris 4096 Sep  5 14:53  /tmp/new
```

Note also that the execute bits (x) must be on, if you want people to be able to use the directory as their current directories.

Using Symbolic and Hard Links

Instead of copying files and directories to different parts of the file system, links can be set up to access that same file from multiple locations. BSD supports both *soft links* (usually called *symbolic links*) and *hard links*.

When you try to open a *symbolic link* that points to a file or change to one that points to a directory, the command you run acts on the file or directory that is the target of that link. The target has its own set of permissions and ownership that you cannot see from the symbolic link. The symbolic link can exist on a different disk partition than the target. In fact, the symbolic link can exist, even if the target doesn't.

> **NOTE** *When you use commands such as* tar *to backup files that include symbolic links, there are ways of choosing whether or not the actual file the symbolic link points to is archived. If you do back up the actual file, restoring the file can cause the link to be overwritten (which may not be what you want). See the* tar *man page for details on different ways of backing up symbolic links.*

A hard link can only be used on files (not directories) and is basically a way of giving multiple names to the same physical file. Every physical file has at least one hard link, which is commonly thought of as the file itself. Any additional names (hard links) that point to that single physical file must be on the same partition as the original target file (in fact, one way to tell that files are hard links is that they all have the same inode number). Changing permission, ownership, date/timestamp, or content of any hard link to a file results in all others being changed as well. However, deleting one link will not remove the file; it will continue to exist until the last link, or technically the last inode, to the file is deleted.

Here are some examples of using the `ln` command to **create hard and symbolic links**:

```
$ touch myfile
$ ln myfile myfile-hardlink
$ ln -s myfile myfile-symlink
```

```
$ ls -li myfile*
292007 -rw-rw-r-- 3 francois francois 0 Mar 25 00:07 myfile
292007 -rw-rw-r-- 3 francois francois 0 Mar 25 00:07 myfile-hardlink
292008 lrwxr-xr-x 2 francois francois 6 Mar 25 00:09 myfile-symlink -> myfile
```

Note that after creating the hard and symbolic link files, we used the `ls -li` command to list the results. The `-li` option shows the inodes associated with each file. You can see that `myfile` and `myfile-hardlink` both have the inode number of 292007 (signifying the exact same file on the hard disk). The `myfile-symlink` symbolic link has a different inode number. And although the hard link simply appears as a file (-), the symbolic link is identified as a link (l) with wide-open permissions. You won't know if you can access the file the symbolic link points to until you try it or list the link target.

Using Device Files

When applications need to communicate with your computer's hardware, they direct data to *device files*. By convention, device files are stored in the /dev directory. Historically, devices were generally divided into block devices (such as storage media) and character devices (such as serial ports and terminal devices). FreeBSD, however, uses only character devices to communicate with the hardware.

Here are examples of device files:

```
$ ls -l /dev/*            List devices
crw-r----- 1 root   operator  0,  94 Jan 29 19:12 acd0    CD drive
crw-r----- 1 root   operator  0,  85 Jan 29 19:12 ad0     Hard Drive
crw--w---- 1 chris  tty       0, 100 Jan 31 06:07 ttyp0   Remote login terminal
crw------- 1 chris  tty       0,  60 Jan 30 07:18 ttyv0   First virtual terminal
crw------- 1 root   wheel     0,  61 Jan 29 19:12 ttyv1   Second virtual terminal
```

Using Named Pipes and Sockets

When you want to allow one process to send information to another process, you can simply pipe (|) the output from one to the input of the other. However, to provide a presence in the file system from which a process can communicate with other processes, you can create *named pipes* or *sockets*. Named pipes are typically used for interprocess communication on the local system while sockets can be used for processes to communicate over a network.

Named pipes and sockets are often set up by applications in the /tmp directory. Here are some examples of named pipes and sockets:

```
$ ls -l /tmp/.TV-chris/tvtimefifo-local /tmp/.X11-unix/X0
prw------- 1 chris chris 0 Sep 26  2007 /tmp/.TV-chris/tvtimefifo-local
srwx------ 1 chris wheel 0 Sep  4 01:30 /tmp/fam-chris/fam-
```

The first listing is a named pipe set up by a TV card player (note the p at the beginning indicating a named pipe). The second listing is a socket set up for interprocess communications.

To **create your own named pipe**, use the mkfifo command as follows:

```
$ mkfifo mypipe
$ ls -l mypipe
prw-r--r--  1 chris chris 0 Sep 26 00:57 mypipe
```

To find out what sockets are currently active on your system, use the sockstat command as follows:

```
$ sockstat
USER       COMMAND    PID    FD PROTO LOCAL ADDRESS       FOREIGN ADDRESS
chris      gnome-term 6514   3  stream -> /tmp/.X11-unix/X0
chris      gnome-term 6514   10 stream -> /tmp/.ICE-unix/2373
root       syslogd    557    4  dgram  /var/run/log
root       syslogd    557    5  dgram  /var/run/logpriv
root       devd       501    4  stream /var/run/devd.pipe
```

Unless you are developing applications, you probably won't need to create named pipes or sockets. Another way to find where named pipes and sockets exist on your system is to use the -type option to the find command, as described later in this chapter.

Setting File and Directory Permissions

The ability to access files, run commands, and change to a directory can be restricted with permission settings for user, group, and other users. When you do a long list (ls -l) of files and directories, the beginning 10 characters shown indicate what the item is (file, directory, character device, and so on) along with whether or not the item can be read, written, or executed. Figure 4-1 illustrates the meaning of those 10 characters.

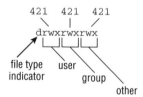

Figure 4-1: Read, write, and execute permissions are set for files and directories.

55

To follow along with examples in this section, create a directory called /tmp/test and a file called /tmp/test/hello.txt. Then do a long listing of those two items, as follows:

```
$ mkdir /tmp/test
$ echo "some text" > /tmp/test/hello.txt
$ ls -ld /tmp/test/ /tmp/test/hello.txt
drwxrwxr-x  2 francois wheel 4096 Mar 21 13:11 /tmp/test
-rw-r--r--  2 francois wheel   10 Mar 21 13:11 /tmp/test/hello.txt
```

After creating the directory and file, the first character of the long listing shows /tmp/test as a directory (d) and hello.txt as a file (-). Other types of files available in BSD that would appear as the first character include character devices (c), block devices (b) or symbolic links (1), named pipes (p), and sockets (s).

The next nine characters represent the permissions set on the file and directory. The first rwx indicates that the owner (francois) has read, write, and execute permissions on the directory. Likewise, the group wheel has the same permission (rwx). Then all other users have only read and execute permission (r-x); the dash indicates the missing write permission. For the hello.txt file, the user and group have read permission (r--) and others have read permission (r--).

When you set out to change permissions, each permission can be represented by an octal number (where read is 4, write is 2, and execute is 1) or a letter (rwx). Generally speaking, read permission lets you view the contents of the directory, write lets you change (add or modify) the contents of the directory, and execute lets you change to (in other words, access) the directory.

If you don't like the permissions you see on files or directories you own, you can change those permissions using the chmod command.

Changing Permissions with chmod

The chmod command lets you change the access permissions of files and directories. Table 4-1 shows several chmod command lines and how access to the directory or file changes.

Table 4-1: Changing Directory and File Access Permission

chmod command (octal or letters)	Original Permission	New Permission	Description
chmod 0700	any	drwx------	The directory's owner can read or write files in that directory as well as change to it. All other users (except root) have no access.

Table 4-1: Changing Directory and File Access Permission (*continued*)

chmod command (octal or letters)	Original Permission	New Permission	Description
chmod 0711	any	drwx--x--x	Same for owner. All others can change to directory, but not view or change files in the directory. This can be useful for server hardening, where you prevent someone from listing directory contents, but allow access to a file in the directory if someone already knows it's there.
chmod go+r chmod 0777	drwx------	drwxr--r--	Adding read permission to a directory may not give desired results. Without execute on, others can't view the contents of any files in that directory.
chmod a=rwx chmod 0000	any	drwxrwxrwx	All permissions are wide open.
chmod a-rwx	any	d---------	All permissions are closed. Good to protect a directory from errant changes. However, backup programs that run as non-root may fail to back up the directory's contents.
chmod 666	any	-rw-rw-rw-	Open read/write permissions completely on a file.
chmod go-rw	-rw-rw-rw-	-rw-------	Don't let anyone except owner view, change, or delete the file.
chmod 644	any	-rw-r--r--	Only the owner can change or delete the file, but all can view it.

The first 0 in the mode line can usually be dropped (so you can use 777 instead of 0777). That placeholder has special meaning. It is an octal digit that can be used on commands (executables) to indicate that the command can run as a set-UID program (4), run as a set-GID program (2), or become a *sticky* program (1). With set-UID and set-GID, the command runs with the assigned user or group permissions (instead of running with permission of the user or group that launched the command).

> **WARNING!** *SUID should not be used on shell scripts. A shell script that is owned by the root user is vulnerable to being exploited, resulting in an attacker gaining access to a shell with root user permissions.*

Having the sticky bit on for a directory keeps users from removing or renaming files from that directory that they don't own (/tmp is an example). Given the right permission settings, however, users can change the contents of files they don't own in a sticky bit directory. The final permission character is t instead of x on a sticky directory. A command with sticky bit on used to cause the command to stay in memory, even while not being used. This is an old UNIX feature that is not supported in most modern BSD, UNIX, and Linux systems.

The -R option is a handy feature of the chmod command. With -R, you can **recursively change permissions of all files and directories starting from a point in the file system.** Here are some examples:

```
# chmod -R 700 /tmp/test    Open permission only to owner below /tmp/test
# chmod -R 000 /tmp/test    Close all permissions below /tmp/test
# chmod -R a+rwx /tmp/test Open all permissions to all below /tmp/test
```

Note that the -R option is inclusive of the directory you indicate. So the permissions above, for example, would change for the /tmp/test directory itself, and not just for the files and directories below that directory.

Setting the umask

Permissions given to a file or directory are assigned originally at the time that item is created. How those permissions are set is based on the user's current *umask* value. Using the umask command, you can **set the permissions given to files and directories** when you create them.

```
$ umask 0066    Make directories drwx--x--x and files -rw-------
$ umask 0077    Make directories drwx------ and files -rw-------
$ umask 0022    Make directories drwxr-xr-x and files -rw-r--r--
$ umask 0777    Make directories d--------- and files ----------
```

Changing Ownership

When you create a file or directory, your user account is assigned to that file or directory. So is your primary group. As root user, you can **change the ownership (user) and group assigned to a file to a different user or group** using the chown and chgrp commands. Here are some examples:

```
# chown chris test/          Change owner to chris
# chown chris:market test/   Change owner to chris and group to market
# chgrp market test/         Change group to market
# chown -R chris test/       Change all files below test/ to owner chris
```

The recursive option to chown (-R) just shown is useful if you need to change the ownership of an entire directory structure. As with chmod, using chown recursively changes permissions for the directory named, along with its contents. You might use chown recursively when a person leaves a company or stops using your web service. You can use chown -R to reassign their entire /home directory to a different user.

Traversing the File System

Basic commands for changing directories (cd), checking the current directory (pwd) and listing directory content (ls) are well known to even casual shell users. So this section focuses on some less-common options to those commands, as well as other lesser-known features for moving around the file system. Here are some quick examples of cd for **moving around the file system:**

```
$ cd                    Change to your home directory
$ cd $HOME              Change to your home directory
$ cd ~                  Change to your home directory
$ cd ~francois          Change to francois' home directory
$ cd -                  Change to previous working directory
$ cd $OLDPWD            Change to previous working directory (bash shell)
$ cd ~/public_html     Change to public_html in your home directory (if it
exists)
$ cd ..                 Change to parent of current directory
$ cd /usr/bin          Change to usr/bin from root directory
$ cd usr/bin           Change to usr/bin beneath current directory
```

If you want to **find out what your current directory is,** use pwd (print working directory):

```
$ pwd
/home/francois
```

Creating *symbolic links* is a way to access a file from other parts of the file system (see the section "Using Symbolic and Hard Links" earlier in this chapter for more information on symbolic and hard links). However, symbolic links can cause some confusion about how parent directories are viewed. The following commands **create a symbolic link** to the /tmp directory from your home directory and show how to tell where you are related to a linked directory:

```
$ cd $HOME
$ ln -s /tmp tmp-link
$ ls -l tmp-link
lrwxrwxrwx 1 francois francois 13 Mar 24 12:41 tmp-link -> /tmp
$ cd tmp-link/
$ pwd
/home/francois/tmp-link
$ pwd -P               Show the permanent location
/tmp
$ pwd -L               Show the link location
/home/francois/tmp-link
$ cd -L ..             Go to the parent of the link location
$ pwd
/home/francois
$ cd tmp-link
$ cd -P ..             Go to the parent of the permanent location
$ pwd
/
```

Using the -P and -L options to pwd and cd, you can **work with symbolically linked directories in their permanent or link locations**, respectively. For example, cd -L .. takes you up one level to your home directory, whereas cd -P .. takes you up one level above the permanent directory (/). Likewise, the -P and -L options to pwd show permanent and link locations.

If you use the csh or bash shells, they can remember a list of working directories for you. Such a list can be useful if you want to return to previously visited directories. That list is organized in the form of a stack. Use pushd and popd to **add and remove directories**.

```
$ pwd
/home/francois
$ pushd /usr/share/man/
/usr/share/man ~
$ pushd /var/log/
/var/log /usr/share/man ~
$ dirs
/var/log /usr/share/man ~
$ dirs -v
 0  /var/log
 1  /usr/share/man
 2  ~
$ popd
/usr/share/man ~
$ pwd
/usr/share/man
$ popd
~
$ pwd
/home/francois
```

The dirs, pushd, and popd commands can also be used to manipulate the order of directories on the stack. For example, pushd -0 pushes the last directory on the stack to the top of the stack (making it the current directory). The pushd -2 command pushes the third directory from the bottom of the stack to the top.

Copying Files

Provided you have write permission to the target directory, copying files and directories can be done with some fairly simple commands. The standard cp command will **copy a file to a new name or the same name in a new directory**, with a new timestamp associated with the new file. Other options to cp let you retain date/timestamps, copy recursively, and prompt before overwriting. Here are some examples:

```
# cd ; mkdir public_html ; touch index.html
# cp -i index.html public_html/          Copy with new timestamp
# cp -il index.html public_html/         Create hard link instead of copy
# cp -Rv public_html/ /mnt/usb/          Copy all files recursively (with
verbose)
```

The above examples show ways of copying files related to a personal web server. In the first cp example above, if an index.html file exists in public_html, you are prompted before overwriting it with the new file. In the next example, the index.html file is hard-linked to a file of the same name in the public_html directory. In that case, because both hard links point to the same file, editing the file from either location will change the contents of the file in both locations. (The link can only be done if public_html/ and your home directory are in the same file system.)

The cp -Rv command copies all files below the public_html/ directory, updating ownership and permission settings to match those of the user running the command. It also uses current date- and timestamps. If, for example, /mnt/usb represented a USB flash drive, that command would be a way to copy the contents of your personal web server to that drive.

The dd command is another way to **copy data**. This command is very powerful because on BSD systems, everything is a file, including hardware peripherals. Here is an example:

```
$ dd if=/dev/zero of=/tmp/mynullfile count=1
1+0 records in
1+0 records out
512 bytes transferred in 0.000253 secs (2022113 bytes/sec)
```

/dev/zero is a special file that generates null characters. In the example just shown, the dd command takes /dev/zero as input file and outputs to /tmp/mynullfile. The count is the number of blocks. By default, a block is 512 bytes. The result is a 512-bytes long file full of null characters. You could use less or vi to view the contents of the file. However, a better tool to view the file would be the od (Octal Dump) command:

```
$ od -vt x1 /tmp/mynullfile      View an octal dump of a file
```

Here's another example of the dd command. This time, we set the block size to 2 bytes and copied 10 blocks (20 bytes):

```
$ dd if=/dev/zero of=/tmp/mynullfile count=10 bs=2
10+0 records in
10+0 records out
20 bytes transferred in 0.000367 secs (54507 bytes/sec)
```

> **WARNING!** *The following dd commands overwrite the contents of your disk partitions. To be on the safe side, examples show data being written to USB drives. That's so you could use something like a USB memory stick, which we presume can be overwritten without harming the contents of your hard drives. Don't try these commands if you have any confusion about the devices you are dealing with.*

The following command line **clones the first partition of the second IDE drive** to the first USB drive. This can be useful for backing up a small partition to a USB memory stick. (Warning, the following command overwrites the contents of your USB drive.)

```
# dd if=/dev/ad1s1 of=/dev/da0s1
```

The next example **makes a compressed backup** of the first partition of the primary master IDE drive. Typically the partition should be unmounted before a backup such as this.

```
# umount /dev/da0s1
# dd if=/dev/da0s1 | gzip > bootpart.gz
```

The following command copies a boot image (diskboot.img) to your USB flash drive (assuming the drive appears as /dev/da0):

```
# dd if=diskboot.img of=/dev/da0
```

This example copies the Master Boot Record from the second IDE hard drive to a file named mymbrfile:

```
# dd if=/dev/ad1s1 of=mymbrfile bs=512 count=1
```

If you add the dd_rescue program to your BSD system (pkg_add -r dd_rescue) you can create an ISO image with a command that is similar to dd but has many options and much more verbose feedback:

```
# dd_rescue /dev/acd0 myimage.iso
dd_rescue: (info): ipos:      139264.0k, opos:      139264.0k, xferd:
139264.0k8.0k
                errs:           0, errxfer:       0.0k, succxfer:
139264.0k
          +curr.rate:     6702kB/s, avg.rate: 8312kB/s, avg.load: 16.6%
```

Changing File Attributes

Files and directories in BSD file systems have read, write, and execute permissions associated with user, group, and others. However, there are also other attributes that can be attached to files and directories that are specific to certain file system types.

If you have added ext2 or ext3 file systems to your BSD system (possibly for Linux compatibility) you have special attributes that you may choose to use. Tools for creating and working with ext2 and ext3 file systems are available in FreeBSD from the e2fsprogs package (pkg_add -r e2fsprogs). See Chapter 7 for information on creating and using ext2 and ext3 file systems.

You can **list ext2/ext3 attributes** with the lsattr command. Most attributes are obscure and not turned on by default. Here's an example of using lsattr to see some files' attributes:

```
# lsattr /mnt/usb/*
------------- /mnt/usb/01.txt
------------- /mnt/usb/02.txt
------------- /mnt/usb/03.txt
------------- /mnt/usb/04.txt
$ lsattr -aR /tmp/ | less       Recursively list all /tmp attributes
```

The dashes represent 13 ext2/ext3 attributes that can be set. None are on by default. Those attributes are the following: a (append only), c (compressed), d (no dump), i (immutable), j (data journaling), s (secure deletion), t (no tail-merging), u (undeletable), A (no atime updates), D (synchronous directory updates), S (synchronous updates), and T (top of directory hierarchy). You can **change these attributes** using the `chattr` command. Here are some examples:

```
# chattr +i /mnt/usb/01.txt
$ chattr +a /mnt/usb/02.txt
$ chattr +d /mnt/usb/03.txt
$ lsattr /mnt/usb/*.txt
----i--------  /mnt/usb/01.txt
-----a-------  /mnt/usb/02.txt
------d------  /mnt/usb/03.txt
```

As shown in the preceding example, with the +i option set, the 01.txt file becomes immutable, meaning that it can't be deleted, renamed, changed, or have a link created to it. Here, this prevents any arbitrary changes to that file. (The root user can't even remove an immutable file without agreeing to override the i attribute.) With +a set, a file can only be appended to and not deleted. If you use the dump command to back up your ext2/ext3 file systems, the +d option can prevent selected files from being backed up.

To **remove an attribute** with `chatter`, use the minus sign (-). For example:

```
# chattr -i /mnt/usb/01.txt
```

> **NOTE** *Crackers who successfully break into a machine will often replace some system binaries (such as* `ls` *or* `ps`*) with corrupt versions and make them immutable. It's a good idea to occasionally check the attributes set for your executables (in* /bin, /usr/bin, /sbin, *and* /usr/sbin, *for example).*

Searching for Files

Your BSD system can be configured to keep a database of all the files in the file system (with a few exceptions defined in /etc/locate.rc) by periodically running the /usr/libexec/locate.updatedb script. The locate command enables you to search that database. The results come back instantly, since the database is searched and not the actual file system. Before locate was available, most BSD users ran the find command to find files in the file system. Both locate and find are covered here.

Generating the locate Database

You can generate the locate database by running the following script:

```
$ /usr/libexec/locate.updatedb
```

63

Note that by running this script as a regular user, the database will only include files that are accessible to all users, as well as that user in particular. You can run this script as root user to gather all files on your computer. But that could pose a security risk by allowing non-root users to see files you might otherwise want hidden from their sites.

After you run the `locate.updatedb` script, the `/var/db/locate.database` is created. You could add that script to a cron job to run periodically. You are now ready to use the `locate` command to search for files.

Finding Files with locate

Because the database contains the name of every node in the file system, and not just commands, you can use `locate` to find commands, devices, man pages, data file or anything else identified by a name in the file system. Here is an example:

```
$ locate atapifd
...
/boot/kernel/atapifd.ko
...
```

The above example found the atapi.ko kernel module. `locate` is case sensitive unless you use the `-i` option. Here's an example:

```
$ locate -i ImageMagick-6
/usr/local/share/ImageMagick-6.3.6
/usr/local/share/ImageMagick-6.3.6/ChangeLog
...
```

Here are some examples using `locate` with regular expressions and with output limits:

```
$ locate *atapi*ko          Locate files with atapi and ko in the name
...
/boot/kernel/atapicam.ko
/boot/kernel/atapicd.ko
/boot/kernel/atapifd.ko
/boot/kernel/atapist.ko
$ locate -l 5 kernel        Limit number of files found to five
/boot/kernel
/boot/kernel/3dfx.ko
/boot/kernel/3dfx_linux.ko
/boot/kernel/aac.ko
/boot/kernel/aac_linux.ko
locate: [show only 5 lines]
```

You can find information about the location and size of the locate database as follows:

```
$ locate -S
Database: /var/db/locate.database
Compression: Front: 21.64%, Bigram: 61.00%, Total: 15.57%
Filenames: 276585, Characters: 13071602, Database size: 2035326
Bigram characters: 793708, Integers: 9379, 8-Bit characters: 0
```

To **update the locate database immediately,** run the `locate.updatedb` command again manually:

```
$ /usr/libexec/locate.updatedb
```

Locating Files with find

Before the days of `locate`, the way to find files was with the `find` command. Although `locate` will come up with a file faster, `find` has many other powerful options for finding files based on attributes other than the name.

> **NOTE** *Searching the entire file system can take a long time to complete. Before searching the whole file system, consider searching a subset of the file system or excluding certain directories or remotely mounted file systems.*

This example searches the root file system (/) recursively for files named `wlan_wep.ko`:

```
$ find / -name "wlan_wep.ko" -print
find: /tmp/fam-root: Permission denied
find: /usr/local/etc/samba: Permission denied
/usr/share/man/man4/wlan_wep.4.gz
/usr/share/man/cat4/wlan_wep.4.gz
/boot/kernel/wlan_wep.ko
```

Running `find` as a normal user can result in long lists of `Permission denied` as `find` tries to enter a directory you do not have permissions to. You can **filter out the inaccessible directories:**

```
$ find / -name wlan_wep.ko 2>&1 | grep -v "Permission denied"
```

Or **send all errors to the /dev/null** bit bucket:

```
$ find / -name wlan_wep.ko 2> /dev/null
```

Because searches with `find` are case sensitive and must match the name exactly (`wlan_wep.ko` won't match other instances of `wlan_wep`), you can **use regular expressions to make your searches more inclusive.** Here's an example:

```
$ find / -name 'wlan_wep*' 2> /dev/null
/boot/kernel/wlan_wep.ko
/boot/GENERIC/wlan_wep.ko
/usr/share/man/man4/wlan_wep.4.gz
...
```

You can also **find files based on timestamps.** This command line finds files in `/usr/bin/` that have been accessed in the past two minutes:

```
$ find /usr/bin/ -amin -2
/usr/bin/
/usr/bin/find
```

This finds files that have not been accessed in /home/chris for over 60 days:

```
$ find /home/chris/ -atime +60
```

Use the -type d option to find directories. The following command line finds all directories under /etc and redirects stderr to the bit bucket (/dev/null):

```
$ find /etc -type d -print 2> /dev/null
```

This command line finds files in /sbin with permissions that match 555:

```
$ find /sbin/ -perm 555
/sbin/adjkerntz
/sbin/atacontrol
...
```

The exec option to find is very powerful, because it lets you **act on the files found with the find command**. The following command finds all the files in /var owned by the user francois (must be a valid user) and executes the ls -l command on each one:

```
$ find /var -user francois -exec ls -l {} \;
```

An alternative to the find command's exec option is xargs:

```
$ find /var -user francois | xargs ls -l
```

There are big differences on how the two commands just shown operate, leading to very different performance. The find -exec spawns the command ls for each result it finds. The xargs command works more efficiently by passing many results as input to a single ls command.

To **negate a search criterion**, place an exclamation point (!) before that criterion. The next example finds all the files that are not owned by the group root and are regular files, and then does an ls -l on each:

```
$ find / ! -group wheel -type f  2> /dev/null | xargs ls -l
```

The next example finds the files in /sbin that are regular files and are not executable by others, then feeds them to an ls -l command:

```
$ find /sbin/ -type f ! -perm o+x  | xargs ls -l
```

Finding files by size is a great way to determine what is filling up your hard disks. The following command line finds all files that are greater than 10 MB (+10M), lists those files from largest to smallest (ls -lS) and directs that list to a file (/tmp/bigfiles.txt):

```
$ find / -xdev -size +10M  | xargs ls -lS > /tmp/bigfiles.txt
```

In this example, the -xdev option prevents any mounted file systems, besides the root file system, from being searched. This is a good way to keep the find command from searching special file systems (such as the /proc file system, if that is mounted) and any remotely mounted file systems, as well as other locally mounted file systems.

Using Other Commands to Find Files

Other commands for finding files include the whereis and which commands. Here are some examples of those commands:

```
$ whereis man
man: /usr/bin/man /usr/share/man/man1/man1.gz
```

The whereis command is useful because it not only finds commands, it also **finds man pages and configuration files associated with a command**. From the example of whereis for the word man, you can see the man executable, its configuration file, and the location of man pages for the man command. The which command is useful when you're looking for the actual location of an executable file in your PATH, as in this example:

```
$ pkg_info -W `which mkfs.ext2`
/usr/local/sbin/mkfs.ext2 was installed by package e2fsprogs-1.40.2_1
```

Finding Out More About Files

Now that you know how to find files, you can get more information about those files. Using less-common options to the ls command lets you list information about a file that you won't see when you run ls without options. Commands such as file help you identify a file's type. With md5sum and sha1sum, you can verify the validity of a file.

Listing Files

Although you are probably quite familiar with the ls command, you may not be familiar with many of the useful options for ls that can help you find out a lot about the files on your system. Here are some examples of **using ls to display long lists** (-1) of files and directories:

```
$ ls -l      Files and directories in current directory
$ ls -la     Includes files/directories beginning with dot (.)
$ ls -lt     Orders files by time recently changed
$ ls -lS     Orders files by size (largest first)
$ ls -li     Lists the inode associated with each file
$ ls -ln     List numeric user/group IDs, instead of names
$ ls -lh     List file sizes in human-readable form (K, M, etc.)
$ ls -lR     List files recursively, from current and subdirectories
```

67

When you list files, there are also ways to **have different types of files appear differently** in the listing:

```
$ ls -F                          Add a character to indicate file type
BSD6.2@      BSD7/   memo.txt   pipefile|   script.sh* xpid.socket=
$ ls -G                          Show file types as different colors
$ ls -C                          Show files listing in columns
```

In the -F example, the output shows several different file types. The BSD6.2@ indicates a symbolic link to a directory, BSD7/ is a regular directory, memo.txt is a regular file (no extra character), pipefile| is a named pipe (created with mkfifo), script.sh* is an executable file, and xpid.socket= is a socket. The next two examples display different file types in different colors and list output in columns, respectively.

Verifying Files

When files such as software packages and CD or DVD images are shared over the Internet, often a sha1sum or md5sum file is published with it. Those files contain checksums that can be used to make sure that the file you downloaded is exactly the one that the repository published.

The following are examples of downloading an ISO image file, then using the md5 and sha256 commands to **verify checksums of the file**:

```
$ wget -c
ftp://ftp.freebsd.org/pub/FreeBSD/releases/i386/ISO-IMAGES/6.3/6.3-RELEASE-i386-
disc1.iso
$ md5 6.3-RELEASE-i386-disc1.iso
MD5 (6.3-RELEASE-i386-disc1.iso) =
      cdb0dfa4b2db3e4c9cc19138f4fb2ada
$ sha256 6.3-RELEASE-i386-disc1.iso
SHA156 (6.3-RELEASE-i386-disc1.iso) =
      15081a56d184a18c7cc3a5c3cd0d7d5b7d9304c9cc1d5fc40d875b0fd3047721
```

Which command you choose depends on whether the provider of the file you are checking distributed md5sum or sha1sum information. FreeBSD offers both md5 and sha1 files. For example, here is what the CHECKSUM.MD5 file for the FreeBSD 6.3 distribution looked like:

```
MD5 (6.3-RELEASE-i386-bootonly.iso) = ab1db0ae643e8c12ddbe855f533b8fae
MD5 (6.3-RELEASE-i386-disc1.iso) = cdb0dfa4b2db3e4c9cc19138f4fb2ada
MD5 (6.3-RELEASE-i386-disc2.iso) = e73a3d9cf5f3bfbf07384ef0a93ae5d5
MD5 (6.3-RELEASE-i386-disc3.iso) = 123840107a5578ce22875c440d41f453
MD5 (6.3-RELEASE-i386-docs.iso) = 17aa87ccfb01f4453d8ce078874029ab
```

With all the ISO files listed in this CHECKSUM.MD5 file contained in the current directory, you can **verify them all at once** using the -c option and the Linux-compatible md5sum command. Here is an example:

```
$ /usr/compat/linux/usr/bin/md5sum -c CHECKSUM.MD5
6.3-RELEASE-i386-bootonly.iso: OK
6.3-RELEASE-i386-disc1.iso: OK
6.3-RELEASE-i386-disc2.iso: OK
6.3-RELEASE-i386-disc3.iso: OK
6.3-RELEASE-i386-docs.iso: OK
```

To **verify only one of the files listed** in the checksum file, you could do something like the following:

```
$ grep bootonly CHECKSUM.MD5 | /usr/compat/linux/usr/bin/md5sum -c
6.3-RELEASE-i386-bootonly.iso: OK
```

If you had a SHA1SUM file instead of an MD5SUM file to check against, you could use the sha1sum command in the same way. By combining the find command described earlier in this chapter with the m5 command, you can verify any part of your file system. For example, here's how to **create an MD5 checksum for every file in the /etc directory** so they can be checked later to see if any have changed:

```
# find /etc -type f -exec md5 {} \; 2>/dev/null > /tmp/md5.list
```

The result of the previous command line is a /tmp/md5.list file that contains a 128-bit checksum for every file in the /etc directory. Later, you could type the following command to see if any of those files have changed:

```
# cd /etc
# /usr/compat/linux/usr/bin/md5sum -c /tmp/md5.list | grep -v 'OK'
./hosts.allow: FAILED
md5sum: WARNING: 1 of 1668 computed checksums did NOT match
```

As you can see from the output only one file changed (hosts.allow). So the next step is to check the changed file and see if the changes to that file were intentional.

Summary

There are dozens of commands for exploring and working with files in BSD. Commands such as chmod can change the permissions associated with a file, whereas commands that include lsattr and chattr can be used to list and change file attributes that are associated with ext2 and ext3 file system types.

To move around the file system, people use the cd command most often. However, to move repeatedly among the same directories, you can use the pushd and popd commands to work with a stack of directories.

Copying files is done with the cp command. However, the dd command can be used to copy files (such as disk images) from a device (such as a CD-ROM drive). For creating directories, you can use the mkdir command.

Instead of keeping multiple copies of a file around on the file system, you can use symbolic links and hard links to have multiple file names point to the same file or directory. Symbolic links can be anywhere in the file system, whereas hard links must exist on the same partition that the original file is on.

To search for files, BSD systems offer the locate and find commands. To verify the integrity of files you download from the Internet, you can use the md5, sha256, md5sum, and sha1sum commands.

5

Manipulating Text

With only a shell available on the first UNIX systems (on which BSD systems were based), using those systems meant dealing primarily with commands and plain text files. Documents, program code, configuration files, e-mail, and almost anything you created or configured was represented by text files. To work with those files, developers created many text manipulation tools.

Despite having graphical tools for working with text, most seasoned BSD users find command line tools to be more efficient and convenient. Text editors such as vi (vim), Emacs, JOE, nano, and Pico are available with most BSD distributions. Commands such as `grep`, `sed`, and `awk` can be used to find, and possibly change, pieces of information within text files.

This chapter explains how to use many popular commands for working with text files in BSD systems. It also explores some of the less common uses of text manipulation commands that you might find interesting.

Matching Text with Regular Expressions

Many of the tools for working with text enable you to use *Regular Expressions*, sometimes referred to as *regex*, to identify the text you are looking for based on some pattern. You can use these strings to find text within a text editor or use them with search commands to scan multiple files for the strings of text you want.

A RegEx search pattern can include a specific string of text (as in a word such as *UNIX*) or a location (such as end of a line or beginning of a word). It can also be specific (find just the word *hello*) or more inclusive (find any word beginning with *h* and ending with *o*).

Appendix C includes reference information for shell metacharacters that can be used in conjunction with Regular Expressions to do the exact kinds of matches you are looking for. This section shows examples of using Regular Expressions with several different tools you encounter throughout this chapter.

Table 5-1 shows some examples using basic Regular Expressions to match text strings.

Table 5-1: Matching Using Regular Expressions

Expression	Matches
a*	a, ab, abc, aecjejich
^a	Any "a" appearing at the beginning of a line
*a$	Any "a" appearing at the end of a line
a.c	3-character strings that begin with a and end with c
[bcf]at	bat, cat, or fat
[a-d]at	aat, bat, cat, dat, but not Aat, Bat, and so on
[A-D]at	Aat, Bat, Cat, Dat, but not aat, bat, and so on
1[3-5]7	137, 147, and 157
\tHello	A tab character preceding the word Hello
\.[tT][xX][Tt]	.txt, .TXT, .TxT or other case combinations

Many examples of Regular Expressions are used in examples throughout this chapter. Keep in mind that not every command that incorporates RegEx uses its features the same way.

Editing Text Files

There are many text editors in the BSD/UNIX world. The most common editor is vi, which can be found on virtually any UNIX system available today. That is why knowing how to at least make minor file edits in vi is a critical skill for any BSD administrator. One day, if you find yourself in a minimalist, foreign BSD, Linux, or other UNIX environment, trying to bring a server back online, vi is the tool that will almost always be there.

On FreeBSD, an improved version of vi is available called vim (install the vim6 package to get it). Vim (Vi IMproved) with the vim6 package will provide the most up-to-date, feature-rich, and user-friendly vi editor. For more details about using vi and vim, refer to Appendix A.

Traditionally, the other popular UNIX text editor has been Emacs and its more graphical variant, XEmacs. Emacs is a powerful multi-function tool that can also act as a mail/news reader or shell, and perform other functions. Emacs is also known for its very complex series of keyboard shortcuts that require three arms to execute properly.

In the mid-1990s, Emacs was ahead of vi in terms of features. Now that Vim is widely available, both can provide all the text-editing features you'll ever need. If you are not already familiar with either vi or Emacs, we recommend you start by learning vi.

Many other command line and GUI text editors are available for BSD systems. Text-based editors that you may find to be simpler than vi and Emacs include JED, JOE, and nano. Start any of those editors by typing its command name, optionally followed by the file name you want to edit. The following sections offer some quick descriptions of how to use each of those editors.

Using the JOE Editor

If you have used classic word processors such as WordStar that worked with text files, you might be comfortable with the JOE editor. To use JOE, install the joe package (as root, type `pkg_add -r joe`). To use the spell checker in JOE, install the aspell package.

With JOE, instead of entering a command or text mode, you are always ready to type. To move around in the file, you can use control characters or the arrow keys. To open a text file for editing, just type **joe** and the file name or use some of the following options:

```
$ joe memo.txt                        Open memo.txt for editing
$ joe -wordwrap memo.txt              Turn on wordwrap while editing
$ joe -lmargin 5 -tab 5 memo.txt      Set left margin to 5 and tab to 5
$ joe +25 memo.txt                    Begin editing on line 25
```

To add text, just begin typing. You can use keyboard shortcuts for many functions. Use arrow keys to move the cursor left, right, up, or down. Use the Delete key to delete text under the cursor or the Backspace key to erase text to the left of the cursor. Press Enter to add a line break. Press Ctrl+K+H to see the help screen. Table 5-2 shows the most commonly used control keys for editing in JOE.

Table 5-2: Control Keys for Editing with JOE

Key Combo	Result
Cursor	
Ctrl+B	Left
Ctrl+P	Up

Continued

73

Table 5-2: Control Keys for Editing with JOE (*continued*)

Key Combo	Result
Cursor (*continued*)	
Ctrl+F	Right
Ctrl+N	Down
Ctrl+Z	Previous word
Ctrl+X	Next word
Search	
Ctrl+K+F	Find text
Ctrl+L	Find next
Block	
Ctrl+K+B	Begin
Ctrl+K+K	End
Ctrl+K+M	Move block
Ctrl+K+C	Copy block
Ctrl+K+W	Write block to file
Ctrl+K+Y	Delete block
Ctrl+K+/	Filter
Misc	
Ctrl+K+A	Center line
Ctrl+T	Options
Ctrl+R	Refresh
File	
Ctrl+K+E	Open new file to edit
Ctrl+K+R	Insert file at cursor
Ctrl+K+D	Save

Table 5-2: Control Keys for Editing with JOE (*continued*)

Key Combo	Result
Goto	
Ctrl+U	Previous screen
Ctrl+V	Next screen
Ctrl+A	Line beginning
Ctrl+E	End of line
Ctrl+K+U	Top of file
Ctrl+K+V	End of file
Ctrl+K+L	To line number
Delete	
Ctrl+D	Delete character
Ctrl+Y	Delete line
Ctrl+W	Delete word right
Ctrl+O	Delete word left
Ctrl+J	Delete line to right
Ctrl+-	Undo
Ctrl+6	Redo
Exit	
Ctrl+K+X	Save and quit
Ctrl+C	Abort
Ctrl+K+Z	Shell
Spell	
Ctrl+[+N	Word (install the proper spelling dictionary for this to work)
Ctrl+[+l	File (install the proper spelling dictionary for this to work)

Using the Pico and Nano Editors

Pico is a popular, very small text editor, distributed as part of the Pine e-mail client. Although Pico is free, it is not truly open source. Therefore, some BSD distributions don't offer Pico (although FreeBSD does offer Pico: `pkg_add -r pico`). As an alternative to Pico, you can use an open source clone of Pico called nano (*nano's another* editor). This section describes the nano editor (`pkg_add -r nano`).

Nano (represented by the `nano` command) is a compact text editor that runs from the shell, but is screen-oriented (owing to the fact that it is based on the curses library). Nano is popular with those who formerly used the Pine e-mail client because nano's editing features are the same as those used by Pine's Pico editor. On the rare occasion that you don't have the vi editor available on a BSD or Linux system (for example, vi isn't available when you are installing a minimal Gentoo Linux), nano may be available. On FreeBSD, nano is part of the nano package and relies on the aspell package for spell checking.

As with the JOE editor, instead of having command and typing modes, you can just begin typing. To **open a text file for editing**, just type **nano** and the file name or use some of the following options:

```
$ nano memo.txt        Open memo.txt for editing
$ nano -B memo.txt     When saving, backup previous to ~.filename
$ nano -m memo.txt     Turn on mouse to move cursor (if supported)
$ nano +83 memo.txt    Begin editing on line 83
```

As with JOE, to **add text**, just begin typing. Use arrow keys to move the cursor left, right, up, or down. Use the Delete key to delete text under the cursor or the Backspace to erase text to the left of the cursor. Press Enter to add a line break. Press Ctrl+G to read help text. Table 5-3 shows the control codes for nano that are described on the help screen.

Table 5-3: Control Keys for Editing with nano

Control Code	Function Key	Description
Ctrl+G	F1	Show help text (Press Ctrl+X to exit help)
Ctrl+X	F2	Exit nano (or close current file buffer)
Ctrl+O	F3	Save current file
Ctrl+J	F4	Justify current text in current paragraph
Ctrl+R	F5	Insert a file into current file
Ctrl+W	F6	Search for text
Ctrl+Y	F7	Go to the previous screen

Table 5-3: Control Keys for Editing with nano (*continued*)

Control Code	Function Key	Description
Ctrl+V	F8	Go to the next screen
Ctrl+K	F9	Cut (and store) the current line or marked text
Ctrl+U	F10	Uncut (paste) previously cut line into file
Ctrl+C	F11	Display current cursor position
Ctrl+T	F12	Start spell checking
Ctrl+_		Go to selected line and column numbers
Ctrl+\		Search and replace text
Ctrl+6		Mark text, starting at cursor (Ctrl+6 to unset mark)
Ctrl+F		Go forward one character
Ctrl+B		Go back one character
Ctrl+Space		Go forward one word
Alt+Space		Go backward one word
Ctrl+P		Go to previous line
Ctrl+N		Go to next line
Ctrl+A		Go to beginning of the current line
Ctrl+E		Go to end of the current line
Alt+9		Go to beginning of current paragraph
Alt+0		Go to end of current paragraph
Alt+\		Go to first line of the file
Alt+/		Go to last line of the file
Alt+]		Go to bracket matching current bracket
Alt+=		Scroll down one line
Alt+-		Scroll down up line

Graphical Text Editors

Just because you are editing text doesn't mean you have to use a text-based editor. One advantage of using a graphical text editor is that you can use a mouse to select menus, highlight text, cut and copy text, or run special plug-ins.

You can expect to have the GNOME text editor (gedit) if your BSD system has the GNOME desktop installed. Features in gedit enable you to check spelling, list document statistics, change display fonts and colors, and print your documents. The KDE desktop also has its own KDE text editor (kedit in the kdeutils package). It includes similar features to the GNOME text editor, along with a few extras, such as the ability to send the current document with kmail or another user-configurable KDE Component.

Vim itself comes with an X GUI version. It is launched with the gvim command, which is part of the vim6 package. If you'd like to turn GUI Vim into a more user-friendly text editor, you can install Cream (pkg_add -r cream).

Other text editors you can install include nedit (with features for using macros and executing shell commands) and leafpad (which is similar to the Windows Notepad text editor). The Scribes text editor (scribes) includes some advanced features for automatic correction, replacement, indentation, and word completion.

Listing, Sorting, and Changing Text

Instead of just editing a single text file, you can use a variety of BSD commands to display, search, and manipulate the contents of one or more text files at a time.

Listing Text Files

The most basic method to display the content of a text file is with the cat command. The cat command concatenates (in other words, outputs as a string of characters) the contents of a text file to your display (by default). You can then use different shell metacharacters to direct the contents of that file in different ways. For example:

```
$ cat myfile.txt                        Send entire file to the screen
$ cat myfile.txt > copy.txt             Direct file contents to another file
$ cat myfile.txt >> myotherfile.txt     Append file contents to another file
$ cat -s myfile.txt                     Discard multiple consecutive blank lines
$ cat -n myfile.txt                     Show line numbers with output
$ cat -b myfile.txt                     Show line numbers only on non-blank lines
```

However, if your block of text is more than a few lines long, using cat by itself becomes impractical. That's when you need better tools to look at the beginning, the end, or page through the entire text.

To view the top of a file, use head:

```
$ head myfile.txt
$ cat myfile.txt | head
```

Both of these command lines use the head command to output the top 10 lines of the file. You can specify the line count as a parameter to display any number of lines from the beginning of a file. For example:

```
$ head -n 50 myfile.txt          Show the first 50 lines of a file
$ ps auwx | head -n 15           Show the first 15 lines of ps output
```

This can also be done using this outdated (but shorter) syntax:

```
$ head -50 myfile.txt
$ ps auwx | head -15
```

You can use the tail command in a similar way to view the end of a file or command output:

```
$ tail -n 15 myfile.txt          Display the last 15 lines in a file
$ tail -15 myfile.txt            Display the last 15 lines in a file
$ ps auwx | tail -n 15           Display the last 15 lines of ps output
```

The tail command can also be used to continuously watch the end of a file as the file is written to by another program. This is very useful for reading live log files when troubleshooting Apache, Sendmail, or many other system services:

```
# tail -f /var/log/messages      Watch system messages live
# tail -f /var/log/maillog       Watch mail server messages live
# tail -f /var/log/auth.log      Watch login attempt messages live
```

Paging Through Text

When you have a large chunk of text and need to get to more than just its beginning or end, you need a tool to page through the text. The original UNIX system pager was the more command:

```
$ ps auwx | more       Page through the output of ps (press spacebar)
$ more myfile.txt       Page through the contents of a file
```

However, more has some limitations. For example, in the line with ps above, more could not scroll up. The less command was created as a more powerful and user-friendly more. The common saying when less was introduced was: "What is less? less is more!" We recommend you no longer use more, and use less instead.

> **NOTE**   The less command has another benefit worth noting. Unlike text editors such as vi, it does not read the entire file when it starts. This results in faster start-up times when viewing large files.

The `less` command can be used with the same syntax as `more` in the examples above:

```
$ ps auwx | less          Page through the output of ps
$ cat myfile.txt | less    Page through the contents of a file
$ less myfile.txt          Page through a text file
```

The `less` command enables you to **navigate** using the up and down arrow keys, PageUp, PageDown, and the spacebar. If you are using `less` on a file (not standard input), press v to open the current file in `vi`. As in `vi`, G takes you to the end of the file. F takes you to the end of the file, and then scrolls the file as new input is added, similar to a `tail -f`.

As in `vi`, while viewing a file with `less`, you can **search for a string** by pressing / (forward slash) followed by the string and Enter. To search for further occurrences, press / and Enter repeatedly. To search backwards, press ? followed by the search string and Enter.

To **scroll forward and back** while using `less`, use the f and b keys, respectively. For example, 10f scrolls forward ten lines and 15b scrolls back 15 lines. Type **d** to scroll down half a screen and **u** to scroll up half a screen.

Paginating Text Files with pr

The `pr` command provides a quick way to format a bunch of text into a form where it can be printed. This can be particularly useful if you want to print the results of some commands, without having to open up a word processor or text editor. With `pr`, you can **format text into pages with header information** such as date, time, file name, and page number. Here is an example:

```
$ ls /usr/ports | sort | pr -4 | less    Paginate ports directory in 4 cols
```

In this example, the `ls` command lists the contents of the /usr/ports directory and pipes that list to the `sort` command, to be sorted alphabetically. Next, that list is piped to the `pr` command, which converts the single-column list into four columns (-4) and paginates it. Finally, the `less` command enables you to page through the text.

Instead of paging through the output, you can **send the output to a file or to a printer**. Here are examples of that:

```
$ ls /usr/ports | sort | pr -4 | less > pkg.txt   Send pr output to a file
$ ls /usr/ports | sort | pr -4 | less | lpr       Send pr output to printer
```

Other **text manipulation** you can do with the `pr` command includes double-spacing the text (-d), or offsetting the text a certain number of spaces from the left margin (for example, -o 5 to indent five spaces from the left).

Searching for Text with grep

The grep command comes in handy when you need to perform more advanced string searches in a file. In fact, the phrase *to grep* has actually entered the computer jargon as a verb, just as *to Google* has entered the popular language. Here are examples of the grep command:

```
$ grep francois myfile.txt          Show lines containing francois
# grep -i ftp /etc/services          Show lines containing FTP
$ ps auwx | grep init                Show init lines from ps output
$ ps auwx | grep "\[*\]"             Show bracketed commands
$ dmesg | grep "[ ]ata\|^ata"        Show ata kernel device information
```

These command lines have some particular uses, beyond being examples of the grep command. By searching /etc/services for ftp you can see port numbers associated with FTP services. Displaying bracketed commands that are output from the ps command is a way to see commands for which ps cannot display options. The last command checks the kernel buffer ring for any ATA device information, such as hard disks and CD-ROM drives.

The grep command can also recursively search a few or a whole lot of files at the same time. The following command recursively searches (-R) files in the /usr/local/etc and /etc directories for the string ftp (-i for any case):

```
$ grep -Ri ftp /usr/local/etc /etc | less
```

Add line numbers (-n) to your grep command to find the exact lines where the search terms occur:

```
$ grep -Rin ftp /etc /usr/local/etc | less
```

To colorize the searched term in the search results, add the --color option:

```
# grep --color -Rin ftp /etc/services | less
```

By default, in a multi-file search, the file name is displayed for each search result. Use the -h option to disable the display of file names. This example searches for the string relay in the files dmesg.today, dmesg.yesterday, and so on:

```
# grep -h acpi /var/log/dmesg*
```

If you want to ignore case when you search messages, use the -i option:

```
# grep -i audio /var/log/messages    Search file for audio (any case)
```

To display only the name of the file that includes the search term, add the -l option:

```
$ grep -Ril FTP /etc
```

To display all lines that do *not* match the string, add the -v option:

```
# grep -v "#" /etc/ttys | less    Show lines that don't contain comments
```

> **NOTE** *When piping the output of* ps *into* grep, *here's a trick to prevent the* grep *process from appearing in the* grep *results:*
>
> ```
> # ps auwx | grep "[i]nit"
> ```

Checking Word Counts with wc

There are times when you need to know the number of lines that match a search string. The wc command can be used to **count the lines** that it receives. For example, the following command lists how many times a specific IP address appears in log files:

```
$ grep 192.198.1.1 /var/log/* | wc -l
```

The wc command has other uses as well. By default, wc **prints the number of lines, words and bytes in a file**:

```
$ wc /usr/local/share/doc/jpeg/README   List counts for a single file
    385    3006   19945 /usr/local/share/doc/README
$ wc /usr/local/share/doc/jpeg/*         List single counts/totals for many files
    385    3006   19945 /usr/local/share/doc/README
    118     813    5364 /usr/local/share/doc/coderules.doc
    ...
   6658   52200  339141 total
```

Sorting Output with sort

It can also be useful to **sort the content of a file or the output of a command**. This can be helpful in bringing order to disorderly output. The following examples list the names of all software packages currently installed, grabs any with gnome in the name, and sorts the results in alphanumeric order (forward and reverse):

```
$ pkg_info | grep gnome | sort      Sort in alphanumeric order
$ pkg_info | grep gnome | sort -r   Sort in reverse alphanumeric order
```

The following command **sorts processes based on descending memory usage** (fourth field of ps output). The -k option specifies the key field to use for sorting. 4,4 indicates that the fourth field and only the fourth field is a key field.

```
$ ps auwx | sort -r -k 4,4
```

The following command line **sorts loaded kernel modules in increasing size order**. The n option tells `sort` to treat the second field as a number and not a string:

```
# kldstat | sort -k 2,2n
```

Finding Text in Binaries with Strings

Sometimes you need to read the ASCII text that is inside a binary file. Occasionally, you can learn a lot about an executable that way. For those occurrences, use `strings` to **extract all the human-readable ASCII text**. Here are some examples:

```
$ strings /bin/ls | grep -i libc    Find occurrences of libc in ls
$ cat /bin/ls | strings             List all ASCII text in ls
$ strings /bin/ls                   List all ASCII text in ls
```

Replacing Text with sed

Finding text within a file is sometimes the first step towards replacing text. Editing streams of text is done using the `sed` command. The `sed` command is actually a full-blown scripting language. For the examples in this chapter, we cover basic text replacement with the `sed` command.

If you are familiar with text replacement commands in vi, `sed` has some similarities. In the following example, you would **replace only the first occurrence per line** of *francois* with *chris*. Here, `sed` takes its input from a pipe, while sending its output to stdout (your screen). The original file itself is not changed:

```
$ cat myfile.txt | sed s/francois/chris/
```

Adding a g to the end of the substitution line, as in the following command, causes every occurrence of *francois* to be changed to *chris*. Also, in the following example, input is directed from the file `myfile.txt` and output is directed to `mynewfile.txt`:

```
$ sed s/francois/chris/g < myfile.txt > mynewfile.txt
```

The next example replaces the first occurrences of `myname` on each line in the `/etc/hosts` file with `yourname`. The output is directed to the `/tmp/hosts` file.

```
$ sed 's/myname/yourname/' < /etc/hosts > /tmp/hosts
```

Although the forward slash is the `sed` command's default delimiter, you can **change the delimiter** to any other character of your choice. Changing the delimiter can make your life easier when the string contains slashes. For example, the previous command line that contains a path could be replaced with either of the following commands:

```
$ sed 's-/nsswitch.conf-/nsswitch.conf and stuff-' < /etc/hosts | grep nss
$ sed 'sD/termios.hD/termios.h and stuffD' < /etc/gettytab | grep termios
```

In the first line shown, a dash (-) is used as the delimiter. In the second case, the letter D is the delimiter.

The sed command can **run multiple substitutions at once,** by preceding each one with -e. Here, in the text streaming from myfile.txt, all occurrences of *francois* are changed to *FRANCOIS* and occurrences of *chris* are changed to *CHRIS*:

```
$ sed -e s/francois/FRANCOIS/g -e s/chris/CHRIS/g < myfile.txt
```

You can use sed to **add newline characters to a stream of text.** The following example is done from the bash shell. Where Enter appears, press the Enter key. The > is on the second line and is generated by bash, not typed in.

```
$ echo aaabccc | sed 's/b/\Enter
> /'
aaa
ccc
```

The trick just shown does not work on the left side of the sed substitution command. When you need to substitute newline characters, it's easier to use the tr command.

Translate or Remove Characters with tr

The tr command is an easy way to **do simple character translations on the fly.** In the following example, new lines are replaced with spaces, so all the files listed from the current directory are output on one line:

```
$ ls | tr '\n' ' '              Replace newline characters with spaces
```

The tr command can be used to **replace one character with another,** but does not work with strings as sed does. The following command replaces all instances of the lowercase letter f with a capital F.

```
$ tr f F < myfile.txt           Replace every f in the file with F
```

You can also use the tr command to simply **delete characters.** Here are two examples:

```
$ ls | tr -d '\n'               Delete new lines (resulting in one line)
$ tr -d f < myfile.txt          Delete every letter f from the file
```

The tr command can do some nifty tricks when you **specify ranges of characters** to work on. Here's an example of capitalizing lowercase letters to uppercase letters:

```
$ echo chris | tr a-z A-Z       Translate chris into CHRIS
CHRIS
```

The same result can be obtained with the following syntax:

```
$ echo chris | tr '[:lower:]' '[:upper:]'     Translate chris into CHRIS
```

Checking Differences Between Two Files with diff

When you have two versions of a file, it can be useful to **know the differences between the two files**. For example, when changing a configuration file, people often leave a copy of the original configuration file. When that occurs, you can use the diff command to discover which lines differ between your new configuration and the original configuration, in order to see what you have done. For example:

```
$ cp /etc/sysctl.conf /etc/sysctl.conf.backup
Make some changes to the sysctl.conf file
$ diff /etc/sysctl.conf /etc/sysctl.conf.backup
```

You can change the output of diff to what is known as *unified format*. Unified format can be easier to read by human beings. It adds three lines of context before and after each block of changed lines that it reports, and then uses + and - to show the difference between the files. The following set of commands creates a file (f1.txt) containing a sequence of numbers (1–7), creates a file (f2.txt) with one of those numbers changed (using sed), and compares the two files using the diff command (type pkg_add -r seq2 to get the seq2 command):

```
$ seq2 -s 1 -e 7 > f1.txt          Send a sequence of 7 number to f1.txt
$ cat f1.txt                       Display contents of f1.txt
1
2
3
4
5
6
7
$ sed s/4/FOUR/ < f1.txt > f2.txt   Change 4 to FOUR and send to f2.txt
$ diff f1.txt f2.txt
4c4                                 Shows line 4 was changed in file
< 4
---
> FOUR
$ diff -u f1.txt f2.txt             Display unified output of diff
--- f1.txt 2007-09-07 18:26:06.000000000 -0500
+++ f2.txt 2007-09-07 18:26:39.000000000 -0500
@@ -1,7 +1,7 @@
1
2
3
```

```
-4
+FOUR
5
6
7
```

The diff -u output just displayed adds information such as modification dates and times to the regular diff output. The sdiff command can be used to give you yet another view. The sdiff command can **merge the output of two** files interactively, as shown in the following output:

```
$ sdiff f1.txt f2.txt
1                                          1
2                                          2
3                                          3
4                                        | FOUR
5                                          5
6                                          6
7                                          7
```

Another variation on the diff theme is vimdiff, which opens the two files side by side in vim and outlines the differences in color. (As root, type pkg_add -r vim6 to install those commands.) Similarly, gvimdiff opens the two files in gvim.

The output of diff -u can be fed into the patch command. The patch command takes an old file and a diff file as input and **outputs a patched file**. Following on the example above, use the diff command between the two files to generate a patch and then apply the patch to the first file:

```
$ diff -u f1.txt f2.txt > patchfile.txt
$ patch f1.txt < patchfile.txt
Hmm...  Looks like a unified diff to me...
The text leading up to this was:
    ...
$ cat f1.txt
1
2
3
FOUR
5
6
7
```

That is how many OSS developers (including kernel developers) distribute their code patches. The patch and diff can also be run on entire directory trees. However, that usage is outside the scope of this book.

Using awk and cut to Process Columns

Another massive text processing tool is the awk command. The awk command is a
full-blown programming language. Although there is much more you can do with
the awk command, the following examples show you a few tricks related to extracting
columns of text:

```
$ ps auwx | awk '{print $1,$11}'           Show columns 1, 11 of ps
$ ps auwx | awk '/francois/ {print $11}'    Show francois' processes
$ ps auwx | grep francois | awk '{print $11}' Same as above
```

The first example displays the contents of the first column (user name) and eleventh
column (command name) from currently running processes output from the ps command (ps auwx). The next two commands produce the same output, with one using
the awk command and the other using the grep command to find all processes owned
by the user named francois. In each case, when processes owned by francois are
found, column 11 (command name) is displayed for each of those processes.

By default, the awk command assumes the delimiter between columns is spaces. You
can specify a different delimiter with the -F option as follows:

```
$ awk -F: '{print $1,$5}' /etc/passwd   Use colon delimiter to print cols
```

You can get similar results with the cut command. As with the previous awk example, we specify a colon (:) as the column delimiter to process information from the
/etc/passwd file:

```
$ cut -d: -f1,5 /etc/passwd             Use colon delimiter to print cols
```

The cut command can also be used with ranges of fields. The following command prints
columns 1 thru 5 of the /etc/passwd file:

```
$ cut -d: -f1-5 /etc/passwd             Show columns 1 through 5
```

Instead of using a dash (–) to indicate a range of numbers, you can use it to print all
columns from a particular column number and above. The following command displays all
columns from column 5 and above from the /etc/passwd file:

```
$ cut -d: -f5- /etc/passwd              Show columns 5 and later
```

We prefer to use the awk command when columns are separated by a varying number of spaces, such as the output of the ps command. And we prefer the cut command when dealing with files delimited by commas (,) or colons (:), such as the
/etc/passwd file.

Converting Text Files to Different Formats

Text files in the UNIX world use a different end-of-line character (\n) than those used in the DOS/Windows world (\r\n). You can view these special characters in a text file with the od command:

```
$ cp /etc/hosts myfile.txt
$ od -c -t x1 myfile.txt
```

So they will appear properly when copied from one environment to the other, it is necessary to **convert the files**. Here are some examples using the unix2dos and dos2unix commands (pkg_add -r unix2dos):

```
$ unix2dos < myfile.txt > mydosfile.txt
$ cat mydosfile.txt | dos2unix > myunixfile.txt
$ file mydosfile.txt myunixfile.txt
mydosfile.txt:    ASCII English text, with CRLF line terminators
myunixfile.txt:   ASCII English text
```

The unix2dos example just shown above converts a BSD or UNIX plain text file (myunixfile.txt) to a DOS or Windows text file (mydosfile.txt). The dos2unix example does the opposite by converting a DOS/Windows file to a BSD/UNIX file. Both dos2unix and unix2dos are in the unix2dos package.

Summary

BSD and UNIX systems traditionally use plain text files for system configuration, documentation, output from commands, and many forms of stored information. As a result, many commands have been created to search, edit, and otherwise manipulate plain text files. Even with today's GUI interfaces, the ability to manipulate plain text files is critical to becoming a power BSD user.

This chapter explores some of the most popular commands for working with plain text files in BSD systems. Those commands include text editors (such as vi, nano, and joe), as well as commands that can edit streaming data (such as sed and awk commands). There are also commands sorting text (sort), counting text (wc), and translating characters in text (tr).

6

Playing with Multimedia

There's no need to go to a GUI tool, if all you need to do is play a song or convert an image or audio file to a different form. There are commands for working with multimedia files (audio or images) that are quick and efficient if you find yourself working from the shell. And if you need to manipulate batches of multimedia files, the same command you use to transform one file can be added to a script to repeat the process on many files.

This chapter focuses on tools for working with audio and digital image files from the shell.

IN THIS CHAPTER

Playing music with play, ogg123, and mpg321

Adjusting audio with alsamixer and aumix

Ripping music CDs with cdparanoia

Encoding music with oggenc, flac, and lame

Converting audio files with sox

Transforming digital images with convert

Working with Audio

There are commands available for BSD systems that can manipulate files in dozens of audio formats. Commands such as ogg123, mpg321, and play can be used to listen to audio files. There are commands for ripping songs from music CDs and encoding them to store efficiently. There are even commands to let you stream audio so anyone on your network can listen to your playlist.

Starting with Audio

Your BSD system may not be configured to play sound when you first install it. If that's the case, you need to load the appropriate drivers for your sound card to work. The drivers for many popular sound cards are already included with FreeBSD. Here is a quick procedure to find and configure sound in FreeBSD:

```
# dmesg | grep -i audio        Check if your sound card was detected
pcm0: <AudioPCI ES1373-B> port 0xdf00-0xdf3f irq 6 at device 7.0 on
pci1
# lspci | grep -i audio        List PCI audio devices (from pciutils
package)
01:07.0 Multimedia audio controller: Ensoniq ES1371 [AudioPCI-97]
(rev 06)
```

Next check the /boot/defaults/loader.conf file to find the module for your card. Don't edit that file! Instead, add entries to /boot/loader.conf to **enable sound and load your sound card's driver**. In my case, I added this and rebooted:

```
sound_load="YES"           # Digital sound system
snd_es137x_load="YES"      # es137x
```

If you are not sure exactly which sound card you have, you can try loading all sound drivers with the line snd_driver_load="YES" instead of the es137x line shown above. After reboot, sound devices in /dev that should now be available include dsp, dsp0.0, audio, audio0.0, mixer0, and sndstat. (The devices you get depend on your sound card.) Type this to see if the sound module was properly configured:

```
$ cat /dev/sndstat        Check your installed audio device
FreeBSD Audio Driver (newpcm)
Installed devices:
pcm0: <AudioPCI ES1373-B> at io 0xdf00 irq 6 kld snd_es137x
     (1p/1r/0v channels duplex default)
```

Some sound commands let you enter a specific device, which is particularly useful if you have multiple sound cards or CD drives. Mixing applications use /dev/mixer0 by default. Your CD device is likely /dev/acd0. For some reason, permissions on /dev/acd0 are closed to all but root, by default. So, as root, you might need to open permissions to let regular users play music from a CD as follows:

```
$ chmod 666 /dev/acd0     Open permissions so any user can play CDs.
```

Next, check out the Adjusting Audio Levels section and then try playing some audio. For the audio players described in the rest of this section, you can install the following packages: sox, vorbis-tools, libvorbis, mpg123, and aumix. For audio ripping and encoding, you can install packages such as cdparanoia and flac. You can use pkg_add -r package to install any of those packages.

Playing Music

Depending on the audio format you want to play, several command line players are available for BSD. The play command (based on the sox facility, described later), can play audio files in multiple, freely available formats. You can use ogg123 to play popular open source music formats, including Ogg Vorbis, Free Lossless Audio Codec (FLAC) and Speex files. The mpg321 player, which is available in the FreeBSD software repository, is popular for playing MP3 music files.

Type play -h to **see audio formats and effects** available to use with play:

```
$ play -help
   ...
Supported file formats: aiff al au auto avr cdr cvs dat vms hcom la lu maud nul
ossdsp prc raw sb sf sl smp sndt sph 8svx sw txw ub ul uw voc vox wav wve
```

```
Supported effects: avg band bandpass bandreject chorus compand copy dcshift
deemph earwax echo echos fade filter flanger highp highpass lowp lowpass mask
mcompand noiseprof noisered pan phaser pick pitch polyphase rate repeat resample
reverb reverse silence speed stat stretch swap synth trim vibro vol
```

Here are some examples of playing files using `play`:

```
$ play inconceivable.wav       Play WAV file (maybe ripped from CD)
$ play *.wav                   Play all WAV files in directory (up to 32)
$ play hi.au vol .6            AU file, lower volume (can lower distortion)
$ play -r 14000 short.aiff     AIFF, sampling rate of 14000 hertz
$ play song.wav speed 2        Speed up playback (to sing like the Chipmunks)
```

If you don't have any audio files available, there's an audio file you can play to get a quick doink here: `/usr/local/lib/firefox/res/samples/test.wav`.

Here are examples for playing Ogg Vorbis (`www.vorbis.com`) files with `ogg123`:

```
$ ogg123 mysong.ogg                                 Play ogg file
$ ogg123 http://vorbis.com/music/Lumme-Badloop.ogg    Play  Web address
$ ogg123 -z *.ogg                                   Play files in pseudo-random order
$ ogg123 -Z *.ogg                                   Same as -z, but repeat forever
$ ogg123 /var/music/                                Play songs in /var/music and sub directories
$ ogg123 -@ myplaylist                              Play songs from playlist
```

A playlist is simply a list of directories or individual Ogg files to play. When a directory is listed, all Ogg files are played from that directory or any of its subdirectories. When playing multiple files, press Ctrl+C to **skip to the next song**. Press Ctrl+C twice to **quit**.

To use the `mpg321` player to play MP3 files, you need to install the mpg321 package (`pkg_add -r mpg321`). Here are examples for playing MP3 audio files with `mpg321`:

```
$ mpg321 yoursong.mp3          Play MP3 file
$ mpg321 -@ mp3list            Play songs from playlist of MP3s
$ cat mp3list | mpg321 -@ -    Pipe playlist to mpg321
$ mpg321 -z *.mp3             Play files in pseudo-random order
$ mpg321 -Z *.mp3             Same as -z, but repeat forever
```

An mpg321 playlist is simply a list of files. You can produce the list using a simple `ls` command and directing the output to a file. Use full paths to the files, unless you plan to use the list from a location from which relative paths make sense.

Adjusting Audio Levels

Open Source Sound System (OSS) is the default sound system for most BSD systems. If you configured sound as described earlier in this chapter, you should be able to adjust audio levels using tools such as `mixer` and `aumix`.

The mixer utility provides a very simple way to adjust audio levels for OSS sound applications. Here are examples of the mixer for **viewing and adjusting audio levels**:

```
$ mixer              Show mixer levels
Mixer vol       is currently set to  88:88
Mixer pcm       is currently set to   0:88
Mixer speaker   is currently set to   0:0
Mixer line      is currently set to   0:0
Mixer mic       is currently set to 100:100
...
$ mixer -s           Output mixer levels in form when you can restore later
vol 10:80 pcm 0:76 speaker 0:0 line 0:0 mic 100:100 cd 100:100 rec 0:0 igain
100:100 ogain 99:99 line1 99:99 phin 100:100 phout 100:100 video 68:68 =rec mic
$ mixer vol -10      Increase volume 10%
$ mixer vol -20      Decrease volume 20%
$ mixer vol 80:60    Set left volume to 80% and right volume to 60%
$ mixer =rec cd      Change recording device to cd
```

The mixer channels you have depend on the channels available on your sound card. Besides volume (vol), you can adjust any of the levels shown above (pcm, speaker, line, and so on) in the same way.

The aumix audio mixing application (aumix packages) can operate in screen-oriented or plain command mode. In plain text you use options to **change or display settings**. Here are examples of aumix command lines:

```
$ aumix                    With no options, aumix runs screen-oriented
$ aumix -q                 Show left/right volume and type for all channels
$ aumix -l q -m q          List current settings for line and mic only
$ aumix -v 80 -m 0         Set volume to 70% and microphone to 0
$ aumix -m 80 -m R -m q    Set mic to 80%, set it to record, list mic
```

When run screen-oriented, aumix displays all available audio channels. In screen-oriented mode, **use keys to highlight and change displayed audio settings**. Use PageUp, PageDown, up arrow, and down arrow keys to select channels. Use right or left arrow keys to increase or decrease volume. Type **m** to mute the current channel. Press the spacebar to **select the current channel as the recording device**. If a mouse is available, you can use it to select volume levels, balance levels, or the current recording channel.

Ripping CD Music

To be able to play your personal music collection from your BSD system, you can use tools such as cdparanoia to rip tracks from music CDs to wave files on your hard disk. The ripped files can then be encoded to save disk space, using tools such as oggenc (Ogg Vorbis), flac (FLAC), or lame (MP3).

> **NOTE**   *There are some excellent graphical tools for ripping and encoding CDs, such as* grip *and* sound-juicer. *Because they are CDDB-enabled, those tools can also use information about the music on the CD to name the output files (artist,*

album, song, and so on). This section, however, describes how to use some of the underlying commands to rip and encode CD music manually.

Using `cdparanoia`, you can check that your CD drive is capable of ripping Compact Disc Digital Audio (CDDA) CDs, retrieve audio tracks from your CD's drive and copy them to hard disk. Start by inserting a music CD in your drive and typing the following:

```
$ cdparanoia -vsQ
    . . .
Checking /dev/acd0 for cdrom...
Verifying CDDA command set...
    . . .
Table of contents (audio tracks only):
track        length                 begin          copy pre ch
===========================================================
   1.     18295 [04:03.70]       0 [00:00.00]    no    no  2
   2.     16872 [03:44.72]   18295 [04:03.70]    no    no  2
    . . .
  11.     17908 [03:58.58]  174587 [38:47.62]    no    no  2
  12.     17342 [03:51.17]  192495 [42:46.45]    no    no  2
TOTAL   209837 [46:37.62]     (audio only)
```

The snipped output shows `cdparanoia` checking the capabilities of /dev/acd0, and verifying that the drive can handle CDDA information. Finally, it prints information about each track. Here are examples of `cdparanoia` command lines for **ripping a CD to hard drive**:

```
$ cdparanoia -B                   Rip tracks as WAV files by track name
$ cdparanoia -B -- "5-7"          Rip tracks 5-7 into separate files
$ cdparanoia -- "3-8" abc.wav     Rip tracks 3-8 to one file (abc.wav)
$ cdparanoia -- "1:[40]-"         Rip tracks 1 from 40 secs in to end
$ cdparanoia -f -- "3"            Rip track 3 and save to AIFF format
$ cdparanoia -a -- "5"            Rip track 5 and save to AIFC format
$ cdparanoia -w -- "1" my.wav     Rip track 1 and name it my.wav
```

Encoding Music

After a music file is ripped from CD, encoding that file to save disk space is usually the next step. Popular encoders include `oggenc`, `flac`, and `lame`, for encoding to Ogg Vorbis, FLAC, and MP3 formats, respectively.

With `oggenc`, you can start with audio files or streams in WAV, AIFF, FLAC, or raw format and convert them to Ogg Vorbis format. Although Ogg Vorbis is a lossy format, the default encoding from WAV files still produces very good quality audio and can result in a file that's about one-tenth the size. Here are some examples of `oggenc`:

```
$ oggenc ab.wav                   Encodes WAV to Ogg (ab.ogg)
$ oggenc ab.flac -o new.ogg       Encodes FLAC to Ogg (new.ogg)
$ oggenc ab.wav -q 9              Raises encoding quality to 9
```

By default, the quality (-q) of the oggenc output is set to 3. You can **set quality** to any number from -1 to 10 (including fractions such as 5.5). You can also add information to the resulting Ogg file, as follows:

```
$ oggenc NewSong.wav -o NewSong.ogg \
    -a Bernstein -G Classical         \
    -d 06/15/1972 -t "Simple Song"   \
    -l "Bernsteins Mass"              \
    -c info="From Kennedy Center"    \
```

The command just shown converts MySong.wav to MySong.ogg. The artist name is Bernstein and the music type is Classical. The date is June 15, 1972, the song title is Simple Song and the album name is Bernsteins Mass. A comment is From Kennedy Center. The backslashes aren't needed if you just keep typing the whole command on one line. However, if you do add backslashes, make sure there are no spaces after the backslash.

The preceding example adds information to the header of the resulting Ogg file. You can **see the header information**, with other information about the file, using ogginfo:

```
$ ogginfo NewSong.ogg
Processing file "NewSong.ogg"...
      ...
Channels: 2
Rate: 44100
Nominal bitrate: 112.000000 kb/s
User comments section follows...
        info=From Kennedy Center
        title=Simple Song
        artist=Bernstein
        genre=Classical
        date=06/15/1972
        album=Bernsteins Mass
Vorbis stream 1:
        Total data length: 3039484 bytes
        Playback length: 3m:25.240s
        Average bitrate: 118.475307 kb/s
Logical stream 1 ended
```

Here you can see that comments were added during encoding. The -c option was used to set an arbitrary field (in this case, info) with some value to the header. Besides the comments information, you can see that this file has two channels and was recorded at a 44100 bitrate. You can also see the data length, playback time, and average bitrate.

The flac command is an encoder similar to oggenc, except that the WAV, AIFF, RAW, FLAC or Ogg file is encoded to a FLAC file. Because flac is a free lossless audio codec, it is a popular encoding method for those who want to save some space, but still want top quality audio output. Using default values, our encoding from WAV to FLAC resulted in files one-half the size, as opposed to one-tenth the size with oggenc. However, the resulting FLAC file will have no loss of quality from the original WAV file, with the OGG file will lose some quality. Here is an example of the `flac` command:

```
$ flac now.wav                    Encodes WAV to FLAC (now.flac)
$ sox now.wav now.aiff            Encodes WAV to AIFF (now.flac)
$ flac now.aiff -o now2.flac      Encodes AIFF to FLAC (now.flac)
$ flac -8 top.wav -o top.flac     Raises compression level to 8
```

Compression level is set to -5 by default. A range from -0 to -8 can be used, with the highest number giving the greatest compression and the lower number giving faster compression time. The `flac` command can also be used to **add an image to the FLAC file.** Here's an example:

```
$ flac hotsong.wav -o hotsong.flac \   Encodes WAV to FLAC (now.flac)
        --picture=cover.jpg            Adds cover.jpg to FLAC file
```

With an image embedded into the FLAC audio file, music players such as Rhythmbox can display the embedded image when the song is playing. So, a CD cover or image from a music video can be used in the FLAC file. (Note that the picture feature is not available for `flac` on all BSD systems.)

To **convert files to MP3 format** using the `lame` command, you must first install the lame package. If lame is not available on your BSD system (there are patent issues associated with MP3 encoding), try the `twolame` command (twolame package). Here are some examples of the `lame` command to encode from WAV and AIFF files:

```
$ lame in.wav                       Encodes WAV to MP3 (in.wav.mp3)
$ lame tune.aiff -o tune.mp3        Encodes AIFF to MP3 (tune.mp3)
$ lame -h -b 64 -m m in.wav out.mp3 High quality, 64-bit, mono mode
$ lame -q 0 in.wav -o abcHQ.mp3     Encode with quality set to 0
```

With `lame`, you can set the quality from 0 to 9 (5 is the default). Setting quality to 0 uses the best encoding algorithms, while setting it to 9 disables most algorithms (but the encoding process moves much faster). As with `oggenc`, you can **add tag information to your MP3 file** that can be used later when you play back the file. Here's an example:

```
$ lame NewSong.wav NewSong.mp3      \
    --ta Bernstein --tg Classical \
    --ty 1972 --tt "Simple Song"   \
    --tl "Bernsteins Mass"          \
    --tc "From Kennedy Center"
```

Like the wav to ogg example shown earlier in this chapter, the command just shown converts MySong.wav to MySong.mp3. As before, the artist name is Bernstein and the music type is Classical. The year is 1972, the song title is Simple Song and the album name is Bernsteins Mass. A comment is From Kennedy Center. The backslashes aren't needed if you just keep typing the whole command on one line. However, if you do add backslashes, make sure there are no spaces after the backslash.

The tag information appears on the screen in graphical MP3 players (such as Rhythmbox and Totem, when they have been enabled to play MP3 format). You can also see tag information when you use command line players, such as the following mpg321 example:

```
$ mpg123 NewSong.mp3
High Performance MPEG 1.0/2.0/2.5 Audio Player for Layer 1, 2, and 3.
   ...
Title  : Simple Song              Artist: Bernstein
Album  : Bernsteins Mass          Year  : 1972
Comment: From Kennedy Center      Genre : Classical

Playing MPEG stream from NewSong.mp3 ...
MPEG 1.0 layer III, 128 kbit/s, 44100 Hz joint-stereo
```

Converting Audio Files

The sox utility is an extremely versatile tool for working with audio files in different freely available formats. Here are a few examples of things you can do with sox:

The following command concatenates two WAV files to a single output file:

```
$ sox head.wav tail.wav output.wav
```

This command mixes two wave files:

```
$ soxmix sound1.wav sound2.wav output.wav
```

To use sox to display information about a file, use the stat effect as follows:

```
$ sox sound1.wav -e stat
Samples read:              208512
Length (seconds):         9.456327
Scaled by:         2147403647.0
Maximum amplitude:        0.200592
Minimum amplitude:        0.224701
Midline amplitude:       -0.012054
Mean    norm:             0.030373
Mean    amplitude:        0.000054
RMS     amplitude:        0.040391
Maximum delta:            0.060852
Minimum delta:            0.000000
Mean    delta:            0.006643
RMS     delta:            0.009028
Rough   frequency:             784
Volume adjustment:           4.450
```

Use `trim` to **delete seconds of sound** from an audio file. For example:

```
$ sox sound1.wav output.wav trim 4        Trim 4 seconds from start
$ sox sound1.wav output.wav trim 2 6      Keep from 2-6 seconds of file
```

The first example deletes the first 4 seconds from `sound1.wav` and writes the results to `output.wav`. The second example takes `sound1.wav`, keeps the section between second 2 and second 6 and deletes the rest, and writes to `output.wav`.

Transforming Images

With directories full of digital images, the ability to manipulate images from the command line can be a huge time saver. The ImageMagick package (available with FreeBSD) comes with some very useful tools for transforming your digital images into forms you can work with. This section shows some commands for manipulating digital images, and provides examples of simple scripts for making those changes in batches.

Getting Information about Images

To **get information about an image**, use the `identify` command, as follows:

```
$ identify p2090142.jpg
p2090142.jpg JPEG 2048x1536+0+0 DirectClass 8-bit 402.037kb
$ identify -verbose p2090142.jpg | less
Image p2090142.jpg
  Format: JPG (Joint Photographic Experts Group JFIF format)
  Standard deviation: 61.1665 (0.239869)
  Colors: 205713
  Rendering intent: Undefined
  Resolution: 72x72
  Units: PixelsPerInch
  Filesize: 402.037kb
  Interlace: None
  Background color: white
  Border color: rgb(223,223,223)
  Matte color: grey74
  Transparent color: black
  Page geometry: 2048x1536+0+0
  Compression: JPEG
  Quality: 44
```

The first command in the preceding example displays basic information about the image (its file name, format, geometry, class, channel depth, and file size). The second command shows every bit of information it can extract from the image. In addition to the information you see in the example, the verbose output also shows creation times, the type of camera used, aperture value, and ISO speed rating.

Converting Images

The `convert` command is the Swiss Army knife of file converters. Here are some ways to manipulate images using the `convert` command. The following examples convert image files from one format to another:

```
$ convert tree.jpg tree.png        Convert a JPEG to a PNG file
$ convert icon.gif icon.bmp        Convert a GIF to a BMP file
$ convert photo.tiff photo.pcx     Convert a TIFF to a PCX file
```

Image types that `convert` supports include JPG, BMP, PCX, GIF, PNG, TIFF, XPM, and XWD. Here are examples of `convert` being used to resize images:

```
$ convert -resize 1024x768 hat.jpg hat-sm.jpg
$ convert -sample 50%x50% dog.jpg dog-half.jpg
```

The first example creates an image (`hat-sm.jpg`) that is 1024×768 pixels. The second example reduced the image `dog.jpg` in half (`50%x50%`) and saves it as `dog-half.jpg`.

You can rotate images from 0 to 360 degrees. Here are examples:

```
$ convert -rotate 270 sky.jpg sky-final.jpg       Rotate image 270 degrees
$ convert -rotate 90 house.jpg house-final.jpg    Rotate image 90 degrees
```

You can add text to an image using the `-draw` option:

```
$ convert -fill black -pointsize 60 -font helvetica   \
    -draw 'text 10,80 "Copyright NegusNet Inc."'   \
    p10.jpg p10-cp.jpg
```

The previous example adds copyright information to an image, using 60-point black Helvetica font to write text on the image. The text is placed 10 points in and 80 points down from the upper left corner. The new image name is `p10-cp.jpg`, to indicate that the new image had copyright information added.

Here are some interesting ways to create thumbnails with the `convert` command:

```
$ convert -thumbnail 120x120 a.jpg a-a.png
$ convert -thumbnail 120x120 -frame 40x40 a.jpg a-b.png
$ convert -thumbnail 120x120 -frame 40x40 -rotate 10 \
        -background red a.jpg a-c.png
```

All three examples create a 120×120 thumbnail. The second adds the `-frame` option to put a border around the thumbnail, so it looks like a picture frame. The last example sets the `-rotate` angle to 10, so that the image looks slightly askew, and fills the background in red. Figure 6-1 shows the results of these three examples.

a-a.png a-b.png a-c.png

Figure 6-1: Use convert to create a regular, framed, and angled thumbnail.

Besides the things you can do to make images useful and manageable, there are also ways of making your images fun and even weird. Here are some examples:

```
$ convert -sepia-tone 75% house.jpg oldhouse.png
$ convert -charcoal 5 house.jpg char-house.png
$ convert -colorize 175 house.jpg color-house.png
```

The -sepia-tone option gives the image an "old west" sort of look. The -charcoal option makes the image look as if the picture was hand-drawn using charcoal. By using the -colorize option, every pixel in the image is modified using the colorize number provided (175 in this case). Figure 6-2 shows the original house picture in the upper-left corner, the sepiatone in the upper right, the charcoal in the lower left, and the colorized house in the lower right.

Figure 6-2: Start with a normal image and sepiatone, charcoal, and colorize it.

99

If you are looking for one more example of weird image conversions, try swirling your image. For example, use this command to get a picture like the one shown in Figure 6-3:

```
$ convert -swirl 300 photo.pcx weird.pcx
```

Figure 6-3: Give your vacation pictures a swirl.

Converting Images in Batches

Most of the image conversions described in this chapter can be done quite easily using a graphical image manipulation tool such the GIMP. However, where the convert commands we described can really shine are when you use them in scripts. So instead of resizing, rotating, writing on, or colorizing a single file, you can do any (or all) of those things to a whole directory of files.

You may want to create thumbnails for your duck decoy collection images. Or perhaps you want to reduce all your wedding photos so they can play well on a digital photo frame. You might even want to add copyright information to every image in a directory before you share them on the Web. All these things can be done quite easily with the convert commands already described and some simple shell scripts.

Here's an example of a script you can run to resize an entire directory of photos to 1024×768 pixels to play on a digital photo frame:

```
$ cd $HOME/myimages
$ mkdir small
$ for pic in `ls *.tif`
do
    echo "converting $pic"
    convert -resize 1024x768 $pic small/sm-$pic
done
```

Before running the script, this procedure changes to the $HOME/myimages directory (which happens to contain a set of high-resolution images). Then it creates a subdirectory to hold the reduced images called small. The script itself starts with a for loop that lists each file ending in .tif in the current directory (you might need to make that .jpg or other image suffix). Then, each file is resized to 1024×768 and copied to the small directory, with sm- added to each file name.

Using that same basic script, you can use any of the `convert` command lines shown earlier, or make up your own to suit your needs. You might be able to convert a whole directory of images in a few minutes that would have taken you hours of clicking in the GUI.

Summary

The shell can provide a quick and efficient venue for working with your audio and digital image files. This chapter describes ways of playing, ripping, encoding, converting, and streaming audio files from the command line. As for digital images, the chapter provides many examples of using the `convert` command for resizing, rotating, converting, writing on, and otherwise manipulating those images.

7

Administering File Systems

File systems provide the structures in which files, directories, devices, and other elements of the system are accessed from your BSD system. FreeBSD primarily uses the UNIX File System (UFS), although it also supports many different types of file systems (ext3, msdos, cd9660, ntfs, and so on) to some extent. FreeBSD can also work with file systems on many different types of media (hard disks, CDs, USB flash drives, ZIP drives, and so on).

Creating and managing disk slices, partitions, and the file systems on partitions are among the most critical jobs in administering a BSD system. That's because if you mess up your file system, you might very well lose the critical data stored on your computer's hard disk or removable media.

This chapter contains commands for partitioning storage media, creating file systems, mounting and unmounting file systems, and checking file systems for errors and disk space.

Understanding File System Basics

Even though there are a lot of different file system types available for FreeBSD systems, there are not many that you need to set up a basic BSD system. If you are coming from a Linux or other UNIX system background, however, you should start by understanding how BSD systems divide up disks into *slices* and *partitions*.

In FreeBSD, the four primary parts into which you can divide a hard disk are called slices. Within each slice that's dedicated to FreeBSD, the disk space can be divided into what are referred to as partitions. You can have multiple partitions within a slice, each representing a different part of the total file system (such as /usr, /var, /tmp, and of course the root partition /).

> **NOTE** *If you are coming from a Linux background, what BSD users call slices are what you refer to as partitions. The reason that Linux systems can have more than four partitions is that they can have extended partitions.*

Setting Up the Disk Initially

Assuming you are starting to set up FreeBSD with a disk you can erase completely, the FreeBSD installer provides you with the opportunity to format your disk. The quick install procedure in Chapter 2 highlights the opportunities you have for setting up your disk for use with FreeBSD. That procedure lets you:

❏ **Create Slices**: Using the fdisk utility, you can choose to dedicate the entire hard disk to either *compatibility mode* (where you can add other operating systems later) or *dedicated mode* (where only a single BSD system can boot from the disk). To install other operating systems, as described later in this chapter, you need to select compatibility mode. (Note that the fdisk utility is different from the utility of the same name you find in DOS or Linux systems.

❏ **Create Partitions**: Within FreeBSD slices, you can create partitions using the bsdlabel utility. Partitions can include the normal UFS file systems and swap space, however.

In the process of creating slices and partitions, you will also install boot code in the master boot record and on the BSD slice itself. Details on using fdisk and bsdlabel to work with slices, partitions, and boot code are contained in this chapter.

Checking Your Disk Setup

If you took the default settings when you installed the FreeBSD system, you might have put the entire BSD system on slice one, consuming the entire hard disk. Within that slice, you might have multiple partitions. For example, the output of the mount command shows how the disk space is divided among several partitions that are then mounted in different places in the file system:

```
$ mount                  Display mounted disk partitions
/dev/ad0s1a on / (ufs, local)
devfs on /dev (devfs, local)
/dev/ad0s1e on /tmp (ufs, local, soft-updates)
/dev/ad0s1f on /usr (ufs, local, soft-updates)
/dev/ad0s1d on /var (ufs, local, soft-updates)
```

Four disk partitions are mounted in the above example. The first partition (a) on the first slice (s1) on the first disk (ad0) accessible from /dev/ad0s1a is mounted on the root file system (/). Partition 4 (/dev/ad0s1d) is mounted on /var, partition 5 (/dev/ad0s1e) is on /tmp, and partition 6 is on /usr. The devfs file system is where the computer's devices can be accessed (/dev directory) and isn't used to store data. One partition not shown here is the swap partition. You can see available swap partitions using the swapinfo command:

```
$ swapinfo -h              Display information about swap partitions
Device           1K-blocks     Used    Avail Capacity
/dev/ad0s1b        487880       0B      476M    0%
```

There is one swap partition in the example above that has 476MB of space available. Next, to get a sense of how the disk space is distributed among the partitions on your hard disk, you can use the df command as follows:

```
$ df -h        Display disk space usage
Filesystem     Size    Used    Avail Capacity  Mounted on
/dev/ad0s1a    496M     39M     417M     9%     /
devfs          1.0K    1.0K      0B    100%     /dev
/dev/ad0s1e    496M     32K     456M     0%     /tmp
/dev/ad0s1f     16G    1.7G      13G    11%     /usr
/dev/ad0s1d    1.2G     19M     1.1G     2%     /var
```

In this example, we assigned 20GB of a 40GB hard drive to the BSD slice (slice 1). The output of df shows how that disk space was divided among the root partition / (496MB), /tmp (496MB), /var (1.2GB) and /usr (16G). This default install expects you to keep most of your applications and data in the /usr partition. In fact, your system's /home directory (where user data are stored) as well as /compat and /sys directories are links to permanent directories in the /usr partition.

The last thing to do for now is show how the disk slices are configured using the fdisk command:

```
# fdisk ad0              Show slice information for the first hard disk
******* Working on device /dev/ad0 *******
parameters extracted from in-core disklabel are:
cylinders=79428 heads=16 sectors/track=63 (1008 blks/cyl)
...
Media sector size is 512
Warning: BIOS sector numbering starts with sector 1
Information from DOS bootblock is:
The data for partition 1 is:
sysid 165 (0xa5),(FreeBSD/NetBSD/386BSD)
    start 63, size 40949622 (19994 Meg), flag 80 (active)
        beg: cyl 0/ head 1/ sector 1;
        end: cyl 1023/ head 254/ sector 63
The data for partition 2 is:
<UNUSED>
The data for partition 3 is:
<UNUSED>
The data for partition 4 is:
<UNUSED>
```

You can see that only the first slice is defined (although they happen to call them partitions here), and it consumes about 20GB of space (19994 Meg). So the other slices are available to be configured later (if needed).

The disk configuration just shown is used for most of the examples in this chapter.

Understanding File System Types

To use FreeBSD, you can get by with very few different file system types. The UNIX File System (UFS) is used for most disk storage needs. As noted earlier, you also should have at least one partition defined as a swap area. However, cases where you might want to use other file system types with FreeBSD include:

❏ **Other Local Operating Systems**: If multiple operating systems (such as Windows or Linux) are installed on your hard disk, you might want to access the data from the partitions containing those systems (even if only to read the data).

❏ **Other Media**: You may have a CD, DVD, backup tape, or other media that contains data formatted in other file system types. Even in cases where FreeBSD can't create file systems of a certain type, it may be able to mount and use those file systems.

Most of the examples in this chapter use UFS file systems to illustrate how a file system is created and managed. However, Table 7-1 lists different file system types and describes when you might want to use them.

Table 7-1: File System Types Supported in FreeBSD

File System Type	Description
ufs	Default file system type used with FreeBSD and other BSD systems.
ext2fs	Most commonly used file system with Linux is ext3. It contains journaling features for safer data and fast reboots after unintended shutdowns. The ext2 file system is the predecessor of ext3, but doesn't contain journaling. Either type can be mounted as an ext2fs in FreeBSD. However, journaling will not be enabled if you mount an ext3 file system using `mount_ext2fs`.
cd9660	File system type used on most data CDs and DVDs. Evolved from the High Sierra file system (which was the original standard used on CD-ROM). May contain Rock Ridge extensions to allow cd9660 file systems to support long filenames and other information (file permissions, ownership, and links).
msdosfs	MS-DOS file system. Can be used to mount older MS-DOS file systems, such as those on old floppy disks.
ntfs	Microsoft New Technology File System (NTFS). Useful when file systems need to share files with most Windows systems (as with dual booting or removable drives).

Table 7-1: File System Types Supported in FreeBSD (*continued*)

File System Type	Description
reiserfs	Journaling file system that used to be the default on some SUSE, Slackware, and other Linux systems. Reiserfs is not well-supported on many BSD systems.
swap	Used on swap partitions to hold data temporarily when RAM is not currently available.
unionfs	Often used on live CDs to give the appearance of being able to write to read-only file systems, while the actual saved data resides in a writeable area (such as a ramdisk).

Besides those file system types listed, there are also what are referred to as *network shared file systems*. Locally, a network shared file system may be a ufs, ntfs, or other normal file system type. However, all or part of those file systems can be shared with network protocols such as Samba (smbfs file system type), NFS (nfs), and NetWare (nwfs).

You can use procedures in the following sections to create, manage, mount, and otherwise use the file system types just described.

Creating and Managing File Systems

FreeBSD gives you the option of either having the installer create a default partitioning and file system scheme or letting you set that all up manually when you first install FreeBSD. It does this by running the sysinstall utility, which in turn uses tools such as bsdlabel and fdisk to actually change your disk slices and partitions.

After your BSD system is installed, you can use sysinstall again to create or change partitions and slices. Or, you can use command-line utilities directly to change and work with your disk partitions and the file systems created on those partitions.

Slicing and Partitioning Hard Disks

Historically, PC hard drives have used a 32-bit PC-BIOS partition table with a Master Boot Record (MBR). This limits the sizes of partitions (referred to as slices in BSD systems) to 2TB and only allows four primary partitions per drive. The use of extended partitions is a way to overcome the four-primary-partition limit. In order to overcome the 2TB limit, PC-BIOS partition tables are being replaced with GPT (GUID Partition Tables).

FreeBSD uses the fdisk utility to create and manage slices. It uses the bsdlabel utility to work with the partitions within each slice. Both have simplified interfaces available through the sysinstall utility.

NOTE *If you prefer to use graphical tools for partitioning, resizing, and otherwise manipulating your hard disk, you can try* gparted *or* qtparted *partitioning tools. The command names and package names are the same for those two tools.*

Changing Disk Slices with sysinstall

To work with your hard disk slices and partitions in various ways, you can run the sysinstall utility. This provides a screen-oriented interface to the fdisk and bsdlabel commands. After starting sysinstall as root user, select the following to work with your disk slices:

Configure ➪ Fdisk   The Disk Slice (PC-style partition) Editor

Here is an example of the sysinstall Fdisk screen:

```
Disk name:      ad0                              FDISK Partition Editor
DISK Geometry:  4983 cyls/255 heads/63 sectors = 80051895 sectors (39087MB)

Offset        Size(ST)        End      Name  PType      Desc  Subtype      Flags
0          63              62        -     12    unused         0
           63    40949622    40949684    ad0s1      8    freebsd       165
     40949685    15631245    56580929    ad0s2      4     ext2fs       131
     56580930     1558305    58139234    ad0s3      4 linux_swap       130
     58139235    21924189    80063423        -     12    unused         0

The following commands are supported (in upper or lower case):
A = Use Entire Disk   G = set Drive Geometry   C = Create Slice    F = `DD' mode
D = Delete Slice      Z = Toggle Size Units     S = Set Bootable    | = Wizard m.
T = Change Type       U = Undo All Changes      W = Write Changes

Use F1 or ? to get more help, arrow keys to select.
```

The following are some selections you can make from the Fdisk screen to **change your BSD slices (PC partitions)**. Keep in mind that your PC partition table will not change until you write the changes to disk (by pressing **w**) Also, note that at any time before a write you can **undo your changes** by typing the following key:

U   *Undo any changes made since previous write*

To **change or delete an existing slice,** use the arrow keys to highlight the slice you want to change or delete. Then type one of the following to change it:

D   *Deletes the highlighted slice*
T   *Change the slice type (PC partition types)*
     Use **165** *(FreeBSD),* **6** *(DOS FAT16),* **7** *(NTFS),* **130** *(Linux swap),* **131** *(Linux)*
S   *Set the current slice as bootable*

To **create a new slice,** use the arrow keys to highlight the unused space entry. Then type the following to start creating the slice:

C   *Create a new slice from unused space*

You are asked to enter the size of the new slice (such as, 10G, 10705M, or 10962094K). Next enter the slice (PC partition) type as 165 for FreeBSD, 6 for DOS, 7 for NTFS, 130 for Linux swap, or 131 for Linux.

Here are some **other things to do with the sysinstall FDISK Partition Editor:**

A   *Assigns the entire disk to the first slice (only do this at first install)*
Z   *Steps through display of slice sizes (standard, KB, MB, and GB)*
G   *Change the geometry of the drive*

When you are done, type the following to **write all changes to the partition table:**

W   *Write changes to partition table*

To exit without saving changes, type **q**. At this point, sysinstall also gives you the option of installing a boot manager on the drive. If your system is running, you probably don't want to mess with the boot manager at this point (so select None).

Changing Disk Slices with fdisk

The fdisk command is a useful BSD tool for listing and changing disk slices. Keep in mind that modifying or deleting slices can cause valuable data to be removed, so be sure of your changes before writing them to disk. To use the fdisk command to **list information about the slices on your hard disk,** type the following commands as root user:

```
# fdisk -p ad0          Display slice table information in config file format
# /dev/ad0
g c79428 h16 s63
p 1 0xa5 63 40949622
p 2 0x83 40949685 15631245
a 2
p 3 0x82 56580930 1558305
# fdisk -s ad0          Display slice table summary information
/dev/ad0: 79428 cyl 16 hd 63 sec
Part        Start        Size Type Flags
   1:          63    40949622 0xa5 0x00
   2:    40949685    15631245 0x83 0x80
   3:    56580930     1558305 0x82 0x00
# fdisk ad0             Long list of disk slices for the first IDE hard disk (ad0)
 ...
The data for partition 1 is:
sysid 165 (0xa5),(FreeBSD/NetBSD/386BSD)
    start 63, size 40949622 (19994 Meg), flag 80 (active)
        beg: cyl 0/ head 1/ sector 1;
        end: cyl 1023/ head 254/ sector 63
The data for partition 2 is:
sysid 131 (0x83),(Linux native)
    start 40949685, size 15631245 (7632 Meg), flag 0
        beg: cyl 1023/ head 254/ sector 63;
        end: cyl 1023/ head 254/ sector 63
The data for partition 3 is:
sysid 130 (0x82),(Linux swap or Solaris x86)
```

109

```
         start 56580930, size 1558305 (760 Meg), flag 0
             beg: cyl 1023/ head 254/ sector 63;
             end: cyl 1023/ head 254/ sector 63
The data for partition 4 is:
<UNUSED>
```

The output just displayed shows three configured partitions and one that is unused. FreeBSD is assigned to the first slice (it contains all BSD partitions, which are described later). The second is a native Linux slice (an entire Debian root file system happens to be installed there). The third slice contains the Linux swap area.

There are several ways you can **change existing slices** using the fdisk command:

> **WARNING!** *Here is where you can do real damage to your existing file systems. Be sure to have backup copies of important data. If you are uncomfortable changing partition tables, try to find an expert to help.*

```
# fdisk -a ad0     Change active slice, to boot from different slice by default
Partition 1 is marked as active
Do you want to change the active partition? [n] y
Supply a decimal value for "active partition" [1] 2     Change slice 2 to active
Are you happy with this choice [n] y
...
2: sysid 131 (0x83),(Linux native)
    start 40949685, size 15631245 (7632 Meg), flag 80 (active)
    ...
Should we write new partition table? [n] y             Write changes to table
```

```
# fdisk -i ad0          Interactively change slice table
******* Working on device /dev/ad0 *******
parameters extracted from in-core disklabel are:
cylinders=79428 heads=16 sectors/track=63 (1008 blks/cyl)
    ...
Do you want to change our idea of what BIOS thinks?[n] n   No to change disk geom
    ...
Data for partition 1 is:
sysid 165 (0xa5),(FreeBSD/NetBSD/386BSD)
    start 63, size 40949622 (19994 Meg), flag 80 (active)
        beg: cyl 0/ head 1/ sector 1;
        end: cyl 1023/ head 254/ sector 63
Do you want to change it? [n] y
Supply a decimal value for "sysid (165=FreeBSD)" [165] 165
Supply a decimal value for "start" [63] 63
Supply a decimal value for "size" [80063361] 80063361
Explicitly specify beg/end address ? [n] y
    ...
Do you want to change the active partition? [n] n
    ...
Should we write new partition table?[n] y    Danger! y writes changes, n doesn't
```

The previous procedure stepped through changing the settings associated with an existing slice (the first slice on your first hard disk). To **create a new slice**, run the same command, stepping past all defined slices, until you get to a slice marked <UNUSED>. Then type **y** and proceed as follows:

```
# fdisk -i ad0
   . . .
The data for partition 4 is:
<UNUSED>
Do you want to change it? [n] y
Supply a decimal value for "sysid (165=FreeBSD)" [165] 165
Supply a decimal value for "start" [58139235] 58139235
Supply a decimal value for "size" [1558305] 1558305
Explicitly specify beg/end address ? [n] n
sysid 165 (0xa5),(FreeBSD/NetBSD/386BSD)
    start 58139235, size 1558305 (760 Meg), flag 0
        beg: cyl 333/ head 13/ sector 1;
        end: cyl 855/ head 11/ sector 63
Are we happy with this entry? [n] y
Partition 2 is marked active
Do you want to change the active partition? [n] n

We haven't changed the partition table yet.  This is your last chance.
   . . .
Should we write new partition table? [n] y
```

The example just shown started at the first available point after the third slice. The file system type was specified as FreeBSD (165). With the new slice created you can go on to partition that slice into smaller sections.

Changing Partitions with sysinstall

BSD systems refer to the separate disk areas within a slice as partitions. Creating separate partitions allows an administrator to assign separate disk space to different parts of the file system. Using the `sysinstall` or `bsdlabel` utilities, you can **list, configure, and change the partitions** within your BSD slice.

> **NOTE**   *Your BSD system is probably not configured to allow you to change disk partitions by default. To open permissions to modify your partitions, type the following command as the root user:* ***sysctl kern.geom.debugflags=16***. *Everything you do after this point should be done with great consideration, since you can very easily make the data on your disk inaccessible.*

Type `sysinstall` as root user. Then select the following to open the FreeBSD Disklabel Editor:

Configure ⮑ Label   The disk Label editor

The following example of the FreeBSD Disklabel Editor displays all BSD slices on the local hard disk:

```
                    FreeBSD Disklabel Editor

Disk: ad0       Partition name: ad0s1   Free: 0 blocks (0MB)
Disk: ad0       Partition name: ad0s4   Free: 1558305 blocks (760MB)


Part     Mount          Size Newfs   Part     Mount          Size Newfs
----     -----          ---- -----   ----     -----          ---- -----
ad0s1a   <none>         512MB *
ad0s1b   swap           476MB SWAP
ad0s1d   <none>        1262MB *
ad0s1e   <none>         512MB *
ad0s1f   <none>       17232MB *

The following commands are valid here (upper or lower case):
C = Create      D = Delete    M = Mount pt.       W = Write
N = Newfs Opts  Q = Finish    S = Toggle SoftUpdates  Z = Custom Newfs
T = Toggle Newfs  U = Undo    A = Auto Defaults   R = Delete+Merge
Use F1 or ? to get more help, arrow keys to select.
```

The previous example shows the first IDE hard disk (ad0) containing two slices (ad0s1 and ad0s4) that are configured as FreeBSD slices. The first slice is where the entire operating system is installed. The second slice contains 760MB of disk space, all of which is currently free.

To **create partitions on a slice using available disk space**, highlight the slice you want (in this case, ad0s4) and press **c**. You are prompted for the following information:

❑ **Partition size**: Identify how much space should be assigned to the partition in blocks, gigabytes (G), or megagytes (M) up to the maximum amount available on the disk.

❑ **File system or swap**: Indicate whether the disk will contain a file system or swap space.

❑ **Mount point**: If it's a file system, specify the point in the file system where the partition will be mounted (for example, /mnt/music). You should create this mount point before creating the partition (as root, type mkdir /mnt/music).

The new partition is created. In this example, here is what the new partition looked like:

```
ad0s4a    /mnt/music    100MB UFS2+S Y
```

You can also **change existing partitions** in different ways. For example, with the partition just created highlighted, here are some ways of changing that partition:

U   *Undo any changes made since previous write*
N   *Add additional UFS newfs options while creating this file system*

M   *Change the mount point to a different place in the file system*
D   *Deletes the highlighted partition*

When you are done making changes, type the following to **write all changes to the disk label**:

W   *Write changes to partition table*

If you want to just exit without saving changes, simply type **Q**.

Changing Partitions with bsdlabel

The bsdlabel provides a command-line alternative to sysinstall for changing the partitions you have on a BSD slice. To **view partition information on a particular BSD slice**, type the following:

```
# bsdlabel ad0s1       Display partition information from a BSD slice
  # /dev/ad0s1:
  8 partitions:
  #        size    offset    fstype   [fsize bsize bps/cpg]
    a:  1048576         0    4.2BSD        0     0     0
    b:   975760   1048576    swap
    c: 40949622         0    unused        0     0     # "raw" part, don't edit
    d:  2584576   2024336    4.2BSD        0     0     0
    e:  1048576   4608912    4.2BSD        0     0     0
    f: 35292134   5657488    4.2BSD        0     0     0
```

There are several ways you can **create or change labels for an existing slice** (don't do this on slices that have data you want to keep):

```
# bsdlabel -n -w ad0s4    Show results of writing a label, but not writing
# bsdlabel -w ad0s4       Writing a standard label to disk 1, slice 4 (ad0s4)
# bsdlabel -e ad0s4       Opens the label for ad0s4 in an editor
```

With the -w option, a standard label is added to the slice. The standard label assigned the entire slice as a single partition. By editing the label (-e), which opens the label in the vi editor, you can identify the file system type as 4.2BSD. Next, you need to create a file system on the new partition.

Creating a UFS File System on a Partition

To **create a UFS file system** on an empty partition, you can use the newfs command. In the example above, because you made the entire label a single partition, you can identify the entire slice as containing the new file system. Here is an example:

```
# newfs -N /dev/ad0s4    Show results of adding UFS files system, but not writing
/dev/ad0s4: 760.9MB (1558304 sectors) block size 16384, fragment size 2048
        using 5 cylinder groups of 183.77MB, 11761 blks, 23552 inodes.
super-block backups (for fsck -b #) at:
 160, 376512, 752864, 1129216, 1505568
# newfs /dev/ad0s4       Write the UFS file system to disk 1, slice 4
```

113

At this point, your file system should be ready to use. Later, we describe more about how to use the `mount` command to mount file systems. For the moment, you could try the following to quickly check that the new file system can be mounted:

```
# mkdir /mnt/music          Create the mount point directory
# mount /dev/ad0s4 /mnt/music   Mount filesystem on disk 1,slice 4 to /mnt/music
```

Working with Linux-Compatible File Systems

Having Linux compatibility software included with FreeBSD makes it possible to have Linux-compatible file systems, such as ext2 and ext3 file systems. Besides including tools (such as `mkfs.ext2` and `mkfs.ext3`) for creating Linux file systems, there are also tools for checking (`fsck.ext2` and `fsck.ext3`) and adjusting parameters (`tune2fs`) of a Linux file system. (You need to add Linux Compatibility during installation to get these features.)

The device examples below create and use the ext2 file system on the third slice of the first IDE hard disk (`/dev/ad0a1`). If instead of working with an IDE drive you are using a SCSI or USB memory stick, the first such disk would be identified as a `da` drive. When you go to create a Linux-compatible file system, you can do so by either creating it to the entire drive (da0) or a slice on that drive (da0s1).

Creating Linux-Compatible File Systems

To **create a Linux-compatible file system in FreeBSD,** you can start by creating a slice dedicated to Linux. Refer to the "Changing Disk Slices with sysinstall" section earlier in this chapter for information on creating a slice. Then assign that slice to a partition type of 131 (Linux ext2fs). You are now ready to make an ext2 or ext3 file system on that partition.

> **NOTE** *If procedures in this chapter don't work, make sure that you have the Linux compatibility feature installed and the Linux driver loaded (`kldload linux`). Keep in mind that ext2 and ext3 support is not particularly stable. For production machines we recommend using the UFS file system in most cases.*

Here are some examples using the `mkfs.ext2` and `mkfs.ext3` commands to **create an ext2 or ext3 file system** on a Linux (ext2fs) slice:

```
# cd /usr/compat/linux/sbin      Change to Linux sbin (or add to your $PATH)
# ./mkfs.ext2 -v /dev/ad0s4      Create ext2 file system on disk 1/slice 4 (ad0s4)
mke2fs 1.38 (30-Jun-2005)
/dev/ad0s4 is not a block special device.
Proceed anyway? (y,n) y
Filesystem label=
OS type: Linux
Block size=4096 (log=2)
Fragment size=4096 (log=2)
97536 inodes, 194788 blocks
```

```
9739 blocks (5.00%) reserved for the super user
First data block=0
Maximum filesystem blocks=201326592
6 block groups
32768 blocks per group, 32768 fragments per group
16256 inodes per group
Superblock backups stored on blocks:
        32768, 98304, 163840
    . . .
# ./mkfs.ext2 -v -c /dev/ad0s4       Verbose and scan for bad blocks
    . . .
/dev/ad0s4 is not a block special device.
Proceed anyway? (y,n) y
    . . .
Running command: badblocks -b 4096 -s /dev/ad0s4 194788
Checking for bad blocks (read-only test): done    788
    . . .
# ./mkfs.ext3 -v -c /dev/ad0s4       Same a previous, but creates ext3 file system
```

Viewing and Changing Linux File System Attributes

Using the tune2fs or dumpe2fs commands you can view attributes of ext2 and ext3 file systems. The tune2fs command can also be used to change file system attributes. Here are examples (both commands produce the same output):

```
# cd /usr/compat/linux/sbin            Change to Linux sbin directory
# ./tune2fs -l /dev/ad0s4  | less      View tunable file system attributes
# ./dumpe2fs -h /dev/ad0s4 | less      Same as tune2fs output
Filesystem volume name:    mypartition
Last mounted on:           <not available>
Filesystem UUID:           86d67872-3c9c-456a-986b-25c802d060c9
Filesystem magic number:   0xEF53
Filesystem revision #:     1 (dynamic)
Filesystem features:       has_journal resize_inode filetype sparse_super
large_file
Default mount options:     (none)
Filesystem state:          clean
Errors behavior:           Continue
Filesystem OS type:        Linux
Inode count:               97536
Block count:               194788
Reserved block count:      9739
Free blocks:               187424
Free inodes:               97525
First block:               0
Block size:                4096
Fragment size:             4096
Reserved GDT blocks:       47
Blocks per group:          32768
Fragments per group:       32768
Inodes per group:          16256
Inode blocks per group:    508
Filesystem created:        Tue Feb 19 00:41:23 2008
```

115

```
Last mount time:          n/a
Last write time:          Tue Feb 19 00:41:25 2008
Mount count:              0
Maximum mount count:      36
Last checked:             Tue Feb 19 00:41:23 2008
Check interval:           15552000 (6 months)
Next check after:         Sun Aug 17 01:41:23 2008
Reserved blocks uid:      0 (user root)
Reserved blocks gid:      0 (group wheel)
```

The output shows a lot of information about the file system. For example, if you have a file system that needs to create many small files (such as a news server), you can check that you don't run out of inodes. Setting the Maximum mount count ensures that the file system is checked for errors after it has been mounted the selected number of times. You can also find dates and times for when a file system was created, last mounted, and last written to.

To change settings on an existing ext2 or ext3 file system, you can use the tune2fs command. The following command changes the number of mounts before a forced file system check:

```
# tune2fs -c 31 /dev/ad0s4      Sets # of mounts before check is forced
tune2fs 1.38 (30-Jun-2005)
Setting maximal mount count to 31
```

If you'd like to switch to forced file system checks based on time interval rather than number of mounts, disable mount count checking by setting it to negative 1 (-1):

```
# tune2fs -c -1 /dev/ad0s4
tune2fs 1.38 (30-Jun-2005)
Setting maximal mount count to -1
```

Use the -i option to enable time-dependent checking. Here are some examples:

```
# tune2fs -i 10 /dev/ad0s4      Check after 10 days
# tune2fs -i 1d /dev/ad0s4      Check after 1 day
# tune2fs -i 3w /dev/ad0s4      Check after 3 weeks
# tune2fs -i 6m /dev/ad0s4      Check after 6 months
# tune2fs -i 0 /dev/ad0s4       Disable time-dependent checking
```

Be sure you always have either mount count- or time-dependent checking turned on.

Creating a Memory Disk File System

If you want to make a file system that is more portable (in other words, not tied to a physical disk), you can create a *memory disk file system*. A memory disk file system is one that sits within a file on an existing file system. You can format it as a file system, mount and unmount it, and even move it around and use it from different computers.

Memory disk file systems are useful for such things as backing up data, creating live CDs, or running dedicated virtual operating systems. In the example that follows, you create a blank 1GB disk image file, format it as a file system, and then mount it to access data on the file system:

```
# dd if=/dev/zero of=mydisk count=2048000    Create zero-filled 1GB file
2048000+0 records in
2048000+0 records out
1048576000 bytes transferred in 56.519717 secs (18552393 bytes/sec)
# du -sh mydisk                              Check memory disk file size
1.0G    mydisk
# mdconfig -a -t vnode -f mydisk -u 2        Identifies mydisk as memory disk file
# bsdlabel -w md2 auto                       Adds BSD label to file
# newfs md2a                                 Creates UFS file system
/dev/md2a: 1000.0MB (2047984 sectors) block size 16384, fragment size 2048
        using 6 cylinder groups of 183.77MB, 11761 blks, 23552 inodes.
super-block backups (for fsck -b #) at:
 160, 376512, 752864, 1129216, 1505568, 1881920
# mkdir /mnt/mydisk                          Creates mount point
# mount /dev/md2a /mnt/mydisk                Mounts memory disk
```

In this procedure, the dd command creates an empty disk image file of 2048000 blocks (about 1 GB). The mdconfig command identifies the mydisk file as the storage area for the memory disk. The bsdlabel command adds the BSD label to the file image. The newfs command creates a UFS file system on that image.

When the virtual file system is mounted, you can access it as you would any file system. When you are done with the file system, leave it and unmount it:

```
# cd /mnt/mydisk              Change to the mount point
# mkdir test                  Create a directory on the file system
# cp /etc/hosts .             Copy a file to the file system
# cd                          Leave the file system
# umount /mnt/mydisk          Unmount the file system
```

With the virtual file system unmounted, you could move it to another system or burn it to a CD to use a file system in another location. If you don't want the file system any more, simply delete the file.

Creating and Using Swap Partitions

Swap partitions are needed in BSD systems to hold data that overflows from your system's RAM. If you didn't create a swap partition when you installed BSD, you can create it later manually. You can **create your swap area** either on a regular disk partition (identify a new partition as swap when you create partitions as described earlier) or in a file formatted as a swap partition.

If you don't have a spare partition, you can **create a swap area within a file** as follows:

```
# dd if=/dev/zero of=/tmp/swapfile00 count=65536
65536+0 records in
65536+0 records out
33554432 bytes transferred in 1.541522 secs (21767079 bytes/sec)
```

117

```
# chmod 600 /tmp/swapfile00
# mdconfig -a -t vnode -f /tmp/swapfile00 -u -0
# swapon /dev/md0
```

The dd command above creates a 32MB file named swapfile00. The chmod command locks down the permissions on the file. The mdconfig command configures the swap file as an md device.

After you have created a swap partition or swap file, you need to **tell the system to use the swap area** you made using the swapon command. This is similar to what happens at boot time. Here are examples:

```
# swapon /dev/md0          Turn swap on for /dev/md0 partition
```

You can use the swapinfo command to **see a list of your swap files and partitions**:

```
# swapinfo          View all swap files and partitions that are on
Filename              1K-blocks     Used     Avail    Capacity
/dev/ad0s1b            487880        0        487880    0%
/dev/md0               32768         0        32768     0%
Total                  520648        0        520648    0%
# swapinfo -h       View all swap files and partitions in megabytes
Device       1K-blocks    Used    Avail  Capacity
/dev/ad0s1b   487880      0B      476M    0%
/dev/md0      32768       0B      32M     0%
Total         520648      0B      508M    0%
# swapinfo -k       View all swap files and partitions in kilobytes
```

To **turn off a swap area**, you can use the swapoff command. Only do this if you are sure your swap area is not being used, because it may crash the system:

```
# swapoff /dev/md0       Turn off swap file
# swapoff /dev/ad0s1b    Turn off swap partition
# swapoff -a             Turn off all swap partitions
```

Mounting and Unmounting File Systems

Before you can use a regular, non-swap file system, you need to attach it to a directory in your computer's file system tree by *mounting* it. Your root file system (/) and other file systems you use on an ongoing basis are typically mounted automatically based on entries in your /etc/fstab file. Other file systems can be mounted manually as they are needed, using the mount command.

Mounting File Systems from the fstab File

When you first install FreeBSD, the /etc/fstab file is usually set up automatically to contain information about your root partition and other partitions. Those partitions can then be set to mount at boot time or be ready to mount manually (with mount points and other options ready to use when a manual mount is done).

Here is an example of a /etc/fstab file:

```
# Device            Mountpoint      FStype      Options        Dump  Pass#
/dev/ad0s1b         none            swap        sw             0     0
/dev/ad0s1a         /               ufs         rw             1     1
/dev/ad0s1e         /tmp            ufs         rw             2     2
/dev/ad0s1f         /usr            ufs         rw             2     2
/dev/ad0s1d         /var            ufs         rw             2     2
/dev/acd0           /cdrom          cd9660      ro,noauto      0     0
/dev/ad0s2          /mnt/debian     ext2fs      rw             0     0
```

All the file systems are mounted automatically, except for the CD drive at /dev/acd0 (as indicated by the noauto option). The root (\), /tmp, /usr, and /var partitions are regular UFS file systems and are mounted read/write (rw). The /dev/ads2 slice (disk slice 2) was added manually in this example to mount the Debian GNU/Linux partition located on that device.

Table 7-2 describes each field in the /etc/fstab file.

Table 7-2: Fields in /etc/fstab File

Field	Description
1	**The device name representing the file system.** This is the device name of the partition to mount (such as /dev/ad0s1a). It can also contain the device name representing a slice (as in /dev/ad0s2 for slice 2) if the entire slice is dedicated to a single file system.
2	**The mount point in the file system.** The file system contains all data from the mount point down the directory tree structure, unless another file system is mounted at some point beneath it.
3	**The file system type.** See Table 7-1 for a list of many common file system types.
4	**mount command options.** Examples of mount options include noauto (to prevent the file system from mounting at boot time) or ro (to mount the file system read-only). Commas must separate options. See the mount command manual page (under the -o option) for information on other supported options.
5	**Dump file system?** This field is only significant if you run backups with dump. Positive numbers signify that the file system should be dumped. A number 1 means that the file system needs to be dumped first (this is used for the root file system). A number 2 assumes that the file system can be dumped at any point after the root file system is checked.
6	**File system check?** The number in this field indicates whether or not the file system needs to be checked with fsck. A zero indicates that the file system should not be checked. As with the dump indicators, number 1 means that the file system needs to be checked first (this is used for the root file system). A number 2 assumes that the file system can be checked at any point after the root file system is checked.

You can create your own entries for any hard disk or removable media partitions you want in the /etc/fstab file. Remote file systems (NFS, Samba, and others) can also contain entries in the /etc/fstab file to automatically mount those file systems at boot time or later by hand.

Mounting File Systems with the mount Command

The mount command is used to view mounted file systems, as well as to mount any local (hard disk, USB drive, CD, DVD, and so on) or remote (NFS, Samba, and so on) file systems. Here are examples of the mount command for **listing mounted file systems**:

```
$ mount                        List mounted remote and local file systems
/dev/ad0s1a on / (ufs, local)
devfs on /dev (devfs, local)
/dev/ad0s1e on /tmp (ufs, local, soft-updates)
/dev/ad0s1f on /usr (ufs, local, soft-updates)
/dev/ad0s1d on /var (ufs, local, soft-updates)
/dev/ad0s2 on /mnt/debian (ext2fs, local)
$ mount -v                     List mounted file systems with file system ids
/dev/ad0s1a on / (ufs, local, fsid 3abeb447a6961229)
devfs on /dev (devfs, local, fsid 00ff000505000000)
/dev/ad0s1e on /tmp (ufs, local, soft-updates, fsid 3abeb447c27d4dec)
/dev/ad0s1f on /usr (ufs, local, soft-updates, fsid 3abeb44746a302f2)
/dev/ad0s1d on /var (ufs, local, soft-updates, fsid 3bbeb44797a19385)
/dev/ad0s2 on /mnt/debian (ext2fs, local, fsid 4f00000008000000)
```

Use the -t option to **list only mounts of a specific file system type**:

```
$ mount -t ufs                 List mounted ufs file systems
/dev/ad0s1a on / (ufs, local)
/dev/ad0s1e on /tmp (ufs, local, soft-updates)
/dev/ad0s1f on /usr (ufs, local, soft-updates)
/dev/ad0s1d on /var (ufs, local, soft-updates)
$ mount -t ext2fs              List mounted ext2 file systems
/dev/ad0s2 on /mnt/debian (ext2fs, local)
```

Here is a simple mount command to **mount a local file system** (the /dev/ad0s4 device) on an existing directory named /mnt/music.

```
# mount /dev/ad0s4 /mnt/music      Mount a local file system
# mount -v /dev/ad0s4 /mnt/music/  Mount file system, more verbose
```

In the examples above, the mount command will either look for an entry for /dev/sda1 in the /etc/fstab file or try to guess the type of file system.

Use -t to **explicitly indicate the type of file system to mount**:

```
# mount -v -t ext2fs /dev/ad0s4 /mnt/music/  Mount an ext2 file system
/dev/ad0s4 on /mnt/music (ext2fs, local, fsid 5e00000008000000)
```

If you're mounting something that is listed in your `fstab` file already, you only need to specify one item: mount point or device. For example, with the following `fstab` entry:

```
/dev/ad0s4        /mnt/music        ext2fs    rw        2 2
```

you can **mount the file system using only some of the options**:

```
# mount -v /dev/ad0s4    Mount file system with device name only
/dev/ad0s4 on /mnt/music (ext2fs, local, fsid 5e00000008000000)
# mount -v /mnt/music    Mount file system with mount point only
/dev/ad0s4 on /mnt/music (ext2fs, local, fsid 5e00000008000000)
```

You can **specify mount options** by adding `-o` and a comma-separated list of options. They are the same options you can add to field 4 of the `/etc/fstab` file. By default, partitions are mounted with read/write access. You can explicitly indicate to **mount a file system as read/write (rw) or read-only (ro)**:

```
# mount -v -t ext2fs -o rw /dev/ad0s4 /mnt/music  Mount read/write
/dev/ad0s4 on /mnt/music (ext2fs, local, fsid 5e00000008000000)
# mount -v -t ext2fs -o ro /dev/ad0s4 /mnt/music  Mount read-only
/dev/ad0s4 on /mnt/music (ext2fs, local, fsid 5e00000008000000)
```

A few other useful `mount` options you can use include:

❑ `noatime`: Does not update the access time on files. Good on file systems with a lot of I/O, such as mail spools and logs.

❑ `noexec`: Prevents execution of binaries located on this file system. Can be used to increase security, for example for `/tmp` in environments with untrusted users.

Just as you can swap to a file, you can **create a file system in a file and then mount it** so you can view its contents as you would any file system. Creating and mounting such a file is described in the "Creating a Memory Disk File System" section earlier in this chapter. A common situation where you might want to **mount a file in loopback** is after downloading a BSD install CD or LiveCD. By mounting that CD image, you can view its contents or copy files from that image to your hard disk.

```
# mdconfig -a -t vnode -f /usr/images/FreeSBIE-2.0.1-RELEASE.iso -u 1
# mkdir /mnt/freesbie
# mount -t cd9660 /dev/md1 /mnt/freesbie
# ls /mnt/freesbie/
.cshrc      boot        etc        media      rescue     tmp
.profile    boot.catalog home       mnt        root       usr
COPYRIGHT   dev         lib        pkg_info.txt sbin       uzip
bin         dist        libexec    proc        sys        var
```

Unmounting File Systems with umount

To **unmount a file system**, use the `umount` command. You can `umount` the file system using the device name or the mount point. You're better off `umounting` with the mount point, to avoid mistyping the device name (many of which are very similar).

121

```
# umount -v /dev/ad0s4          Unmount by device name
/dev/sda1 umounted
# umount -v /mnt/music          Unmount by mount point
/tmp/diskboot.img umounted
```

If the device is busy, the unmount will fail. A common reason for an unmount to fail is that you have a shell open with the current directory of a directory inside the mount:

```
# umount -v /mnt/mymount/
umount: unmount of /mnt/music failed: Device busy
```

Checking File Systems

File systems are traditionally checked when the system first boots up. Settings in the /etc/fstab file are used to determine which file systems are checked before they are mounted. The fsck command, which actually depends on a set of file system-specific fsck commands, not only can check for consistency problems in a file system, it can also interactively repair those problems when necessary.

After file systems are mounted and users are allowed to access the system, fsck can be run again with the -B flag to do background checking. You can run fsck at any time to check, and possibly repair, a file system.

Instead of having fsck try to figure out the file system type you are checking, you can run the file system-specific commands directly on your file systems. These commands include fsck_ufs and fsck_msdosfs.

The following example shows how to **check a UFS file system** by simply adding the device name of the disk partition you want to check with the fsck_ufs command:

```
# fsck_ufs /dev/ad0s4           Check UFS file system of inconsistencies
** /dev/ad0s4
** Last Mounted on /mnt/extra
** Phase 1 - Check Blocks and Sizes
** Phase 2 - Check Pathnames
** Phase 3 - Check Connectivity
** Phase 4 - Check Reference Counts
** Phase 5 - Check Cyl groups
377 files, 864 used, 373871 free (15 frags, 46732 blocks, 0.0% fragmentation)
```

This example shows a file system check on slice four of IDE disk 1 (/dev/ad0s4). The slice is not currently mounted, so if fixes needed to be done to the disk, they could be. Here are some other examples of options you can use when checking a file system with the fsck_ufs command:

```
# fsck_ufs -B /dev/ad0s1f        Run check in the background
# fsck_ufs -B -f ad0s1f          Force file system check, even if marked clean
```

```
** /usr/.snap/fsck_snapshot
** Last Mounted on /usr
** Phase 1 - Check Blocks and Sizes
** Phase 2 - Check Pathnames
** Phase 3 - Check Connectivity
** Phase 4 - Check Reference Counts
** Phase 5 - Check Cyl groups
198317 files, 1814392 used, 6730360 free (25136 frags, 838153 blocks, 0.3%
fragmentation)
# fsck_ufs -d /dev/ad0s1a     Print commands without executing (debug mode)
# fsck_ufs -y /dev/ad0s1c     Make fsck say yes to any questions (like repairs)
```

If you want to check a DOS file system, you can use the fsck_msdos command. In this example, the second partition on a USB memory stick (/dev/da0s2) contains a DOS file system. You can create that DOS partition originally using the newfs_msdos command. (Note that memory sticks and SCSI drives device names begin with da, as opposed to IDE disks which are named ad.)

```
# newfs_msdos /dev/md2a        Create DOS file system on USB device 1, slice 2
# fsck_msdosfs /dev/da0s2      Check DOS partition (on 2nd slice, 1st da device)
** /dev/da0s2 (NO WRITE)
** Phase 1 - Read and Compare FATs
** Phase 2 - Check Cluster Chains
** Phase 3 - Checking Directories
** Phase 4 - Checking for Lost Files
2712 files, 610448 free (38153 clusters)
MARK FILE SYSTEM CLEAN? no

***** FILE SYSTEM IS LEFT MARKED AS DIRTY *****
```

Note that the file system was listed as NO WRITE, because it was currently mounted. So it could not be marked as clean. The file system could be marked as clean after unmounting the file system and running fsck_msdosfs again:

```
# umount /dev/da0s2
# fsck_msdosfs /dev/da0s2      Run check again after unmounting
** /dev/da0s2
** Phase 1 - Read and Compare FATs
** Phase 2 - Check Cluster Chains
** Phase 3 - Checking Directories
** Phase 4 - Checking for Lost Files
2712 files, 610448 free (38153 clusters)
```

If fsck encounters errors during the file system check (and you have not indicated -y to automatically respond yes and continue), you can interactively say whether or not you want to fix the errors. Here is an example:

```
# fsck_msdosfs /dev/da0s2          Check a file system that has errors
** /dev/da0s2
** Phase 1 - Read and Compare FATs
```

```
** Phase 2 - Check Cluster Chains
** Phase 3 - Checking Directories
/hello.txt starts with free cluster
Truncate? [yn] y
** Phase 4 - Checking for Lost Files
2713 files, 610448 free (38153 clusters)
MARK FILE SYSTEM CLEAN? [yn] y
MARKING FILE SYSTEM CLEAN

***** FILE SYSTEM WAS MODIFIED *****
```

In the example just shown, the file hello.txt was open in a text editor when the memory stick containing the file was unplugged. This subsequent file system check showed the error, and I was able to correct it by typing **y**.

Finding Out About File System Use

Running out of disk space can be annoying on your desktop system and potentially a disaster on your servers. To determine how much disk space is available and how much is currently in use, you can use the df command. To check how much space particular files and directories are consuming, use the du command.

The df command provides **utilization summaries of your mounted file systems**. Using the -h option, you can have the data (which is shown in bytes by default) converted to kilobytes (K), megabytes (M) and gigabytes (G), to make that output more human-readable:

```
$ df -h          Display space on file systems in human readable form
Filesystem    Size   Used  Avail Capacity  Mounted on
/dev/ad0s1a   496M   39M   417M    9%      /
devfs         1.0K   1.0K    0B  100%      /dev
/dev/ad0s1e   496M   32M   456M    0%      /tmp
/dev/ad0s1f    16G   3.5G   12G   23%      /usr
/dev/ad0s1d   1.2G   19M   1.1G    2%      /var
/dev/ad0s2    7.3G  593M   6.4G    8%      /mnt/debian
/dev/da0s1     48M  856K    45M    2%      /mnt/da0s1
```

Every file that is physically saved to a file system is represented by an inode. If your file system has many small files, it's possible that you might run out of inodes. To have the df command **check inode utilization** use the -i option:

```
$ df -hi         Display how many inodes are available and used
Filesystem    Size   Used  Avail Capacity  iused    ifree  %iused  Mounted on
/dev/ad0s1a   496M   39M   417M    9%       1117    64673     2%    /
devfs         1.0K   1.0K    0B  100%          0        0   100%    /dev
/dev/ad0s1e   496M   34K   456M    0%         17    65773     0%    /tmp
/dev/ad0s1f    16G   3.5G   12G   23%     198316  2015570     9%    /usr
/dev/ad0s1d   1.2G   19M   1.1G    2%       2523   162339     2%    /var
```

If you have network mounts (such as Samba or NFS), these will show up, too, in your df output. To limit df output to local file systems, use the -l (as in local) option:

```
$ df -hl            Display disk space only for local file systems
```

To display output for a particular file system type, use the -T option:

```
$ df -ht ufs        Only display ufs file system types
Filesystem      Size    Used    Avail Capacity  Mounted on
/dev/ad0s1a     496M    39M     417M    9%      /
   ...
```

To check for disk space usage for particular files or directories in a file system, use the du command. The following command was run as the user named francois:

```
$ du -h /home/            Show disk space usage for /home directory
du: /home/chris: Permission denied
4.0K    /home/francois/Mail
52K     /home/francois
64K     /home/
```

The output shows that access to another home directory's disk use (in this case /home/chris) was denied for security reasons. So the next examples will show how to avoid permission issues and get totals that are correct by using the root user account. This is clearly visible when we use -s to summarize

```
$ du -sh /home     Regular user is denied space totals to others' homes
du: /home/chris: Permission denied
du: /home/horatio199: Permission denied
64K     /home
# du -sh /home     You can display summary disk use as root user
1.6G    /home
```

You can specify multiple directories with the -c option and total them up:

```
# du -sch /home /var     Show directory and total summaries
1.6G    /home
111M    /var
1.7G    total
```

You can combine du with the find command to check out disk space in all directories beneath a point in your directory structure. Use the following command to view the disk space used in directories beneath the /var file system:

```
# find /var -maxdepth 1 -type d -exec du -sh {} \;
 44M    /var
2.0K    /var/account
8.0K    /var/at
```

125

```
 2.0K    /var/audit
  ...
438K     /var/log
 86K     /var/mail
 4.0K    /var/msgs
 53K     /var/named
 2.0K    /var/preserve
```

Summary

Creating and managing file systems is a critical part of BSD system administration. Most BSD systems use the UNIX File System (UFS) as the primary file system type for storing data. However, most BSD systems can mount and use data from a variety of file system types, including ext2, ext3, ntfs, msdos, reiserfs, and unionfs. It can also work with network file systems, such as NFS, nwfs, and smbfs.

You can partition hard disks with commands such as `fdisk` and `bsdlabel`. Tools for working with file systems include those that create file systems (`newfs`), mount/unmount file systems (`mount` and `umount`), and check for problems (`fsck`). To see how much space has been used in file systems, use the `df` and `du` commands.

8

Backups and Removable Media

Data backups in UNIX were traditionally done by running commands to archive and compress the files to backup, then writing that backup archive to tape. Choices for archive tools, compression techniques, and backup media have grown tremendously in recent years. Tape archiving has, for many, been replaced by techniques for backing up data over the network, to other hard disks, or to CDs, DVDs, or other low-cost removable media.

This chapter details some useful tools for backing up and restoring your critical data. The first part of the chapter details how to use basic tools such as tar, gzip, and rsync for backups.

IN THIS CHAPTER

Creating backup archives with tar

Compressing backups with gzip, bzip2, and lzop

Backing up over the network with SSH

Doing network backups with rsync

Making backup ISO images with mkisofs

Burning backup images to CD or DVD with cdrecord and growisofs

Backing Up Data to Compressed Archives

If you are coming from a Windows background, you may be used to tools such as WinZip and PKZIP, which both archive and compress groups of files in one application. BSD systems offer separate tools for gathering groups of files into a single archive (such as tar) and compressing that archive for efficient storage (gzip, bzip2, and lzop). However, you can also do the two steps together by using additional options to the tar command.

Creating Backup Archives with tar

The tar command, which stands for *tape archiver*, dates back to early UNIX systems. Although magnetic tape was the common medium that tar wrote to originally, today, tar is most often used to create an archive file that can be distributed using a variety of media.

The fact that the `tar` command is rich in features is reflected in the dozens of options available with `tar`. The basic operations of `tar`, however, are used to create a backup archive (-c), extract files from an archive (-x), and update files in an archive (-u). You can also append files to (-r or -A) or list the contents of an archive (-t).

NOTE *Although the* `tar` *command is available on nearly all UNIX and BSD systems, it behaves differently on many systems. For example, Solaris does not support* -z *to manage* `tar` *archives compressed in gzip format. The* `Star` *(pronounced ess-tar) command supports access control lists (ACLs) and file flags (for extended permissions used by Samba).*

As part of the process of creating a `tar` archive, you can add options that compress the resulting archive. For example, add -j to compress the archive in `bzip2` format or -z to compress in `gzip` format. By convention, regular `tar` files end in `.tar`, while compressed `tar` files end in `.tar.bz2` (compressed with `bzip2`) or `.tar.gz` (compressed with `gzip`). If you compress a file manually with `lzop` (see www.lzop.org), the compressed `tar` file should end in `.tar.lzo`. (As root, type `pkg_add -r lzop` to install `lzop`.)

In addition to being used for backups, `tar` files are popular ways to distribute source code and binaries from software projects. That's because you can expect every BSD and UNIX -like system to contain the tools you need to work with `tar` files.

NOTE *One quirk of working with the* `tar` *command comes from the fact that* `tar` *was created before there were standards regarding how options are entered. Although you can prefix* `tar` *options with a dash, it isn't always necessary. So you might see a command that begins* `tar` `xvf` *with no dashes to indicate the options.*

A classic example for using the `tar` *command might combine old-style options and pipes for compressing the output; for example:*

```
$ tar cf - *.txt | gzip -c > myfiles.tar.gz Make archive, zip it and output
```

The example just shown illustrates a two-step process you might find in documentation for old UNIX systems. The `tar` command creates (c) an archive from all .txt files in the current directory. Instead of writing to the default tape device (/dev/sa0), the f option says to direct output to a file (or in this case, "-" for standard output). The output is piped to the `gzip` command and output to stdout (-c), and then redirected to the `myfiles.tar.gz` file. Note that `tar` is one of the few commands that doesn't require that options be preceded by a dash (-).

New tar versions, on modern BSD systems, can **create the archive and compress the output** in one step:

```
$ tar czf myfiles.tar.gz *.txt    Create gzipped tar file of .txt files
$ tar czvf myfiles.tar.gz *.txt   Be more verbose creating archive
a textfile1.txt
a textfile2.txt
```

In the examples just shown, note that the new archive name (`myfiles.tar.gz`) must immediately follow the `f` option to `tar` (which indicates the name of the archive). Otherwise the output from `tar` will be directed to the default tape device (`/dev/sa0`) or stdout (if you use "-" instead of a file name). The `z` option says to do `gzip` compression and `v` produces verbose descriptions of processing.

When you want to **return the files to a file system** (unzipping and untarring), you can also do that as either a one-step or two-step process, using the `tar` and optionally the `gunzip` command:

```
$ gunzip -c myfiles.tar.gz | tar xf -        Unzips and untars archive
```

Or try the following command line instead:

```
$ gunzip myfiles.tar.gz ; tar xf myfiles.tar   Unzips then untars archive
```

This command removes the `tar.gz` file, leaving only the `.tar` file. To do that same procedure in one step, you could use the following command:

```
$ tar xzvf myfiles.tar.gz
x textfile1.txt
x textfile2.txt
```

The result of the previous commands is that the archived `.txt` files are copied from the archive to the current directory. The `x` option extracts the files, `z` uncompresses (unzips) the files, `v` makes the output and `f` indicates that the next option is the name of the archive file (`myfiles.tar.gz`).

Using Compression Tools

Compression is an important aspect of working with backup files. It takes less disk space on your backup medium (CD, DVD, tape, and so on) or server to store compressed files. It also takes less time to transfer the archives to the media or download the files over a network.

Although compression can save a lot of storage space and transfer times, it can significantly increase your CPU usage. You can consider using hardware compression on a tape drive (see www.amanda.org/docs/faq.html#id346016).

> **NOTE** *See the man page of the* `mt` *command for details on how compression can be set via software for most magnetic tape drives.*

In the examples shown in the previous section, `tar` calls the `gzip` command. But `tar` can work with many compression tools. Out of the box on FreeBSD, `tar` will work with `gzip` and `bzip2`. A third compression utility we add to our toolbox is the `lzop` command, which can be used with `tar` in a different way. The order of these tools from fastest/least compression to slowest/most compression is: `lzop`, `gzip`, and `bzip2`.

If you are archiving and compressing large amounts of data, the time it takes to compress your backups can be significant. So you should be aware that, in general, `bzip2` may take about five times longer than `lzop` and only give you twice the compression. However, with each compression command, you can choose different compression levels, to balance the need for more compression with the time that compression takes.

To use the `tar` command with **bzip2 compression**, use the `-j` option. You can add the bzip2 package with `pkg_add -r bzip2` if it does not exist:

```
$ tar cjvf myfiles.tar.bz2 *.txt    Create archive, compress with bzip2
```

You can also **uncompress (-j) a bzip2 compressed file** as you extract files (`-x`) using the `tar` command:

```
$ tar xjvf myfiles.tar.bz2   Extract files, uncompress bzip2 compression
```

The `lzop` compression utility is a bit less integrated into `tar`. Before you can use `lzop`, you need to install the `lzop` package. To do **lzop compression**, you can pipe the output of `tar` to `lzop` as follows:

```
# pkg_add -r lzop
$ tar -cf - *.txt | lzop > myfiles.tar.lzo    Create lzop compressed tar archive
$ lzop -d < myfiles.tar.lzo | tar -xf -       Extract lzop-compressed tar archive
```

In the previous examples, the command line reverses the old syntax of `tar` with a switch before the command. For normal use and in other examples, we used the modern syntax of `tar` with no switch.

> **NOTE** *You may encounter* `.rar` *compressed files in the RAR format. This format seems to be popular in the world of peer-to-peer networks. RAR is a proprietary format so there is no widespread compressing tool. There is a rar package available in the FreeBSD ports system (/usr/ports/archivers/rar). The unrar command, on the other hand, has a binary package available with FreeBSD.*

Compressing with gzip

As noted, you can **use any of the compression commands alone** (as opposed to within the `tar` command line). Here are some examples of the `gzip` command to create and work with `gzip`-compressed files:

```
$ gzip myfile                gzips myfile and renames it myfile.gz
```

The following command provides the same result, with verbose output:

```
$ gzip -v myfile             gzips myfile with verbose output
myfile: 86.0% -- replaced with myfile.gz
$ gzip -tv myfile.gz         Tests integrity of gzip file
myfile.gz:    OK
$ gzip -lv myfile.gz         Get detailed info about gzip file
```

```
method   crc    date   time     compressed      uncompr.  ratio uncompressed_name
defla  0f27d9e4 Jul 10 04:48       46785         334045   86.0% myfile
```

Use any one of the following commands to **compress all files in a directory**:

```
$ gzip -rv mydir        Compress all files in a directory
mydir/file1: 39.1% -- replaced with mydir/file1.gz
mydir/file2: 39.5% -- replaced with mydir/file2.gz
$ gzip -1 myfile        Fastest compression time, least compression
$ gzip -9 myfile        Slowest compression time, most compression
```

Add a dash before a number from 1 to 9 to set the compression level. As illustrated above, -1 is the fastest (least) and -9 is the slowest (most) compression. The default for gzip is level 6. The lzop command has fewer levels: 1, 3 (default), 7, 8, and 9. Compression levels for bzip2 behave differently.

To **uncompress a gzipped file**, you can use the gunzip command. Use either of the following examples:

```
$ gunzip -v myfile.gz       Unzips myfile.gz and renames it myfile
myfile.gz:       86.0% -- replaced with myfile
$ gzip -dv myfile.gz        Same as previous command line
```

Although the examples just shown refer to zipping regular files, the same options can be used to compress tar archives.

Compressing with bzip2

The **bzip2 command** is considered to provide the highest compression among the compression tools described in this chapter. Here are some examples of bzip2:

```
$ bzip2 myfile          Compresses file and renames it myfile.bz2
$ bzip2 -v myfile       Same as previous command, but more verbose
  myfile:  9.529:1, 0.840 bits/byte, 89.51% saved, 334045 in, 35056 out.
$ bunzip2 myfile.bz2    Uncompresses file and renames it myfile
$ bzip2 -d myfile.bz2   Same as previous command
$ bunzip2 -v myfile.bz2 Same as previous command, but more verbose
  myfile.bz2: done
```

Compressing with lzop

The lzop command behaves differently from gzip and bzip2. The lzop command is best in cases where compression speed is more important than the resulting compression ratio. When lzop compresses the contents of a file it leaves the original file intact (unless you use -U), but creates a new file with a .lzo suffix. Use either of the following examples of the **lzop command to compress a file called myfile**:

```
$ lzop -v myfile            Leave myfile, create compressed myfile.lzo
compressing myfile into myfile.lzo
$ lzop -U myfile            Remove myfile, create compressed myfile.lzo
```

With **myfile.lzo** created, choose any of the following commands to **test, list, or uncompress** the file:

```
$ lzop -t myfile.lzo          Test the compressed file's integrity
$ lzop --info myfile.lzo      List internal header for each file
$ lzop -l myfile.lzo          List compression info for each file
method   compressed  uncompr. ratio uncompressed_name
LZO1X-1     59008      99468  59.3% myfile
$ lzop --ls myfile.lzo        Show contents of compressed file as ls -l
$ cat myfile | lzop > x.lzo   Compress standin and direct to stdout
$ lzop -dv myfile.lzo         Leave myfile.lzo, make uncompressed myfile
```

Unlike gzip and bzip2, lzop has no related command for unlzopping. Always just use the -d option to lzop to uncompress a file. If fed a list of file and directory names, the lzop command will compress all files and ignore directories. The original file name, permission modes, and timestamps are used on the compressed file as were used on the original file.

Listing, Joining, and Adding Files to tar Archives

So far, all we've done with tar is create and unpack archives. There are also options for listing the contents of archives, joining archives together, adding files to an existing archive, and deleting files from an archive.

To **list an archive's contents,** use the -t option:

```
$ tar tvf myfiles.tar            List files from uncompressed archive
-rw-r--r-- root/root   9584 2008-07-05 11:20:33 textfile1.txt
-rw-r--r-- root/root   9584 2008-07-09 10:23:44 textfile2.txt
$ tar tzvf myfiles.tgz           List files from gzip compressed archive
```

If the archive were a tar archive compressed with lzop and named myfile.tar.lzo, you could **list that tar/lzo file's contents** as follows:

```
$ lzop -d < myfiles.tar.lzo | tar -tf -     List lzo/tar archives
```

Use the -r option to **add one or more files to an existing archive.** In the following example, myfile is added to the archive.tar archive file:

```
$ tar rvf archive.tar myfile    Add a file to a tar archive
```

You can use wildcards to **match multiple files to add** to your archive:

```
$ tar rvf archive.tar *.txt     Add multiple files to a tar archive
```

Backing Up Over Networks

After you have backed up your files and gathered them into a `tar` archive, what do you do with that archive? The primary reason for having a backup is in case something happens (such as hard disk crash) where you need to restore files from that backup. Methods you can employ to keep those backups safe include:

❑ **Copying backups to removable media** such as tape, CD, or DVD (as described later in this chapter)

❑ **Copying them to another machine** over a network

Fast and reliable networks, inexpensive high-capacity hard disks, and the security that comes with moving your data off-site have all made network backups a popular practice. For an individual backing up personal data or for a small office, combining a few simple commands may be all you need to create efficient and secure backups. This approach represents a direct application of the UNIX philosophy: joining together simple programs that do one thing to get a more complex job done.

Although just about any command that can copy files over a network can be used to move your backup data to a remote machine, some utilities are especially good for the job. Using OpenSSH tools such as `ssh` and `scp`, you can set up secure password-less transfers of backup archives and encrypted transmissions of those archives.

Tools such as the `rsync` command can save resources by backing up only files (or parts of files) that have changed since the previous backup. With tools such as `unison` (`www.cis.upenn.edu/~bcpierce/unison/`), you can back up files over a network from Windows, as well as BSD systems.

The following sections describe some of these techniques for backing up your data to other machines over a network.

> **NOTE** *A similar tool that might interest you is the* `rsnapshot` *command* (`pkg_add -r rshapshot`). *The* `rsnapshot` *command* (`www.rsnapshot.org/`) *can work with with* `rsync` *to make configurable hourly, daily, weekly or monthly snapshots of a file system. It uses hard links to keep a snapshot of a file system, which it can then sync with changed files.*

Backing Up tar Archives Over ssh

OpenSSH (`www.openssh.org/`) provides tools to securely do remote login, remote execution, and remote file copy over network interfaces. By setting up two machines to share encryption keys, you can transfer files between those machines without entering passwords for each transmission. That fact lets you create scripts to back up your data from an SSH client to an SSH server, without any manual intervention.

From a central BSD system, you can **gather backups from multiple client machines** using OpenSSH commands. The following example runs the `tar` command on a remote site (to archive and compress the files), pipes the `tar` stream to standard output, and uses the `ssh` command to catch the backup locally (over `ssh`) with `tar`:

```
$ mkdir mybackup ; cd mybackup
$ ssh francois@server1 'tar cf - myfile*' | tar xvf -
francois@server1's password: ******
myfile1
myfile2
```

In the example just shown, all files beginning with `myfile` are copied from the home directory of francois on server1 and placed in the current directory. Note that the left side of the pipe creates the archive and the right side expands the files from the archive to the current directory. (Keep in mind that ssh might overwrite local files if they exist, which is why we created an empty directory in the example.)

To reverse the process and **copy files from the local system to the remote system**, we run a local `tar` command first. This time, however, we add a `cd` command to put the files in the directory of our choice on the remote machine:

```
$ tar cf - myfile* | ssh francois@server1 \
        'cd /home/francois/myfolder; tar xvf -'
francois@server1's password: ******
myfile1
myfile2
```

In this next example, we're not going to untar the files on the receiving end, but instead **write the results to tgz files:**

```
$ ssh francois@server1 'tar czf - myfile*' | cat > myfiles.tgz
$ tar cvzf - myfile* | ssh francois@server1 'cat > myfiles.tgz'
```

The first example takes all files beginning with `myfile` from the francois user's home directory on server1, tars and compresses those files, and directs those compressed files to the `myfiles.tgz` file on the local system. The second example does the reverse by taking all files beginning with `myfile` in the local directory and sending them to a `myfiles.tgz` file on the remote system.

The examples just shown are good for copying files over the network. Besides providing compression they also enable you to use any `tar` features you choose, such as incremental backup features.

Backing Up Files with rsync

A more feature-rich command for doing backups is `rsync`. What makes `rsync` so unique is the `rsync` algorithm, which compares the local and remote files one small block at a time using checksums, and only transfers the blocks that are different. This algorithm is so efficient that it has been reused in many backup products. To add the rsync package, you can use `pkg_add -r rsync`.

The `rsync` command can work either on top of a remote shell (`ssh`), or by running an `rsyncd` daemon on the server end. The following example uses `rsync` over ssh to mirror a directory:

```
$ rsync -avz --delete chris@server1:/home/chris/pics/ chrispics/
```

The command just shown is intended to mirror the remote directory structure (`/home/chris/pics/`) to a directory on the local system (`chrispics/`). The `-a` says to run in archive mode (recursively copying all files from the remote directory), the `-z` option compresses the files, and `-v` makes the output verbose. The `--delete` tells `rsync` to delete any files on the local system that no longer exist on the remote system.

For on-going backups, you can have `rsync` do seven-day incremental backups. Here's an example:

```
# mkdir /mnt/backups
# rsync --delete --backup                          \
    --backup-dir=/mnt/backups/backup-`date +%A` \
    -avz chris@server1:/home/chris/Personal/      \
    /mnt/backups/current-backup/
```

When the command just shown runs, all the files from `/home/chris/Personal` on the remote system server1 are copied to the local directory `/mnt/backups/current-backup`. The first time the command is run, all files are backed up to the current-backup directory. The next time the command runs (on the next day), all files modified that day are copied to a directory named after the current day of the week, such as `/mnt/backups/backup-Monday`. Over a week, seven directories will be created that reflect changes over each of the past seven days.

Another trick for rotated backups is to use hard links instead of multiple copies of the files. This two-step process consists of rotating the files, then running `rsync`:

```
# rm -rf /mnt/backups/backup-old/
# mv /mnt/backups/backup-current/ /mnt/backups/backup-old/
# rsync --delete --link-dest=/mnt/backups/backup-old -avz \
    chris@server1:/home/chris/Personal/ /mnt/backups/backup-current/
```

In the previous procedure, the existing `backup-current` directory replaces the `backup-old` directory, deleting the two-week-old full backup with last-week's full backup. When the new full backup is run with `rsync` using the `--link-dest` option, if any of the files being backed up from the remote `Personal` directory on server1 existed during the previous backup (now in `backup-old`), a hard link between the file in the `backup-current` directory and `backup-old` directory is created.

You can save a lot of space by having hard links between files in your `backup-old` and `backup-current` directory. For example, if you had a file named `file1.txt` in both directories, you could check that both were the same physical file by listing the files' inodes as follows:

```
$ ls -i /mnt/backups/backup*/file1.txt
260761   /mnt/backups/backup-current/file1.txt
260761   /mnt/backups/backup-old/file1.txt
```

Backing Up with unison

Although the `rsync` command is good to back up one machine to another, it assumes that the machine being backed up is the only one where the data is being modified. What if you have two machines that both modify the same file and you want to sync those files? Unison is a tool that will let you do that.

It's common for people to want to work with the same documents on their laptop and desktop systems. Those machines might even run different operating systems. Because unison is a cross-platform application, it can let you **sync files** that are on both BSD and Windows systems. In FreeBSD, to use unison you must install the unison package (type the `pkg_add -r unison` command).

With unison, you can define two *roots* representing the two paths to synchronize. Those roots can be local or remote over ssh. For example:

```
$ unison /home/francois ssh://francois@server1//home/fcaen
$ unison /home/francois /mnt/backups/francois-homedir
```

Unison contains both graphical and command-line tools for doing unison backups. It will try to run the graphical version by default. This may fail if you don't have a desktop running or if you're launching unison from within screen. To **force unison to run in command line mode**, add the `-ui text` option as follows:

```
$ unison /home/francois ssh://francois@server1//home/fcaen -ui text
Contacting server...
francois@server1's password:
Looking for changes
    Waiting for changes from server
Reconciling changes
local           server1
newfile ---->            memo.txt  [f] y
Propagating updates
    ...
```

The unison utility will then compare the two roots and for each change that occurred since last time, ask you what you want to do. In the example above, there's a new file called `memo.txt` on the local system. You are asked if you want to proceed with the update (in this case, copy `memo.txt` from the local machine to server1). Type **y** to do the updates.

If you trust unison, add `-auto` to make it take default actions without prompting you:

```
$ unison /home/francois ssh://francois@server1//home/fcaen -auto
```

There is no man page for unison. However, you can see `unison` options with the `-help` option. There is a manual in `/usr/local/share/doc/unison`. You can also display and page through the `unison` manual using the `-doc all` option as shown here:

```
$ unison -help               See unison options
$ unison -doc all | less      Display unison manual
```

If you find yourself synchronizing two roots frequently, you can **create a profile**, which is a series of presets. In graphical mode, the default screen makes you create profiles. Profiles are stored in `.prf` text files in the `~/.unison/` directory. They can be as simple as the following:

```
root = /home/francois
root = ssh://francois@server1//home/fcaen
```

If this is stored in a profile called `fc-home.prf` you can invoke it simply with the following command line:

```
$ unison fc-home
```

Backing Up to Removable Media

The capacity of CDs and DVDs, and the low costs of those media, has made them attractive options as computer backup media. Using tools that commonly come with BSD systems, you can gather files to back up into CD or DVD images and burn those images to the appropriate media.

Command-line tools such as `mkisofs` (for creating CD images) and `cdrecord` (for burning images to CD or DVD) once provided the most popular interfaces for making backups to CD or DVD. Now there are many graphical front ends to those tools you could also consider using. For example, GUI tools for mastering and burning CDs/DVDs include K3b (the KDE CD and DVD Kreator) and Nautilus (GNOME's file manager that offers a CD-burning feature). Other GUI tools for burning CDs include gcombust, X-CD-Roast, and graveman.

The commands for creating file system images to back up to CD or DVD, as well as to burn those images, are described in this section. To get the `mkisofs` and `cdrecord` commands you need to install the cdrtools package (`pkg_add -r cdrtools`).

Creating Backup Images with mkisofs

Most data CDs and DVDs can be accessed on both Windows and BSD systems because they are created using the ISO9660 standard for formatting the information on those discs. Because most modern operating systems need to save more information about file and directories than the basic ISO9660 standard includes, extensions to that standard were added to contain that information.

Using the mkisofs command, you can back up the file and directory structure from any point in your BSD file system and produce an ISO9660 image. That image can include the following kinds of extensions:

❏ **System Use Sharing Protocol** (SUSP) are records identified in the Rock Ridge Interchange Protocol. SUSP records can include UNIX -style attributes, such as ownership, long file names, and special files (such as character devices and symbolic links).

❏ **Joliet** directory records store longer file names in a form that makes them usable to Windows systems.

❏ **Hierarchical File System** (HFS) extensions allow the ISO image to appear as an HFS file system, which is the native file system for Macintosh computers. Likewise, Data and Resource forks can be added in different ways to be read by Macs.

When you set out to create your ISO image, consider where you will ultimately need to access the files you back up using mkisofs (BSD, Linux, Windows, or Macs). After the image is created, it can be used in different ways, the most obvious of which is to burn the image to a CD or DVD.

Besides being useful in producing all or portions of a BSD file system to use on a portable medium, mkisofs is also useful for creating live CDs/DVDs. It does this by adding boot information to the image that can launch a BSD kernel or other operating system, bypassing the computer's hard drive.

Because most BSD users store their personal files in their home directories, a common way to use mkisofs to back up files is to back up everything under the /home directory. Here are some examples of using mkisofs to create an ISO image from all files and directories under the /home directory:

```
# cd /tmp
# mkisofs -o home.iso /home              Create basic ISO9660 image
# mkisofs -o home2.iso -J -R /home       Add Joliet Rock Ridge extensions
# mkisofs -o home3.iso -J -R -hfs /home  Also add HFS extensions
```

In each of the three examples above, all files and directories beneath the /home directory are added to the ISO image (home.iso). The first example has no extensions, so all file names are converted to DOS-style naming (8.3 characters). The second example uses Joliet and Rock Ridge extensions, so file names and permissions should appear as they did on the original BSD system when you open the ISO on a BSD, Linux, or Windows system. The last example also makes the files on the image readable from a Mac file system.

You can **have multiple sources added to the image**. Here are some examples:

```
# mkisofs -o home.iso -R -J music/ docs/ \   Multiple directories/files
        chris.pdf /var/spool/mail
# mkisofs -o home.iso -J -R              \   Graft files on to the image
    -graft-points Pictures/=/var/pics/   \
    /home/chris
```

The first example above shows various files and directories being combined and placed on the root of the ISO image. The second example grafts the contents of the /var/pics directory into the /home/chris/Pictures directory. As a result, on the CD image the /Pictures directory will contain all content from the /var/pics directory. Use the -graft option if backing up files from multiple directories causes name duplication errors.

Adding information into the header of the ISO image can help you identify the contents of that image later. This is especially useful if the image is being saved or distributed online, without a physical disc you can write on. Here are some examples:

```
# mkisofs -o /tmp/home.iso -R -J          \   Add header info to ISO
    -p www.handsonhistory.com             \
    -publisher "Swan Bay Folk Art Center" \
    -V "WebBackup"                        \
    -A "mkisofs"                          \
    -volset "All web site material on November 2, 2008" \
    /home/chris
```

In the example above, -p indicates the preparer ID, which could include a phone number, mailing address or web site for contacting the preparer of the ISO image. With the option -publisher, you can indicate a 128-character description of the preparer (possibly the company or organization name). The -V indicates the volume ID. Volume ID is important because in some operating systems this volume ID is used to mount the CD when it is inserted. For example, in the command line shown above, the CD would be mounted on /media/WebBackup in FreeBSD and other BSD systems. The -A option can be used to indicate the application used to create the ISO image. The -volset option can contain a string of information about a set of ISO images.

When you have created your ISO image, and before you burn it to disc, you **can check the image** and make sure you can access the files it contains. Here are ways to check it out:

```
# isoinfo -d -i home.iso        Display header information
CD-ROM is in ISO 9660 format
System id: FreeBSD
Volume id: WebBackup
Volume set id: All Website material on November 2, 2008
Publisher id: Swan Bay Folk Art Center
Data preparer id: www.handsonhistory.com
```

```
Application id: mkisofs
Copyright File id:
Abstract File id:
Bibliographic File id:
Volume set size is: 1
Volume set sequence number is: 1
Logical block size is: 2048
Volume size is: 23805
Joliet with UCS level 3 found
Rock Ridge signatures version 1 found
```

You can see a lot of the information entered on the mkisofs command line when the image was created. If this had been an image that was going to be published, we might also have indicated the locations on the CD of a copyright file (-copyright), abstract file (-abstract), and bibliographic file (-biblio). Provided that the header is okay, you can next try accessing files on the ISO image by mounting it:

```
# mkdir /mnt/myimage                           Create a mount point
# mdconfig -a -t vnode -f home.iso -u 0   Create a memory disk device for ISO
# mount -t cd9660 /dev/md0 /mnt/myimage   Mount the ISO
# ls -l /mnt/myimage                          Check the ISO contents
# umount /mnt/myimage                         Unmount the image when done
```

Besides checking that you can access the files and directories on the ISO, make sure that the date- and timestamps, ownership, and permissions are set as you would like. That information might be useful if you need to restore the information at a later date.

Burning Backup Images with cdrecord

The cdrecord command is the most popular BSD command line tool for burning CD and DVD images. After you have created an ISO image (as described earlier) or obtained one otherwise (such as downloading an install CD or live CD from the Internet), cdrecord makes it easy to put that image on a disc. To use cdrecord, you must have the cdrtools package installed and you need to load the driver required by your CD burner. For example:

```
# pkg_add -r cdrtools
# kldload /boot/kernel/atapicam.ko
```

There is no difference in making a CD or DVD ISO image, aside from the fact that a DVD image can obviously be bigger than a CD image. Check the media you have for their capacity. A CD can typically hold 650 MB, 700 MB, or 800 MB, whereas mini CDs can hold 50 MB, 180 MB, 185 MB, or 193 MB. Single-layer DVDs hold 4.7 GB while double-layer DVDs can hold 8.4 GB.

> **NOTE**   *Keep in mind, however, that CD/DVD manufacturers list their capacities based on 1000 KB per 1 MB, instead of 1024 KB. Type* du --si home.iso *to list the size of your ISO instead of* du -sh *as you would normally, to check if your ISO will fit on the media you have.*

Before you begin burning your image to CD or DVD, check that your drive supports CD/DVD burning and determine the address of the drive. Use the `--scanbus` option to `cdrecord` to do that:

```
# cdrecord --scanbus          Shows a drive that cannot do burning
scsibus0:
       0,0,0   0) 'SAMSUNG ' 'DVD-ROM SD-616E ' 'F503' Removable CD-ROM
       0,0,0   1) *
       0,0,0   2) *
               ...
# cdrecord --scanbus          Shows a drive that can burn CDs or DVDs
scsibus0:
       0,0,0   0) 'LITE-ON ' 'DVDRW SOHW-1633S' 'BS0C' Removable CD-ROM
       0,0,0   1) *
       0,0,0   2) *
               ...
```

In the two examples shown, the first indicates a CD/DVD drive that only supports reading and cannot burn CDs (DVD-ROM and CD-ROM). The second example shows a drive that can burn CDs or DVDs (DVDRW). Insert the medium you want to record on. Assuming your drive can burn the media you have, here are some simple `cdrecord` commands for burning a CD or DVD images:

```
# cdrecord -blank=fast ...          Blank a CDRW disc in fast mode
# cdrecord -dummy home.iso ...      Test burn without actually burning
# cdrecord -v home.iso ...          Burn CD (default settings) in verbose
# cdrecord -v -e d speed=24 home.iso... Set specific speed
# cdrecord -pad home.iso ...        Can't read track so add 15 zeroed sectors
# cdrecord -eject home.iso          Eject CD/DVD when burn is done
# cdrecord -/dev/cdrw home.iso...   Identify drive by device name (may differ)
# cdrecord dev=0,2,0 home.iso       Identify drive by SCSI name
```

The `cdrecord` command can also burn multi-session CDs/DVDs. Here is an example:

```
# cdrecord -multi home.iso      Start a multi-burn session
# cdrecord -msinfo              Check the session offset for next burn
Using /dev/cdrom of unknown capabilities
0,93041
# mkisofs -J -R -o new.iso \    Create a second ISO to burn
   -C 0,93041 /home/chris/more  Indicate start point and new data for ISO
# cdrecord new.iso              Burn new data to existing CD
```

You can use multiple -multi burns until the CD is filled up. For the final burn, don't use -multi, so that the CD will be closed.

Making and Burning DVDs with growisofs

Using the `growisofs` command you can combine the two steps of gathering files into an ISO image (mkisofs) and burning that image to DVD (cdrecord). Besides saving a step, the `growisofs` command also offers the advantage of keeping a session open by default until you close it, so you don't need to do anything special for multi-burn sessions.

Here is an example of some `growisofs` commands for a **multi-burn session**:

```
# growisofs -Z /dev/cd0 -R -J /home/chris    Master and burn to DVD
# growisofs -Z /dev/cd0 -R -J /home/francois  Add to burn
# growisofs -M /dev/cd0=/dev/zero             Close burn
```

If you want to add options when creating the ISO image, you can simply add `mkisofs` options to the command line. (For example, see how the `-R` and `-J` options are added in the above examples.)

If you want to **burn a DVD image using growisofs**, you can use the **-dvd-compat** option. Here's an example:

```
# growisofs -dvd-compat -Z /dev/cd0=image.iso  Burn an ISO image to DVD
```

The `-dvd-compat` option can improve compatibility with different DVD drives over some multi-session DVD burning procedures.

Summary

BSD and its predecessor UNIX systems handled data backups by combining commands that each handled a discrete set of features. Backups of your critical data can still be done in this way. In fact, many of the tools you can use will perform more securely and efficiently than ever before.

The tape archiver utility (`tar` command) has expanded well beyond its original job of making magnetic tape backups of data files. Because nearly every BSD, Linux, and UNIX system includes `tar`, it has become a standard utility for packaging software and backing up data to compressed archives. Those archives can then be transported and stored in a variety of ways.

To move backed up data to other machines over a network, you can use remote execution features of OpenSSH tools (such as `ssh`). You can also use an excellent utility called `rsync`. With `rsync`, you can save resources by only backing up files (or parts of files) that have changed.

Inexpensive CDs and DVDs have made those media popular for doing personal and small-office backups. The `mkisofs` command can create file systems of backed up data in ISO9660 format that can be restored on a variety of systems (BSD, Linux, Windows, or Mac). After `mkisofs` command has created an ISO image, the image can be burned to CD or DVD using the `cdrecord` or `growisofs` commands.

9

Checking and Managing Running Processes

When an executable program starts up, it runs as a process that is under the management of your BSD system's process table. Every BSD system provides all the tools you need to view and change the processes running on your system.

The ps and top commands are great for viewing information on your running processes. There are literally dozens of options to ps and top to help you view process information exactly the way you want to. The pgrep command can further help find the process you want.

There are commands such as nice and renice for raising and lowering processor priority for a process. You can move processes to run in the background (bg command) or back to the foreground (fg command).

Sending signals to a process is a way of changing its behavior or killing it altogether. Using the kill and killall commands, you can send signals to processes by PID or name, respectively. You can also send other signals to processes to do such things as reread configuration files or continue on with a stopped process.

To run commands at scheduled times or so they are not tied to your shell session, you can use the at and batch commands. To run commands repetitively at set times, there are the cron and anacron facilities.

Listing Active Processes

To see which processes are currently running on a system, most people use the `ps` and `top` commands. The `ps` command gives you a snapshot (in a simple list) of processes running at the moment. The `top` command offers a screen-oriented, constantly updated listing of running commands, sorted as you choose (by CPU use, I/O, UID, and so on).

> **NOTE** *To see all the output shown in the following examples, you need to mount the proc file system. One way to do that is to add the following line to your /etc/fstab file (as root user):*
>
> ```
> proc    /proc    procfs  rw     0 0
> ```
>
> *Then type the following command (as root user):*
>
> ```
> # mount  /proc
> ```

Viewing Active Processes with ps

Every BSD system (as well as every system derived from UNIX, such as Linux, Mac OS X, and others) includes the `ps` command. Over the years, however, many slightly different versions of `ps` have appeared, offering slightly different options. Because `ps` dates back to the first UNIX systems, it also supports non-standard ways of entering some options (for example, allowing you to drop the dash before an option in some cases).

The different uses of `ps` shown in this chapter will work on FreeBSD, OpenBSD, NetBSD, and most other UNIX and Linux systems. Here are some examples you can run to **show processes running for the current user** (Table 9-1 contains column descriptions of `ps` output):

```
$ ps                       List processes of current user at current shell
 PID TT  STAT    TIME  COMMAND
 010 v0  I+   0.00.09  -sh (sh)
1117 v2  S    0.00.02  -sh (sh)
1125 v2  R+   0.00.00  ps
$ ps -U chris              Show all chris' running processes (simple output)
 PID TT  STAT    TIME  COMMAND
1132 ??  S    0:00.01  sshd: chris@ttyp0 (sshd)
 810 v0  I+   0.00.09  -sh (sh)
1117 v2  S    0.00.02  -sh (sh)
1125 v2  R+   0.00.00  ps -U chris
1133 p0  Ss+  0.00.00  -sh (sh)
 ...
$ ps -U chris -u          Show all chris' running processes (with CPU/MEM)
USER     PID %CPU %MEM  VSZ  RSS  TT  STAT STARTED    TIME COMMAND
chris   1132  0.0  1.3 6252 3312  ??  S     4:52PM  0:00.03 sshd: chris@ttyp0
chris    810  0.0  0.6 1756 1400  v0  I+    3:30PM  0:00.09 -sh (sh)
chris   1117  0.0  0.6 1752 1396  v2  I+    4:45PM  0:00.05 -sh (sh)
chris   1133  0.0  0.6 1756 1396  p0  Ss    4:52PM  0:00.03 -sh (sh)
chris   1204  0.0  0.4 1460 1036  p0  R+    5:07PM  0:00.00 ps -U chris -u
 ...
```

```
$ ps -fU chris          Show all chris' running processes (with PID)
  PID  TT  STAT      TIME COMMAND
 1132  ??  S      0:00.06 sshd: chris@ttyp0 (sshd)
  810  v0  I+     0:00.09 -sh (sh)
 1117  v2  I+     0:00.05 -sh (sh)
 1133  p0  Ss     0:00.03 -sh (sh)
 1211  p0  R+     0:00.00 ps -fU chris
 . . .
$ ps -vU chris          Show all chris' running processes (with SL and RE)
  PID STAT       TIME  SL  RE PAGEIN   VSZ   RSS  LIM TSIZ %CPU %MEM COMMAND
 1132 S       0:00.16   0 127      0  6252  3312    -  168  0.0  1.3 sshd: chris
  810 I+      0:00.09 127 127      2  1756  1400    -  100  0.0  0.6 -sh (sh)
 1133 Ss      0:00.08   0 127      0  1756  1400    -  100  0.0  0.6 -sh (sh)
 1244 I+      0:00.02  47 110      0  1752  1392    -  100  0.0  0.6 -sh (sh)
 1264 R+      0:00.01   0   0      0  1460  1044    -   24  0.0  0.4 ps -vU
 . . .
```

These examples illustrate some of the processes from a user logged in locally and remotely (over sshd). The first example above shows ps alone being run from a Terminal window, so you only see the processes for the current shell running in that window. Other examples let you display different information for each process. The SL and RE columns show how many seconds the process has been sleeping and how long it has been in core memory, respectively (127 means forever).

Here are ps examples showing output for **every process currently running on the system:**

```
$ ps -x | less        Show running processes, even without controlling terminals
  PID  TT  STAT      TIME COMMAND
    0  ??  WLs    0:00.00 [swapper]
    1  ??  ILs    0:00.01 /sbin/init --
    2  ??  DL     0:00.49 [g_event]
 . . .
$ ps -xl | less       Show long listing of processes
  UID  PID PPID CPU PRI NI   VSZ   RSS MWCHAN STAT  TT       TIME COMMAND
    0    0    0   1  96  0     0     0 -      WLs   ??    0:00.00 [swapper]
    0    1    0   0   8  0   772   388 wait   ILs   ??    0:00.01 /sbin/init
    0    2    0   0  -8  0     0     8 -      DL    ??    0:00.49 [g_event]
 . . .
$ ps -xj | less       Show running process, with user name/process group
USER   PID PPID PGID  SID JOBC STAT  TT       TIME COMMAND
root     0    0    0    0    0 WLs   ??    0:00.00 [swapper]
root     1    0    1    1    0 ILs   ??    0:00.01 /sbin/init --
root     2    0    0    0    0 DL    ??    0:00.56 [g_event]
 . . .
$ ps -aux | less    Show running process, long BSD style
USER    PID %CPU %MEM   VSZ   RSS  TT  STAT STARTED       TIME COMMAND
root     10 99.0  0.0     0     8  ??  RL   3:30PM  209:34.30 [idle]
root      0  0.0  0.0     0     0  ??  WLs  3:30PM    0:00.00 [swapper]
root      1  0.0  0.2   772   388  ??  ILs  3:30PM    0:00.01 /sbin/init --
 . . .
$ ps auwx           Show every running process, long BSD style, wide format
$ ps auwwx          Show every running process, long BSD style, unlimited width
```

The previous two commands are useful if you want to see the entire output of ps entries. If output goes beyond your column width, it will wrap instead of truncating.

Some processes start up other processes. For example, a web server (httpd daemon) will spin off multiple httpd daemons to wait for requests to your web server. You can **view the hierarchy of processes (in a tree view)** using the pstree command (as root, type pkg_add -r pstree to install it):

```
$ pstree              Show processes alphabetically in tree format
-+= 00000 root [swapper]
 |-+= 00001 root /sbin/init --
 | |--= 00121 root adjkerntz -i
   . . .
 | |-+= 00739 root /usr/sbin/sshd
 | | \-+= 01129 root sshd: chris [priv] (sshd)
 | |    \-+- 01132 chris sshd: chris@ttyp0 (sshd)
 | |       \-+= 01133 chris -sh (sh)
 | |          \-+= 01999 chris pstree
 | |             \-+- 02000 chris sh -c ps -axwwo user,pid,ppid,pgid,command
 | |                \--- 02001 chris ps -axwwo user,pid,ppid,pgid,command
   . . .
```

The "tree" example just shown illustrates a different way of displaying the hierarchy of processes. The sshd processes show a running Secure Shell Daemon with a user logging in over the network, resulting in a bash shell (and eventually a ps command) starting.

If you prefer personalized views of ps output, you can select exactly which columns of data to display with ps using the -o option. Table 9-1 shows available column output and the options to add to -o to have each column print with ps.

Table 9-1: Selecting and Viewing ps Column Output

Option	Column Head	Description
%cpu	%CPU	Percentage of CPU use
%mem	%MEM	Percentage memory use
acflag	ACFLG	Accounting flag
args	COMMAND	Command and arguments
comm	COMMAND	Command only
command	COMMAND	Command and arguments (same as args)
cpu	CPU	Short-term CPU usage factor (for scheduling)
etime	ELAPSED	Elapsed runtime

Table 9-1: Selecting and Viewing ps Column Output (*continued*)

Option	Column Head	Description
flags	F	Process flags, in hexadecimal (same as f)
inblk	INBLK	Total blocks read (same as inblock)
jid	JID	Jail ID
jobc	JOBC	Job control count
ktrace	KTRACE	Tracing flags
label	LABEL	MAC label
lim	LIM	Memory use limit
lockname	LOCK	Lock currently blocked on (as a symbolic name)
logname	LOGIN	Login name of user who started the session
lstart	STARTED	Time started
majflt	MAJFLT	Total page faults
minflt	MINFLT	Total page reclaims
msgrcv	MSGRCV	Total messages received (pipes/sockets reads)
msgsnd	MSGSND	Total messages sent (pipes/sockets writes)
mwchan	MWCHAN	Wait channel or lock currently blocked on
nice	NI	Nice value (same as ni)
nivcsw	NIVCSW	Total involuntary context switches
nsigs	NSIGS	Total signals taken (same as nsignals)
nswap	NSWAP	Total swaps in and out
nvcsw	NVCSW	Total voluntary context switches
nwchan	NWCHAN	Wait channel (as an address)
oublk	OUBLK	Total blocks written (same as oublock)
paddr	PADDR	Swap address
pagein	PAGEIN	Pageins (same as majflt)

Continued

Table 9-1: Selecting and Viewing ps Column Output (*continued*)

Option	Column Head	Description
pgid	PGID	Process group number
pid	PID	Process ID
ppid	PPID	Parent process ID
pri	PRI	Scheduling priority
re	RE	Core residency time in seconds (127 means infinity)
rgid	RGID	Real group ID
rgroup	RGROUP	Group name (associated with real group ID)
rss	RSS	Resident set size
rtprio	RTPRIO	Real-time priority (101 means it's not a realtime process)
ruid	RUID	Real user ID
ruser	RUSER	User name (associated with real user ID)
sid	SID	Session ID
sig	PENDING	Pending signals (same as pending)
sigcatch	CAUGHT	Caught signals (same as caught)
sigignore	IGNORED	Ignored signals (same ignored)
sigmask	BLOCKED	Blocked signals (same as blocked)
sl	SL	Sleep time in seconds (127 means infinity)
start	STARTED	Time started
state	STAT	Symbolic process state (same as stat)
svgid	SVGID	Saved gid from a setgid executable
svuid	SVUID	Saved UID from a setuid executable
tdev	TDEV	Control terminal device number
time	TIME	Accumulated CPU time, user + system (same as cputime)

Table 9-1: Selecting and Viewing ps Column Output (*continued*)

Option	Column Head	Description
tsid	TSID	Control terminal session ID
tsiz	TSIZ	Text size in Kbytes
tt	TT	Control terminal name, two letter abbreviation
tty	TTY	Full name of control terminal
uprocp	UPROCP	Process pointer
ucomm	UCOMM	Name to be used for accounting
uid	UID	Effective user ID
upr	UPR	Scheduling priority from system call (same as usrpri)
user	USER	User name (from user ID)
vsz	VSZ	Virtual size in Kbytes (same as vsize)
wchan	WCHAN	Wait channel as a symbolic name
xstat	XSTAT	Exit or stop status (stopped or zombie processes only)

Note that some values that are meant to print user names may still print numbers (UIDs) instead, if the name is too long to fit in the given space. To see the values, use ps -L:

```
$ ps -L          List column options for ps output
%cpu %mem acflag acflg args blocked caught comm command cpu cputime emul etime f
flags ignored inblk inblock jid jobc ktrace label lim lockname login logname
lstart lwp majflt minflt msgrcv msgsnd mwchan ni nice nivcsw nlwp nsignals nsigs
nswap nvcsw nwchan oublk oublock paddr pagein pcpu pending pgid pid pmem ppid
pri re rgid rgroup rss rtprio ruid ruser sid sig sigcatch sigignore sigmask sl
start stat state svgid svuid tdev time tpgid tsid tsiz tt tty ucomm uid upr
uprocp user usrpri vsize vsz wchan xstat
```

Using a comma-separated list of column options, you can produce your custom output. Here are some examples of **custom views of running processes:**

```
$ ps -xo ppid,user,%mem,tsiz,vsz,comm     Display process ID, user, memory, etc.
 PPID USER  %MEM TSIZ  VSZ COMMAND
 1129 chris 1.3  168  6252 sshd
$ ps -xo ppid,user,start,time,%cpu,args  Display PID, user, start, time, etc.
 PPID USER  STARTED     TIME %CPU COMMAND
 1129 chris 4:52PM   0:00.82  0.0 sshd: chris@ttyp0 (sshd)
```

149

```
$ ps -xo ppid,user,nice,cputime,args        Display PID, user, nice, CPU time, etc.
PPID USER  NI     TIME COMMAND
1129 chris  0  0:00.84 sshd: chris@ttyp0 (sshd)
$ ps -xo ppid,user,stat,tty,sid,etime,args  Display PID, user, tty, sid, etc.
PPID USER  STAT TTY     SID     ELAPSED COMMAND
1129 chris S    ??     1129    06:39:23 sshd: chris@ttyp0 (sshd)
```

Here are a few other **extraneous examples of the ps command**:

```
$ ps -aux -r | less                             Sort by CPU usage
USER     PID %CPU %MEM  VSZ  RSS TT  STAT STARTED       TIME COMMAND
root      10 87.4  0.0    0    8 ??  RL    3:30PM 503:12.85 [idle]
root    2551  7.8  0.4 1384  916 v3  R    11:55PM   0:02.50 find .
root       4  1.0  0.0    0    8 ??  DL    3:30PM   0:08.73 [g_down]
$ ps -m | less                                  Sort by memory usage
USER     PID %CPU %MEM  VSZ  RSS TT  STAT STARTED       TIME COMMAND
root    1307  0.0  1.2 4928 3004 v3  I     5:31PM   0:00.58 -csh (csh)
root     745  0.0  1.1 3504 2804 ??  Ss    3:30PM   0:01.04 sendmail:
$ ps -t ttyp0                                   Show ttyp0 processes
 PID  TT  STAT    TIME COMMAND
1133  p0  Ss   0:00.38 -sh (sh)
2595  p0  R+   0:00.00 ps -t ttyp0
$ ps -p 1129 -o pid,ppid,time,args              Display info for PID 1129
 PID  PPID    TIME COMMAND
1129   739 0:08.08 sshd: chris [priv] (sshd)
$ ps -U chris,francois -o pid,ruser,tty,stat,args   See info for two users
PID RUSER     TTY     STAT COMMAND
1132 chris     ??      S   sshd: chris@ttyp0 (sshd)
2480 francois  ??      S   sshd: francois@ttyp1 (sshd)
```

Watching Active Processes with top

If you want to **see the processes running on your system on an on-going basis,** you can use the `top` command. The `top` command runs a screen-oriented view of your running processes that is updated continuously. If you start the `top` command with no options, it displays your system's uptime, tasks, CPU usage, and memory usage, followed by a list of your running processes, sorted by CPU usage. Here's an example:

```
$ top
last pid: 2697;  load averages:  0.04,  0.03,  0.00         up 0+08:44:46
00:14:17
58 processes:  1 running, 57 sleeping
CPU states:  0.0% user,  0.0% nice,  0.8% system,  0.0% interrupt, 99.2% idle
Mem: 58M Active, 97M Inact, 73M Wired, 12M Cache, 34M Buf, 1508K Free
Swap: 484M Total, 484M Free

  PID USERNAME    THR PRI NICE   SIZE    RES STATE   TIME  WCPU COMMAND
 2696 chris         1  96    0 25352K 15520K select  0:03 2.05% gtali
 2618 chris         1  96    0 80392K 14300K select  0:03 0.05% Xorg
 2652 chris         3  20    0 34244K 21356K kserel  0:07 0.00% nautilus
 2650 chris         1  96    0 26564K 16688K select  0:04 0.00% gnome-panel
```

Here are examples of other options you can use to start top to continuously display running processes:

```
$ top -s 5          Change update delay to 5 seconds (from default 3)
$ top -U francois   Only see processes of effective user name francois
$ top -S            Display system processes, as well as other processes
$ top -d 10         Refresh the screen 10 times before quitting
$ top -b            Run in non-interative non-screen-oriented batch mode
```

This last example (top -b) formats the output of top in a way that is suitable for output to a file, as opposed to redrawing the same screen for interactive viewing. This can be used to create a log of processes, for example, when hunting down that runaway process that eats up all your resources in the middle of the night. Here's how to run top and log the output for 10 hours:

```
$ top -b -d 12000 > myprocesslog &
```

When top is running, you can update and sort the process list in different ways. To immediately update the process list, press Space. Press C to sort by CPU and weighted CPU time. Press I to have idle processes displayed or not displayed. Or, press m to toggle between CPU and IO modes. While in IO mode, press o to select the order in which data is sorted.

There are several ways to change the behavior of top as it's running. Press s and type a number representing seconds to change the delay between refreshes. Press u and enter a user name to display only processes for the selected user. To view only a select number of processes, type n and type the number you want to see. Press Ctrl-L at any point to redraw the screen.

You can act on any of the running processes in different ways. To signal (kill) a running process, type k followed by the PID of the process you want to send the signal to. This sends the default 15 signal (TERM), which allows the process to close in an orderly way. To give a process higher or lower run priority, type r and then add a negative number (to increase priority) or a positive number (to reduce priority), followed by the process ID of the process you want to change.

If you want to find more information about how to use top, type ? during a top session. The man page also has a lot of information about how to use top:

```
$ man top          View the top man page
```

When you are done using top, type q to exit.

Finding and Controlling Processes

Changing a running process first means finding the process you want to change, then modifying the processing priority or sending the process a signal to change its behavior. If you are looking for a particular process, you might find it tough to locate it in a large list of processes output by ps or top. The pgrep command offers ways of searching through your active processes for the ones you are looking for. The renice command lets you change the processing priority of running processes. The `kill`, `pkill`, and `killall` commands let you send signals to running processes (including signals to end those processes).

Using pgrep to Find Processes

In its most basic form, you can use `pgrep` to search for a command name (or part of one) and produce the process ID of any process that includes that name. For example:

```
$ pgrep init          Show PID for any process including 'init' string
2617
1
```

Because we know there is only one `init` command running, we next use the `-1` option to see each process's command name (to learn why two processes showed up):

```
$ pgrep -l init       Show PID and name for any process including 'init' string
2617 xinit
1 init
```

You can also **search for processes that are associated with a particular user:**

```
$ pgrep -lu chris     List all processes owned by user chris
2803 vim
2552 bash
2551 sshd
```

Probably the most useful way to use `pgrep` is to have it **find the process IDs of the running processes and pipe those PIDs to another command** to produce the output. Here are some examples (look for other commands if `metacity` or `firefox` isn't running):

```
$ ps -p `pgrep metacity`      Search for metacity and run ps (short)
  PID TT   STAT     TIME COMMAND
 2617 ??   Is    00:07.02 /usr/local/bin/metacity --sm-client-id=default0
$ ps -fp `pgrep xinit`        Search for xinit and run ps (full)
  PID  TT  STAT     TIME COMMAND
 2617  v2  I+     0:00.01 /usr/X11R6/bin/xinit /home/chris/.xinitrc
# renice -5 `pgrep firefox`   Search for firefox, improve its priority
20522: old priority 0, new priority -5
20557: old priority 0, new priority -5
```

Any command that can take a process ID as input can be combined with `pgrep` in these ways. As the previous example of `pgrep` illustrates, you can use commands such as `renice` to change how a process behaves while it is running.

Using fuser to Find Processes

Another way to locate a particular process is by what the process is accessing. The `fuser` command (as root, type `pkg_add -r fuser`) can be used to find which processes have a file or a socket open at the moment. After the processes are found, `fuser` can be used to send signals to those processes. The `fuser` command is most useful for finding out if files are being held open by processes on mounted file systems (such as local hard disks or Samba shares). Finding those processes allows you to close them properly (or just kill them if you must) so the file system can be unmounted cleanly.

Here are some examples of the fuser command for **listing processes that have files open on a selected file system:**

```
# fuser -cu /home       Output of processes with /home open (with user name)
/home:     575x(root)   649x(root)   656x(root)   739x(root)   745x(root)
749x(smmsp)   755x(root)   802cx(root)   805x(root)   806x(root)   807x(root)
808x(root)   809x(root)   810c(chris)   1122x(root)   1129x(root)   1132x(chris)
1133c(chris)   1537cx(root)   2629x(chris)   2632x(chris)   2639x(chris)
2660x(chris)   3300x(root)   3316x(root)   3320x(root)
```

The example just shown displays the process ID for running processes associated with /home. Each may have a file open, a shell open, or be a child process of a shell with the current directory in /home or its subdirectories. The -c causes /home to be treated as the mount point (so anything below that point is matched) and -u causes the owner of each process to be listed.

Letters between the process IDs and user names indicate how the files being held open are being used. In these examples, an x indicates that the file is the executable text of the process, and a c says that the file is the current working directory of the process. Other possible letters include r (file is in the process's root directory), j (file is the jail root of the process), t (file is the kernel tracing file of the process), y (the process uses the file as its controlling tty), m (file is mmapped), w (the file is open for writing), a (file is open as append only), s (file has a shared lock), and e (file has an exclusive lock).

Here are other examples using `fuser` to **show processes with files open:**

```
# fuser -c -m /boot   Show PIDs/symbols for processes opening /boot
# fuser -u /boot       Show PIDs/symbols/user of /boot, not subdirectories
```

After you know which processes have files open, you can close those processes manually or kill them. Close processes manually if at all possible, since simply killing processes can leave files in an unclean state! Here are examples of using `fuser` to **kill or send other signals to all processes with files open to a file system:**

```
# fuser -k /tmp/my.txt   Kill processes with /tmp/my.txt open (SIGKILL)
```

Even after a process is running, you can change its behavior in different ways. With the `renice` command, shown earlier, you can adjust a running process's priority in your system's scheduler. With the `nice` command, you can determine the default priority and also set a higher or lower priority at the time you launch a process.

Another way you can change how a running process behaves is to send a signal to that process. The `kill` and `killall` commands can be used to send signals to running processes. Likewise, the `pkill` command can send a signal to a process.

Adjusting Processor Priority with nice

Every running process has a *nice* value that can be used to tell the BSD process scheduler what priority should be given to that process. Positive values of niceness actually give your process a lower priority. The concept came about during the days of large, multi-user UNIX systems where you could be "nice" by running a non-urgent process at lower priority so other users had a shot at the CPU.

Niceness doesn't enforce scheduling priority, but is merely a suggestion to the scheduler.

The default nice value is 0. You can use the nice command to run a process at a higher or lower priority than the default. The priority number can range from –35 (most favorable scheduling priority) to 19 (least favorable scheduling priority). Although the root user can raise or lower any user's nice value, a regular user can only lower the priorities of a process (setting a higher nice value).

> **WARNING!** *Proceed with caution when assigning negative nice values to processes. This can possibly crash your machine if critical system processes lose their high priority.*

Here are a few examples of starting a command with nice to **change a command's nice value:**

```
$ nice -n 12 nroff -man a.roff | less    Format man pages at low priority
# nice -n -10 designer                   Launch QT Designer at higher priority
```

When a process is already running, you can **change the process's nice value using the renice command.** Here are some examples of the renice command:

```
$ renice +2 -u francois            Renice francois' processes +2
$ renice +5 4737                   Renice PID 4737 by +5
# renice -3 `pgrep -u chris spamd`  Renice chris' spamd processes -3
9688: old priority -1, new priority -3
20279: old priority -1, new priority -3
20282: old priority -1, new priority -3
```

The backticks are use used in the previous command line to indicate that the output of the pgrep command (presumably PIDs of spamd daemons run by chris) be fed to the renice command.

The niceness settings for your processes are displayed by default when you run top. You can also see niceness settings using -o nice when you produce custom output from the ps command.

Running Processes in the Background and Foreground

When you run a process from a shell, it is run in the foreground by default. That means that you can't type another command until the first one is done. By adding an ampersand (&) to the end of a command line, you can run that command line in the background. Using the fg, bg, and jobs commands, along with various control codes, you can move commands between background and foreground.

In the following sequence of commands, we start the GIMP image program from a Terminal window. After that is a series of control keys and commands to stop and start the process and move it between foreground and background:

```
$ gimp                              Run gimp in the foreground
<Ctrl+Z>                            Stop process and place in background
[1]+  Stopped          gimp
$ bg 1                              Start process running again in background (bash)
$ bg %1                             Start process running again in background (sh)
$ fg 1                              Continue running process in foreground (bash)
$ fg %1                             Continue running process in foreground (sh)
gimp
<Ctrl+C>                            Kill process
```

Note that processes placed in the background are given a job ID number (in this case, 1). By placing a percentage sign in front of the number (for example, %1), you can identify a particular background process to the bg and fg commands or with the bash shell; simply type the number with the command (as in fg 1). With one or more background jobs running at the current shell, you can use the jobs command to manage your background jobs:

```
$ jobs                      Display background jobs for current shell
[1]      Running               gimp &
[2]      Running               xmms &
[3]-     Running               gedit &
[4]+     Stopped               gtali
$ jobs -1                   Display PID with each job's information
[1]   31676 Running            gimp &
[2]   31677 Running            xmms &
[3]- 31683 Running             gedit &
[4]+ 31688 Stopped             gtali
$ jobs -1 %2                Display information only for job %2
[2]   31677 Running            xmms &
```

The processes running in the jobs examples might have been done while you were logged in (using ssh) to a remote system, but wanted to run remote GUI applications on your local desktop. By running those processes in the background, you can have multiple applications running at once, while still having those applications associated with your current shell.

> **NOTE** With fg or bg, if you don't indicate which process to act on, the current job is used. The current job has a plus sign (+) next to it.

The fg and bg commands manipulate running processes by moving those processes to the foreground or background. Another way to manipulate running commands is to send signals directly to those processes. A common way to send signals to running processes is with the kill and killall commands.

Killing and Signaling Processes

You can stop or change running processes by sending signals to those processes. Commands such as kill and killall can send signals you select to running processes, which as their names imply, is often a signal to kill the process.

155

Signals are represented by numbers (9, 15, and so on) and strings (SIGKILL, SIGTERM, and so on). Table 9-2 shows standard signals you can send to processes in BSD systems.

Table 9-2: Standard Signals to Send to Processes

Signal Number	Signal Name	Description
1	SIGHUP	Hang up from terminal or controlling process died
2	SIGINT	Interrupt program
3	SIGQUIT	Quit program
4	SIGILL	Illegal instruction
5	SIGTRAP	Trace trap
6	SIGABRT	Abort sent from abort function
7	SIGEMT	Emulate instruction executed
8	SIGFPE	Floating point exception
9	SIGKILL	Kill signal
10	SIGBUS	Bus error
11	SIGSEGV	Segmentation violation
12	SIGSYS	Non-existent system call invoked
13	SIGPIPE	Pipe broken (nothing to read write to pipe)
14	SIGALRM	Timer signal from alarm system call
15	SIGTERM	Termination signal
16	SIGURG	Discard signal
17	SIGSTOP	Stop the process
18	SIGTSTP	Stop typed at terminal
19	SIGCONT	Continue if process is stopped
20	SIGCHLD	Child status changed
21	SIGTTIN	Terminal tries to read background process
22	SIGTTOU	Terminal tries to write to background process

The `kill` command can send signals to processes by process ID or job number while the `killall` command can signal processes by command name. Here are some examples:

```
$ kill 28665            Send SIGTERM to process with PID 28665
$ kill -9 4895          Send SIGKILL to process with PID 4895
$ kill -SIGCONT 5254    Continue a stopped process (pid 5254)
$ kill %3               Kill the process represented by job %3
$ killall spamd         Kill all spamd daemons currently running
$ killall -SIGHUP sendmail  Have sendmail processes reread config files
```

The SIGKILL (9) signal, used generously by trigger-happy novice administrators, should be reserved as a last resort. It does not allow the targeted process to exit cleanly but forces it to end abruptly. This can potentially result in loss or corruption of data handled by that process. The SIGHUP signal was originally used on UNIX systems to indicate that a terminal was being disconnected from a mainframe (such as from a hang-up of a dial-in modem). However, daemon processes, such as sendmail and httpd, were implemented to catch SIGHUP signals as an indication that those processes should reread configuration files.

Running Processes Away from Current Shell

If you want a process to continue to run, even if you disconnect from the current shell session, there are several ways to go about doing that. You can use the nohup command to run a process in a way that it is impervious to a hang-up signal:

```
$ nohup mylongscript.sh &     Run mylongscript.sh with no ability to interrupt
# nohup nice -9 gcc hello.c &  Run gcc uninterrupted and higher priority
```

Using nohup is different than running the command with an ampersand alone because with nohup the command will keep running, even if you exit the shell that launched the command.

The nohup command was commonly used in the days of slow processors and dial-up connections (so you didn't have to stay logged into an expensive connection while a long compile completed). Also, today using tools such as screen (described in Chapter 13) you can keep a shell session active, even after you disconnect your network connection to that shell.

Scheduling Processes to Run

Commands associated with the cron facility can be used to set a command to run at a specific time (including now) so that it is not connected to the current shell. The at command runs a command at the time you set. Enter the at command, type the commands you want to run at the later time, and press Ctrl-D to queue the job:

```
# at now +1 minute           Start command running in one minute
at> ls -R /usr/ports > /tmp/portlist.txt
at> <Ctrl+D> <EOT>
job 5 at Thu Mar 20 20:37:00 2008
# at teatime                 Start command at 4pm today
```

```
# at now +5 days          Start a command in five days
# at 06/25/08             Start a command at current time on June 25, 2008\
```

Another way to run a command that's not connected with the current shell is with the `batch` command. With `batch`, you can **set a command to start as soon as the processor is ready** (load average below .8):

```
# batch                  Start command running immediately
at> find /mnt/isos | grep jpg$ > /tmp/mypics
at> <Ctrl+D> <EOT>
```

Note that after the `at` or `batch` commands you see a secondary `at>` prompt. Type the command you want to run at that prompt and press Enter. After that, you can continue to enter commands. When you are done, press Ctrl+D on a line by itself to queue the commands you entered to run.

When the commands are entered, you can **check the queue of at and batch jobs that are set** to run by typing the `atq` command:

```
$ atq
Date                          Owner     Queue     Job#
Tue Dec 29 16:00:00 CST 2008  root      c         4
Sat Aug  2 19:24:00 CST 2008  root      c         5
```

Regular users can't view queued jobs. The root user can see everyone's queued at jobs. If you want to **delete an at job from the queue,** use the `atrm` command:

```
# atrm 5                  Delete at job number 5
```

The `at` and `batch` commands are for queuing up a command to run as a one-shot deal. You can use the cron facility to **set up commands to run repeatedly.** These commands are scripted into cron jobs, which are scheduled in crontab files. There is one system crontab file (`/etc/crontab`). Also, each user can create a personal crontab file that can launch commands at times that the user chooses. To **create a personal crontab file,** type the following:

```
$ crontab -e            Create a personal crontab file
```

The `crontab -e` command opens your crontab file (or creates a new one) using the `vi` text editor. Here are examples of several entries you could add to a crontab file:

```
15 8 * * Mon,Tue,Wed,Thu,Fri mail chris < /var/project/stats.txt
* * 1 1,4,7,10 * find /doc | grep .doc$ > /var/sales/documents.txt
```

The first crontab example shown sends a mail message to the user named `chris` by directing the contents of `/var/project/stats.txt` into that message. That mail command is run Monday through Friday at 8:15 am. In the second example, on the first day of January, April, July, and October the `find` command runs to look for every `.doc` file in `/doc` and sends the resulting list of files to `/var/sales/documents.txt`.

The last part of each crontab entry is the command that is run. The first five fields represent the time and date the command is run. The fields from left to right are: minute (0 to 59), hour (0 to 23), day of the month (0 to 31), month (0 to 12 or Jan, Feb, Mar, Apr, May, Jun, Jul, Aug, Sep, Oct, Nov, or Dec), and day of the week (0 to 7 or Sun, Mon, Tue, Wed, Thu, Fri, or Sat). An asterisk (*) in a field means to match any value for that field.

Here are some other options with the crontab command:

```
# crontab -eu chris          Edit another user's crontab (root only)
$ crontab -l                 List contents of your crontab file
15 8 * * Mon,Tue,Wed,Thu,Fri mail chris < /var/project/stats.txt
* * 1 1,4,7,10 * find / | grep .doc$ > /var/sales/documents.txt
$ crontab -r                 Delete your crontab file
```

An alternative to the cron facility is the anacron facility (pkg_add -r anacron). With anacron, as with cron, you can configure commands to run periodically. However, anacron is most appropriate for machines that are not on all the time. If a command is not run because the computer was off during the scheduled time, the next time the computer is on, the anacron facility makes sure that the commands that were missed during the down time are run after the system resumes.

Summary

Watching and working with the processes that run on your BSD system are important activities to make sure that your system is operating efficiently. Using commands such as ps and top, you can view the processes running on your system. You can also use pgrep to search for and list particular processes.

With commands such as nice and renice, you can adjust the recommended priorities at which selected processes run. When a process is running, you can change how it is running or kill the process by sending it a signal from the kill or killall commands.

After launching a command from the current shell, you can set that command's process to run in the background (bg) or foreground (fg). You can also stop and restart the process using different control codes.

To schedule a command to run at a later time, you can use the at or batch commands. To set up a command to run repeatedly at set intervals, you can use the cron or anacron facilities.

10

Managing the System

Without careful management, the demands on your BSD system can sometimes exceed the resources you have available. Being able to monitor your system's activities (memory, CPU, and device usage) over time can help you make sure that your machine has enough resources to do what you need it to. Likewise, managing other aspects of your system, such as the device drivers it uses and how the boot process works, can help avoid performance problems and system failures.

This chapter is divided into several sections that relate to ways of managing your FreeBSD or other BSD system. The first section can help you monitor the resources (processing power, devices, and memory) on your BSD system. The next section describes how to check and set your system clock. Descriptions of the boot process and subsequent run levels follow. The last sections describe how to work with the kernel and related device drivers, as well as how to view information about your computer's hardware components.

Monitoring Resources

FreeBSD, OpenBSD, NetBSD, and other UNIX-like systems do a wonderful job of keeping track of what they do. If you care to look, you can find lots of information about how your CPU, hard disks, virtual memory, and other computer resources are being used.

You can use commands to view information about how your computer's virtual memory, processor, storage devices, and network interfaces are being used on your system. There are commands that can monitor several different aspects of your system's resources. Because this book is not just a man page, however, we have divided up the following sections by topic (monitoring memory, CPU, storage devices) rather than by the commands that do them (`top`, `vmstat`, and `iostat`).

> **NOTE** *Many of the applications described in this section are installed by default in FreeBSD. To use commands that collect a history of system activity, such as* `sar` (http://pagesperso-orange.fr/sebastien.godard/), *however, you need to install the bsdsar package or compile bsdsar from source.*

Monitoring Memory Use

Few things will kill system performance faster than running out of memory. Commands such as `top` let you see basic information about how your RAM and swap are being used. The `vmstat` command gives detailed information about memory use and can run continuously.

The `top` command provides a means of watching the currently running processes, with those processes sorted by CPU usage or memory (see Chapter 9 for a description of `top` for watching running processes). However, you can also use `top` to **watch your memory usage in a screen-oriented way.** Here is an example:

```
$ top
last pid:  1619;  load averages:  0.61,  0.85,  0.62  up 0+02:23:09  17:23:49
85 processes:  2 running, 83 sleeping
CPU states: 37.5% user,  0.0% nice, 15.4% system,  0.8% interrupt, 46.3% idle
Mem: 76M Active, 31M Inact, 79M Wired, 2476K Cache, 34M Buf, 53M Free
Swap: 484M Total, 25M Used, 459M Free, 5% Inuse

  PID USERNAME    THR PRI NICE   SIZE    RES STATE    TIME   WCPU COMMAND
 1618 chris         3 117    0 51964K 35352K RUN      0:07  7.96% totem
 1462 chris         1  96    0 85016K 15968K select   0:33  5.66% Xorg
 1491 chris         1  98    0 12812K  8008K select   0:05  1.03% metacity
 1494 chris         1  96    0 27880K 12088K select   0:08  0.44% gnome-panel
```

To exit `top`, press **q**. The `top` command shows the total memory usage for RAM (`Mem:`) and swap space (`Swap:`). However, because `top` is screen oriented and provides on-going monitoring, you can watch memory usage change every two seconds (by default). The most useful column to analyze a process' memory usage is RES, which shows the process' actual physical RAM usage, also known as *resident size*. Run `top -ores` and running processes will be **displayed in resident memory use order** (to sort by the RES column):

```
$ top -ores
     . . .
  PID USERNAME    THR PRI NICE   SIZE    RES STATE    TIME   WCPU COMMAND
 1673 chris         3 112    0 56288K 38660K RUN      0:22  0.00% totem
 1615 chris         1  96    0 27060K 15428K select   0:03  0.00% kview
 1462 chris         1 100    0 84900K 13388K select   1:51 10.60% Xorg
 1496 chris         3  20    0 33072K 10928K kserel   0:05  0.00% nautilus
```

To see the **total size of memory consumed by a process** (including text, data, and stack), you can sort by the SIZE column. To do that, type top -osize:

```
$ top -osize
   . . .
  PID USERNAME     THR PRI NICE   SIZE    RES STATE     TIME   WCPU COMMAND
 1462 chris          1 100     0 85036K 12528K RUN      3:41 10.94% Xorg
 1764 chris          3 114     0 56124K 38712K RUN      0:31  0.00% totem
 1496 chris          3  20     0 33072K  8100K kserel   0:05  0.00% nautilus
 1494 chris          1  96     0 27880K  9384K select   0:10  0.00% gnome-panel
```

For a more detailed view of your virtual memory statistics, use the vmstat command. With vmstat you can **view memory use over a given time period**, for example, since the previous reboot or using a sample period. The following example shows vmstat redisplaying statistics every three seconds:

```
$ vmstat 3
procs       memory      page                     disks    faults      cpu
 r b w      avm    fre flt  re pi  po  fr    sr ad0 da0   in    sy    cs us sy id
 5 2 3   259816  12604 258   1  0   0 183   107   0   0 1482   795  1154 23  5 72
12 2 0   265996  14592 540  28 33  11 404  1014  46   0 1596  8713  2204 59 41  0
 5 2 0   277480  16672 695  25 12  11 602  3228  39   0 1621 10092  2071 71 29  0
 7 2 0   314596  13460 763 115 48  11 1043 13440 66   0 1661  8582  1741 79 21  0
 3 2 0   351960  11916 428 132 56  32 542  5951 109   0 1520 39546  1665 76 21  3
 5 2 0   356944   9032 387 112 31  32 499  5395  73   0 1481 20600  1248 66 34  0
 6 2 0   359284   9312 164  20 11  22 315  3501 100   0 1645 39330  1544 60 40  0
 4 84 0  361076   8884 284  15 18  11 276  1773  43   0 1646 22994  1602 84 16  0
```

To exit vmstat, press Ctrl+C. The vmstat example shows a 30-second time period where a handful of applications are started. Because the swap area resides on the hard disk, you can see that activity on the disk device (ad0) increases as the amount of paging increases. You can see the amount of free pages of space going down under the fre column.

Here are some other options for using vmstat:

```
$ vmstat -c 5          Display output five times, then exit
$ vmstat -z            Display memory in kernel zone allocator (by zone)
```

The previous example shows several options associated with the vmstat command. The -c option displays a set number of output lines before exiting (five in this case). The -z option lets you see kernel zone allocator memory use.

With commands such as ps and top, you can see how much memory each application is consuming on your system. The kernel itself, however, has its own memory cache to keep track of its resources called the *kernel slab*. You can use the vmstat to **display kernel slab memory cache statistics** as follows:

```
$ vmstat -m | less     Page through kernel slab memory cache
     Type    InUse MemUse HighUse Requests  Size(s)
```

163

```
      DEVFS1   105   27K     -    105   256
       DEVFS    12    1K     -     13   16,128
   pfs_nodes    20    3K     -     20   128
 pfs_vncache     2    1K     -     33   32
        GEOM    90   10K     -    480   16,32,64,128,256,512,1024,2048,4096
      isadev    19    2K     -     19   64
        cdev    32    4K     -     32   128
```

The slab memory cache information shows each cache type, the number of objects active for that cache type, amount of memory used, the number of requests to the cache, and the size of the cache.

Monitoring CPU Usage

An overburdened CPU is another obvious place to look for performance problems on your system. The vmstat command, as shown earlier, can produce basic statistics relating to CPU usage (user activity, system activity, idle time, I/O wait time, and time stolen from a virtual machine). The iostat command, however, can generate more detailed reports of CPU utilization. If you want a more interactive way of watching CPU usage, you can use the systat utility. The top command can be used to view which processes are consuming the most processing time.

Here are two examples of using iostat to display a CPU utilization report:

```
$ iostat -w 3        CPU stats every 3 seconds (starting apps)
       tty              ad0            da0           pass0              cpu
 tin tout  KB/t tps  MB/s   KB/t tps  MB/s   KB/t tps  MB/s  us ni sy in id
   8   70 12.42   3  0.04   0.11   0  0.00   0.00   0  0.00  35  0 10  1 54
 384   77  0.00   0  0.00   0.00   0  0.00   0.00   0  0.00  20  0  5  1 74
 405   26 17.63  49  0.84   0.00   0  0.00   0.00   0  0.00  42  0 13  2 43
 333   26 14.03  76  1.04   0.00   0  0.00   0.00   0  0.00  67  0 28  4  1
 232   26 15.76  41  0.63   0.00   0  0.00   0.00   0  0.00  71  0 28  1  0
 291   26 11.14  26  0.28   0.00   0  0.00   0.00   0  0.00  65  0 34  2  0
$ iostat -w 3        CPU stats every 3 seconds (copying files)
       tty              ad0            da0           pass0              cpu
 tin tout  KB/t tps  MB/s   KB/t tps  MB/s   KB/t tps  MB/s  us ni sy in id
   7   53 19.67   3  0.06   0.11   0  0.00   0.00   0  0.00  48  0  9  1 42
   0   77 127.56 85 10.54   0.00   0  0.00   0.00   0  0.00   3  0 22  2 72
   0   26 123.48 90 10.81   0.00   0  0.00   0.00   0  0.00   4  0 20  2 73
   0   26 128.00 91 11.37   0.00   0  0.00   0.00   0  0.00   5  0 18  1 75
   0   26 125.10 81  9.89   0.00   0  0.00   0.00   0  0.00   4  0 19  2 74
   0   26 125.76 95 11.62   0.00   0  0.00   0.00   0  0.00   5  0 21  2 72
   0   26 126.75 102 12.66  0.00   0  0.00   0.00   0  0.00   6  0 26  2 67
```

The first iostat example above starts with a quiet system, then several applications started up. You can see that most of the processing to start the applications is being done in user space. The second iostat example shows a case where several large files are copied from one hard disk to another. The result is a high percentage of time being spent at the system level, also known as *kernel space* (in this case, reading from and writing to disk partitions). Note that the file copies also result in a higher amount of time in idle mode waiting for I/O requests to complete (id column).

Here is an example of using iostat to print CPU utilization reports for a set number of instances:

```
$ iostat -w 2 -C 10      Repeat every 2 seconds for 10 times
```

The systat command provides a screen-oriented interface for viewing information about your CPU usage (as well as other performance-related items). One advantage of systat over other tools is that CPU usage and disk activity are visually represented by bars of Xs that go across the screen. Here is an example of systat for displaying CPU and disk information:

```
$ systat -iostat      View CPU usage continuously (copy large files)
                        /0   /1   /2   /3   /4   /5   /6   /7   /8   /9   /10
      Load Average
               /0   /10  /20  /30  /40  /50  /60  /70  /80  /90  /100
cpu   user|XX
      nice|
   system|XXXXXXXXXXX
interrupt|X
      idle|XXXXXXXXXXXXXXXXXXXXXXXXXXXXXXXXXXXX


               /0   /10  /20  /30  /40  /50  /60  /70  /80  /90  /100
ad0   MB/sXXXXX
       tps|XXXXXXXXXXXXXXXXXXXXXXXXXXXXXXXXXXXXXXXXXXXXXXX
 ...
$ systat -iostat      View CPU usage continuously (busy desktop)
                        /0   /1   /2   /3   /4   /5   /6   /7   /8   /9   /10
      Load Average   ||||
               /0   /10  /20  /30  /40  /50  /60  /70  /80  /90  /100
cpu   user|XXXXXXXXXXXXXXXXXXXXXXXXXXXXXXXXXXX
      nice|
   system|XXXXXXX
interrupt|X
      idle|XXXXXXXX


               /0   /10  /20  /30  /40  /50  /60  /70  /80  /90  /100
ad0   MB/s
       tps|
  ...
```

The first systat -iostat example above shows CPU and disk activity while large files are being copied from one file system to another, illustrated as bar graphs of Xs. Most of the CPU time is spent in system mode, with a fair amount of idle time (waiting for disk I/O). The disk (ad0) information is displayed in megabytes per second and transactions per second.

The second systat -iostat example above shows CPU and disk activity while windows are being moved around on an X desktop. There is less idle time, since there is

165

little or no disk activity (as you can see by the ad0 line below). Most of the processing is happening in user mode.

If you want to find out specifically which processes are consuming the most processing time, you can use the top -mcpu command. Type top, then press c to toggle between CPU usage and weighted CPU usage:

```
$ top -mcpu                    Display running processes and sort by CPU usage
last pid:  3803;  load averages:  0.88,  0.39,  0.20
up 0+12:02:11  03:02:51
119 processes: 3 running, 110 sleeping, 0 zombie
CPU states: 67.9% user,  0.0% nice, 24.2% system,  3.0% interrupt,  5.0% idle
Mem: 130M Active, 17M Inact, 82M Wired, 12M Cache, 34M Buf, 648K Free
Swap: 484M Total, 59M Used, 426M Free, 12% Inuse, 52K In

  PID USERNAME    THR PRI NICE   SIZE    RES STATE    TIME   WCPU COMMAND
 3803 chris         1 109    0 28388K 15728K RUN      0:02 39.03% epiphany
 1462 chris         1  98    0 92452K 20200K select 201:28 11.96% Xorg
 1509 chris         1  96    0 26260K  8960K select  17:16  1.12% wnck-applet
 1491 chris         1  96    0 13228K  7464K select   0:50  0.63% metacity
 3777 chris         6  20    0 47540K 25936K kserel   0:13  0.10% evolution-2.8
```

The full output would show many more processes, all sorted by current weighted CPU usage (WCPU column). In this example, the Epiphany web browser (39.03%) and the Xorg display server (11.96%) are consuming most of the CPU. If you decided you wanted to kill the Epiphany process, you could type k and the process ID of Epiphany (3803) to kill the process (if for some reason you couldn't just close the Epiphany window normally).

If you want **information about the processor itself,** you can view the output from the dmesg command and step through the output until you find the CPU information. Here is an example:

```
$ dmesg | less     View CPU information
  . . .
CPU: Intel Pentium III (648.03 MHz 686-class CPU)
  Origin = "GenuineIntel"  Id = 0x683  Stepping = 3
  Features=0x387f9ff<FPU,VME,DE,PSE,TSC,MSR,PAE,MCE,CX8,SEP,MTRR,PGE,
    MCA,CMOV,PAT,PSE36,PN,MMX,FXSR,SSE>
```

Despite being an older processor (Intel Pentium III, 650MHz), the machine actually runs FreeBSD quite well. Interesting things to note about your CPU are the flags that represent features that it supports. Some features in FreeBSD require particular CPU extensions, associated with those flags, be on for the FreeBSD feature to work. For example, using large amounts of RAM may require that the pae flag be set.

Monitoring Storage Devices

Basic information about storage space available to your BSD file systems can be seen using commands such as du and df (as described in Chapter 7). If you want details about how your storage devices are performing, however, commands such as `gstat` and `iostat` can be useful.

Some of the same kind of output from the `iostat` command shown earlier can be used to tell if bottlenecks occur while doing disk reads and writes. Here's an example:

```
$ iostat -x              Show disk statistics by disk
                         extended device statistics
device    r/s    w/s    kr/s    kw/s wait svc_t   %b
ad0       1.5    1.1    42.3    39.4    0 18.4    1
...
```

The output of `iostat` shown above reflects processing that occurs when a large amount of data is copied from one partition to another on the hard disk (ad0). The columns show reads per second (r/s), writes per second (w/s), kilobytes read per second (kr/s), kilobytes written per second (kw/s), and length of the transactions queue (wait). They also show the duration of transactions, on average, in milliseconds (svc_t) and percentage of time the device had one or more transactions outstanding (%b).

To watch statistics about disk activity in real time, you can use the `gstat` command. Here is an example:

```
dT: 0.503s  w: 0.500s
 L(q)  ops/s   r/s   kBps   ms/r    w/s   kBps    ms/w   %busy Name
   2     95     42   5346   19.9     54   5616    26.3    98.0| ad0
   2     95     42   5346   20.0     54   5616    26.4    98.0| ad0s1
   0      0      0      0    0.0      0      0     0.0     0.0| da0
   0      0      0      0    0.0      0      0     0.0     0.0| ad0s1a
   0      0      0      0    0.0      0      0     0.0     0.0| ad0s1b
   0      0      0      0    0.0      0      0     0.0     0.0| ad0s1c
   1     54      0      0    0.0     54   5616    26.8   101.9| ad0s1d
   0      0      0      0    0.0      0      0     0.0     0.0| ad0s1e
   1     42     42   5346   20.3      0      0     0.0    84.6| ad0s1f
   0      0      0      0    0.0      0      0     0.0     0.0| da0s1
   0      0      0      0    0.0      0      0     0.0     0.0| da0s2
   0      0      0      0    0.0      0      0     0.0     0.0| acd0
```

In the `gstat` example just shown, the display you see is updated every half-second (0.500s). A large amount of data is being written from one partition (ad0s1f) to another (ad0sd). Total activity on the disk is displayed on the ad0 line, while total activity on the disk slice (there is only one) is shown on the ad0s1 line. It's easy to tell when bottlenecks occur because numbers in the %busy column go from green (0–59% activity), to purple (60–79% activity) to red (80–100% activity).

Here are a few other examples of `gstat` command lines:

```
# gstat -a              Only show disk devices with some activity
dT: 0.502s  w: 0.500s
 L(q)  ops/s   r/s   kBps   ms/r    w/s   kBps    ms/w   %busy Name
   1    100     52   6184   16.7     48   6120    4.3    91.6| ad0
```

167

```
   1    100    52  6184  16.7     48  6120    4.4   91.6|  ad0s1
   0     48     0     0   0.0     48  6120    4.5   21.5|  ad0s1d
   1     52    52  6184  16.9      0     0    0.0   87.7|  ad0s1f
# gstat  -I 4s          Update display every 4 seconds
```

If you want to find out what files and directories are currently open on your storage devices, you can use the `lsof` command. This command can be particularly useful if you are trying to unmount a file system that keeps telling you it is busy. You can check what open file is preventing the unmount and decide if you want to kill the process holding that file open and force an unmount of the file system. Here is an example of `lsof`:

```
# lsof | less      List processes holding files and directories open
COMMAND     PID   USER   FD    TYPE    DEVICE   SIZE/OFF    NODE NAME
init          1   root   cwd   VDIR     0,87        512       2 /
init          1   root   rtd   VDIR     0,87        512       2 /
init          1   root   txt   VREG     0,87     514792   49395 /sbin/init
adjkerntz   123   root   cwd   VDIR     0,87        512       2 /
adjkerntz   123   root   rtd   VDIR     0,87        512       2 /
  ...
sh         1443   chris  cwd   VDIR     0,92              2536 2775585 /home/chris
```

The first files shown as being open are those held open by the `init` process (the first running process on the system). The `adjkerntz` process runs next, to adjust local time. Files held open by other system processes (such as `devd`) and daemons (such as `sshd` and `syslogd`) follow after `init`. Eventually, you will see files held open by individual users (which are probably the ones you are interested in if you are unable to unmount a disk partition).

When you are looking at the `lsof` output, you want to see the name of the file or directory that is open (NAME), the command that has it open (COMMAND) and the process ID of that running command (PID). As is often the case when a file system you want to unmount is being held open, the `/home` file system is being held open by a `sh` shell (in the example above, `/home/chris` is the `sh` shell's current working directory). In fact, instead of piping `lsof` output to `less` or `grep`, here are a few other ways you can find what you are looking for from `lsof` output:

```
# lsof -c csh         List files open by C shell (csh) shells
# lsof -d cwd         List directories open as current working directory
# lsof -u chris       List files and directories open by user chris
# lsof /var           List anything open on /var file system
# lsof +d /var/log    List anything open under /var/log directory
```

Mastering Time

Keeping correct time on your BSD system is critical to the system's proper functioning. You can have the time set on your BSD system in several different ways. System time can be viewed and set manually (with the `date` command) or automatically (with ntpdate or the ntpd service). Another time-related command is uptime, which lets you see how long your system has been up.

Changing Time Zone

Your BSD system's time zone is set based on the contents of the /etc/localtime file. You can set a new time zone immediately by copying the file representing your time zone from a subdirectory of /usr/share/zoneinfo. For example, to change the current time zone to that of America/Chicago, you could do the following:

```
# cp /usr/share/zoneinfo/America/Chicago /etc/localtime
```

This can also be accomplished by creating a symlink:

```
# ln -s /usr/share/zoneinfo/America/Chicago /etc/localtime
```

In FreeBSD, there is also tool called tzsetup that lets you select your local time zone.

Displaying and Setting Your Time and Date

The date command is the primary command-based interface for viewing and changing date and time settings, if you are not having that done automatically with NTP. Here are examples of date commands for **displaying dates and times** in different ways:

```
$ date                           Display current date, time and time zone
Tue Aug 12 01:26:50 CDT 2008
$ date '+%A %B %d %G'            Display day, month, day of month, year
Tuesday August 12 2008
$ date '+The date today is %F.'  Add words to the date output
The date today is 2008-08-12.
$ date "+TIME: %H:%M:%S%nDATE: %Y-%m-%d"  Display TIME and DATE on separate lines
TIME: 06:29:10
DATE: 2008-12-18
$ date -v1d -v+1m -v -1d -v-mon      Display the last Monday in the month
Mon Dec 29 09:18:32 CST 2008
$ date -u                        Display Coordinated Universal Time (UTC)
Mon Dec 29 15:19:12 UTC 2008
```

Although our primary interest in this section is time, since we are on the subject of dates as well, the cal command is a quick way to **display dates by month**. Here are examples:

```
$ cal               Show current month calendar (today is highlighted)
    October 2008
Su Mo Tu We Th Fr Sa
          1  2  3  4
 5  6  7  8  9 10 11
12 13 14 15 16 17 18
19 20 21 22 23 24 25
26 27 28 29 30 31
```

```
$ cal 2008                   Show whole year's calendar
                                2008

       January                 February                   March
Su Mo Tu We Th Fr Sa    Su Mo Tu We Th Fr Sa    Su Mo Tu We Th Fr Sa
       1  2  3  4  5                    1  2                        1
 6  7  8  9 10 11 12     3  4  5  6  7  8  9     2  3  4  5  6  7  8
13 14 15 16 17 18 19    10 11 12 13 14 15 16     9 10 11 12 13 14 15
20 21 22 23 24 25 26    17 18 19 20 21 22 23    16 17 18 19 20 21 22
27 28 29 30 31          24 25 26 27 28 29       23 24 25 26 27 28 29
                                               30 31

...
$ cal -j                     Show Julian calendar (numbered from January 1)
        October 2008
 Su  Mo  Tu  We  Th  Fr  Sa
             275 276 277 278
279 280 281 282 283 284 285
286 287 288 289 290 291 292
293 294 295 296 297 298 299
300 301 302 303 304 305
```

The date command can also be used to change the system date and time. (Be careful, however, because randomly changing the date could crash your system.) Here are examples:

```
# date 0812152100            Set date/time to Aug, 12, 2:21PM, 2008
Mon Dec 15 21:00:00 CST 2008
# date -v +2H                   Adjust time to 2 hours later
Sun Aug 12 11:42:33 CDT 2008
# date -v +3m                   Adjust date/time to one month earlier
Wed Nov 12 11:42:38 CDT 2008
```

The next time you boot FreeBSD, the system time will be reset based on the value of your hardware clock (or your NTP server, if NTP service is enabled). And the next time you shut down, the hardware clock will be reset to the system time, in order to preserve that time while the machine is powered off. One way to make sure that you always get the correct time set for your system is to use the Network Time Protocol (NTP).

Using Network Time Protocol to Set Date/Time

When you install FreeBSD, you are given the opportunity to set your time zone and whether your system clock reflects local or UTC time. Your system will display the date and time based on your hardware clock and time zone. As noted earlier, one way to make sure that your system's time doesn't drift is to use Network Time Protocol (NTP).

The ntpd daemon is installed with the FreeBSD system. To have your FreeBSD system synchronize time with a time server on the network, all you need to do is create a configuration file and enable the ntpd service. Edit the /etc/ntp.conf file to create at least a server and driftfile entry. For example:

```
server pool.ntp.org
driftfile /var/db/ntpd.drift
restrict default ignore
```

To enable the Network Time Protocol service (ntpd daemon), you can add the following lines to your /etc/rc.conf file:

```
ntpd_enable="YES"              # Run ntpd Network Time Protocol (or NO).
ntpd_program="/usr/sbin/ntpd"  # path to ntpd, if you want a different one.
ntpd_config="/etc/ntp.conf"    # ntpd(8) configuration file
ntpd_sync_on_start="YES"       # Sync time on ntpd startup,
                               #   even if offset is high
ntpd_flags="-p /var/run/ntpd.pid -f /var/db/ntpd.drift"   # Options to ntpd
```

Actually, all you need to do is add the ntpd_enable and ntpd_sync_on_start lines and make sure they are set to YES. The other ntpd lines are set by default (in the /etc/defaults/rc.conf file) and are just shown here for your information. The next time your system starts, your system time will be set based on information gathered from the NTP server and your local time zone settings. If you prefer to start the ntpd daemon manually, you could type the following:

```
# /usr/sbin/ntpd -p /var/run/ntpd.pid -f /var/db/ntpd.drift -c /etc/ntp.conf
```

When the ntpd service is set up to run, the resulting setup turns your machine into a time server, listening on UDP port 123. Unless you have very specific needs (and your own GPS or atomic clock), running ntpd on your machine can be both a waste of resources and a security risk. For that reason, some system administrators prefer using ntpdate (often in a daily cronjob) to set their system time via NTP:

```
# ntpdate pool.ntp.org          Set date/time immediately from pool.ntp.org
15 Aug 00:37:12 ntpdate[9706]:
adjust time server 66.92.68.11 offset 0.009204 sec
```

If you try running ntpdate while ntpd is running, you will get the following error:

```
# ntpdate pool.ntp.org
15 Aug 00:37:00 ntpdate[9695]: the NTP socket is in use, exiting
```

Note that the ntpdate command has been marked as deprecated and will disappear in the future. It has been replaced by the following options of ntpd:

```
# ntpd -qg
```

The -q option tells ntpd to exit after setting the clock (as opposed to keep running as a daemon). The -g option prevents ntpd from panicking if the system clock is off by more than 1000 seconds.

NOTE *You can set your computer's hardware clock in the BIOS. How your BSD system interprets your hardware clock depends on several things. If the* /etc/wall_cmos_clock *file exists, BSD assumes that the hardware clock should be interpreted as local time. If not, the time is interpreted as UTC time. Based on your hardware clock and time zone, the running adjkerntz process adjusts the kernel clock and stores that information. Type* sysctl machdep.adjkerntz *to see that offset.*

Checking Uptime

A matter of pride among BSD and other Linux and UNIX enthusiasts is how long they can keep their systems running without having to reboot. BSD systems have been known to run for years without having to reboot. The time that a BSD system has been running since the previous reboot is referred to as *uptime*. You can **check your system's uptime** as follows:

```
$ uptime                  Check how long your system has been running
  6:53pm  up 196 days, 14:25,  3 users,  load average: 1.66, 0.88, 0.35
```

The output of uptime shows the current time, how many days and hours the system has been up and how many users are currently logged in. After that, uptime shows the system load over the past 1-, 5-, and 15-minute time periods.

Managing the Boot Process

When a PC (*x86*) first starts up, the basic input/output system (BIOS) looks to its boot order settings to determine where to find the operating system to boot. Typically, if a bootable medium has not been inserted into a removable drive (CD, DVD, floppy disk, and so on), the BIOS looks to the master boot record (MBR) on the first bootable hard disk. At this point, for most BSD systems, control of the boot process is handed to the *boot loader*.

FreeBSD and other BSD and UNIX systems have a choice of boot loaders. By default, however, FreeBSD uses the boot0 boot loader. By configuring boot0, you not only can have your computer boot FreeBSD exactly as you would like, but you can also configure it to boot other operating systems installed on your computer. Or you can choose to use a different boot loader (such as GRUB, described later) to direct the boot process.

A BSD system boots up in several stages. The first is actually the stage where the BIOS starts to initialize the hardware and find the master boot record, usually on hard disk, where the boot0 boot loader takes over. Next, boot1 starts and uses bsdlabel to find boot2. Next boot2 starts, which passes control to the boot loader or directly to the kernel. At the end of that, with FreeBSD you should see a boot prompt that is similar to the following:

```
F1 FreeBSD
Default: F1
```

When a BSD system is selected to boot from the boot loader, the boot loader goes to the partition you asked to boot and either boots a secondary boot loader or loads the kernel. In the final stage of the bootstrapping process in FreeBSD, the kernel is booted, the rc scripts start up system services, and you are presented with a prompt or display manager screen to login.

The following sections describe commands for modifying the boot loader and start-up scripts associated with your BSD system.

Using the boot0 Boot Loader

The /boot/boot0 file contains the default boot image used by FreeBSD. If you want to replace your boot image with one that you compile yourself, you can do that with the boot0cfg command. However, the boot0cfg command can also be used to view or change settings related to the current boot loader.

> **NOTE**   *When referring to disks in the following examples, IDE disks begin with ad and SCSI disks begin with da. So the first IDE disk is ad0, the second is ad1, and so on. Likewise with SCSI disks named da0, da1, and so on. The first slice on IDE disk 1 is ad0s1.*

Here are some examples using the boot0cfg command to check and change your boot image:

```
# boot0cfg -v ad0         Display information about boot0 loader on IDE disk 1
#    flag    start chs    type      end chs      offset        size
1    0x80      0:  1: 1   0xa5    1023:254:63       63      40949622

version=1.0  drive=0x80  mask=0xf  ticks=182
options=packet,update,nosetdrv
default_selection=F1 (Slice 1)
```

The output from boot0cfg -v shows you information about how boot0 is set up on the selected disk (in this case, the first disk, ad0). In this case, only one slice (1) on the first disk (0x80) is bootable. The slice starts at cylinder 0, head 0, and sector 0. It ends at cylinder 1023, head 254, and sector 63. The type of the slice is 0Xa5 (used with FreeBSD, NetBSD, and 386BSD).

After the version number (1.0), the output shows that the BIOS will be told to boot the first hard disk (0x80), that four disk slices are enabled (0xf), and that the boot prompt timeout is set to 182 ticks (about 10 seconds). The three options say to use the disk packet (BIOS INT 0x13 extension) interface for disk I/O (packet), allow the master boot record to be updated by the boot manager (update), and don't force the drive containing the disk referenced by -d option to be used.

Now that you see the settings, here is how you can make changes to the boot0 boot loader.

WARNING! *If you mess up your boot loader, your computer could become temporarily unbootable. I recommend that you have a rescue CD available to correct the problem if your system becomes unbootable.*

```
# boot0cfg -B ad0          Install /boot/boot0, no slice table change
# boot0cfg -b /root/boot0 ad0   Install specific boot0 boot manager file
# boot0cfg -t 364 ad0      Change timeout to 20 seconds (364 ticks)
```

So far, the examples show a case where there is a single 40GB hard drive with 20GB assigned to FreeBSD on a single slice. However, there may be cases where you have multiple bootable operating systems on the same or multiple hard disks.

For example, here are a few tips for installing multiple operating systems on the same computer:

❑ **Windows** — If possible, always try to install Windows first. At least some versions of Windows are a bit antisocial, thinking they own your machine, and will probably overwrite your master boot record (without making your BSD system bootable). With Windows installed first, that system can easily be added to your BSD boot loader so any OS can boot.

❑ **Linux** — Most Linux systems will happily coexist with FreeBSD or other BSD systems. When you install Linux, just tell the installer to put the Linux boot loader (probably GRUB) on the partition containing the /boot directory (often just the / partition). You can then tell the installer not to overwrite the master boot record (which I presume contains your BSD boot0 boot loader).

To illustrate a computer that dual boots with FreeBSD and Debian GNU/Linux, we installed FreeBSD first (slice 1). Then we installed Debian, putting the operating system on slice 2 and making a separate slice containing a swap partition for Linux. We installed the GRUB boot loader during the Debian installation on slice 2, which GRUB referred to as hd0,1. (for disk 1, partition 2).

NOTE *Before things get more confused here, we need to clear up some terminology. In BSD, you can divide the disk into up to four parts referred to as slices. Within a BSD slice, you can further divide the disk into what are called partitions. In Linux, what BSD refers to as slices are called partitions. You can have more than the four primary partitions in Linux because it allows what are called extended partitions. For clarity, and because this is a BSD book, we are trying to use the BSD slice, partition terminology.*

Anyway, with FreeBSD and Debian Linux installed, here's what output from the boot loader with two bootable operating systems looks like:

```
# boot0cfg -v ad0          Display information about boot0 loader (mutiple OS)
#    flag     start chs   type      end chs      offset        size
```

```
1    0x80        0:  1: 1    0xa5   1023:254:63            63    40949622
2    0x00   1023:254:63      0x83   1023:254:63      40949685    15631245
3    0x00   1023:254:63      0x82   1023:254:63      56580930     1558305

version=1.0  drive=0x80  mask=0xf  ticks=182
options=packet,update,nosetdrv
default_selection=F1 (Slice 1)
```

You can see from the output that there are two more slices assigned. Slice 2 is a Linux partition type (0x83) and slice 3 is a swap type (0x82). Slice 2 is bootable.

You can use the fdisk command to see more details about the types and sizes of each slice:

```
# fdisk ad0                    Display disk slice information
******* Working on device /dev/ad0 *******
    . . .
The data for partition 1 is:
sysid 165 (0xa5),(FreeBSD/NetBSD/386BSD)
    start 63, size 40949622 (19994 Meg), flag 80 (active)
        beg: cyl 0/ head 1/ sector 1;
        end: cyl 1023/ head 254/ sector 63
The data for partition 2 is:
sysid 131 (0x83),(Linux native)
    start 40949685, size 15631245 (7632 Meg), flag 0
        beg: cyl 1023/ head 254/ sector 63;
        end: cyl 1023/ head 254/ sector 63
The data for partition 3 is:
sysid 130 (0x82),(Linux swap or Solaris x86)
    start 56580930, size 1558305 (760 Meg), flag 0
        beg: cyl 1023/ head 254/ sector 63;
        end: cyl 1023/ head 254/ sector 63
The data for partition 4 is:
<UNUSED>
```

The fdisk output helps to see more details about each slice. Here are some ways that you can work with those slices. To change the default slice to boot to slice 2, type this:

```
# boot0cfg -v -s 2 ad0            Set slice 2 as default slice
    . . .
default_selection=F2 (Slice2)
```

If you have multiple hard disks, you can also tell the computer's BIOS to look for the boot loader on a hard disk other than the first hard disk (0x80). For example, type this to have the computer's BIOS look for a boot loader on the second hard disk (0x81):

```
# boot0cfg -v -d 0x81 ad0         Look for boot loader on second drive (0x81)
    . . .
 version=1.0  drive=0x81  mask=0xf  ticks=182
```

Using bsdlabel to Check Out Partitions

When you first installed FreeBSD, the sysinstall installer created partitions on your BSD disk slice. To display and work with those partitions within a particular BSD disk slice, you can use the bsdlabel command. Assuming that the first slice of your disk contains your BSD slice, type the following command **to see the partitions on the slice**:

```
# bsdlabel ad0s1        Display partitions on BSD disk 0, slice 1
  # /dev/ad0s1:
  8 partitions:
  #        size    offset    fstype   [fsize bsize bps/cpg]
    a:  1048576         0    4.2BSD    2048 16384     8
    b:   975760   1048576      swap
    c: 40949622         0    unused       0     0    # "raw" part, don't edit
    d:  2584576   2024336    4.2BSD    2048 16384 28552
    e:  1048576   4608912    4.2BSD    2048 16384     8
    f: 35292134   5657488    4.2BSD    2048 16384 28552
```

The output from BSD label shows the different BSD partitions within the first slice of the first IDE hard drive (ad0s1). You can better **see how these partitions relate to how you use your file system** by running the df command to display mounted partitions:

```
# df -h      Display mounted partitions
Filesystem     Size    Used   Avail Capacity  Mounted on
/dev/ad0s1a    496M     39M    418M     8%    /
devfs          1.0K    1.0K      0B   100%    /dev
/dev/ad0s1e    496M     16K    456M     0%    /tmp
/dev/ad0s1f     16G    1.7G     13G    11%    /usr
/dev/ad0s1d    1.2G     19M    1.1G     2%    /var
```

As you can see, of the eight partitions, partition a, d, e, and f are mounted on the root (/), /var, /tmp, and /usr directories, respectively. Partition b is the swap partition. Partition c is the "raw" part and should not be modified. (The devfs file system, /dev, provides access to the computer's hardware devices.)

Because the discussion in this chapter relates to the boot process, refer to Chapter 7 for information on other uses of the bsdlabel and tdisk commands for creating and modifying disk slices and partitions.

Changing to the GRUB boot loader

There is no reason you have to use the boot0 boot loader to boot your BSD system. In fact, these days, many people use the Grand Unified Boot Loader (GRUB), especially in situations where they are booting multiple operating systems, such as Linux. GRUB has some fancy features, such as splash screens and menus for selecting and editing boot options.

There is a grub package available with FreeBSD. Or you can configure GRUB from one of the other systems installed on your computer, if they have it. To **install GRUB in FreeBSD**, type the following:

```
# pkg_add -r grub        Install the grub package
```

Next, **set up your GRUB files** by creating /boot/grub directory and copying the GRUB files you need there.

```
# mkdir /boot/grub        Create the /boot/grub directory
# cp -Rf /usr/local/share/grub/i386-freebsd/ /boot/grub Copy files to /boot/grub
```

Next you need to create a menu.lst file, using any text editor, to tell GRUB what to boot and how. In this example, the FreeBSD system and the Debian GNU/Linux system described earlier are set up to boot from the GRUB boot screen.

```
default=0
timeout 15

title FreeBSD
rootnoverify (hd0,0)
makeactive
chainloader +1

title Debian GNU/Linux
root (hd0,1)
chainloader +1
```

The default operating system to boot is the first one (default=0), FreeBSD. GRUB will pause for 15 seconds (timeout 15) before booting the default operating system. Because boot loaders are installed on both the FreeBSD and Debian partitions, an easy way to configure the two systems to boot is with chainloader. That will let you see a secondary boot screen for each of those two systems.

Now you need to overwrite the hard disk's master boot record. Because you will probably be unable to write to your hard disk's MBR by default, run the following sysctl command to **make it possible to overwrite the MBR**:

```
# sysctl kern.geom.debugflags=16
```

Once you have the menu.list file created and are able to write to the master boot record, you can install it to the master boot record using the grub-install command. Type the following **to install GRUB to the master boot record** on disk ad0:

> **WARNING!** *You are about to overwrite your computer's master boot record. If you did something wrong in your menu.lst file, grub-install will probably fail. However, if the write completed with information that you think won't work, you can always put the old* boot0 *loader back by typing* **boot0cfg -B ad0**.

177

```
# grub-install /dev/ad0
Installation finished. No error reported.
This is the contents of the device map /boot/grub/device.map.
Check if this is correct or not. If any of the lines is incorrect,
fix it and re-run the script `grub-install'.

(fd0)   /dev/fd0
(hd0)   /dev/ad0
root (hd0,1)
chainloader +1
```

At this point you should be able to reboot your computer and see the GRUB screen after control is passed off from the BIOS.

Instead of using chainloader, you can **be more specific about the next stage of the boot process.** For BSD systems, you can call the loader program directly. For Linux systems, you can identify the location of the kernel to boot. Here are examples:

```
title FreeBSD
root (hd0,0,a)
kernel /boot/loader

title     Debian GNU/Linux, kernel 2.6.18-4-686
root      (hd0,1)
kernel    /boot/vmlinuz-2.6.18-4-686 root=/dev/hda2 ro
initrd    /boot/initrd.img-2.6.18-4-686
```

In the example just shown, selecting the FreeBSD title from the GRUB boot screen will run /boot/loader from hard disk (disk 0, slice 0, and partition a). The Debian title will boot the selected kernel directly to the selected kernel (vmlinuz) and initial RAM disk (initrd.img).

You can do other things with GRUB as well. For example, you can **use an image as a splash screen for when GRUB boots.** Create a 16-color, 640 × 480 image, save it to XPM format. Do this in the GNU Image Manipulation Program (The GIMP) by selecting Image ⇨ Mode ⇨ Index, then setting the number of colors to 16. Next, gzip the image and copy it to the /boot/grub directory. For example, if you created an image named splash.xpm.gz, you could identify the image as your spash screen by adding this line to the menu.1st file:

```
splashimage=(hd0,0,a)/boot/grub/splash.xpm.gz
```

Controlling System Services

Many BSD administrators leave the basic start-up features alone and focus on configuring and enabling system services. Most of the optional services are represented by start-up scripts in the /etc/rc.d directory. The service is actually turned on and configured in the /etc/rc.conf file.

Some services are turned on in /etc/rc.conf based on selections you made when you ran sysinstall to install FreeBSD. For example, here is how my /etc/rc.conf file looked just after installation:

```
hostname="myhost.localdomain"
ifconfig_fxp0="DHCP"
linux_enable="YES"
local_startup="/usr/local/etc/rc.d"
sshd_enable="YES"
```

As you can see, the hostname is set, the Ethernet interface is started using DHCP, and Linux compatibility is enabled. Additional rc.d scripts are enabled from the /usr/local/etc/rc.d directory and the Secure Shell service is started, so people can log in to the machine over the LAN.

Many of the services you can enable are network services and are described in some detail in Chapter 14. At this point, however, I would recommend you go through the default rc.conf file (/etc/defaults/rc.conf) and look at the services and features you can enable in there. Copy the lines representing the features you want to the /etc/rc.conf file. Features you change from NO to YES will start and run as you configure them.

Starting and Stopping Your System

Although you can use the init command to start and stop your BSD system, including init 0 (shut down) and init 6 (reboot), there are also specific commands for stopping BSD. The advantages of commands such as halt, reboot, or shutdown are that they include options to let you **stop some features before shutdown occurs**. For example:

> **WARNING!** *Don't try the following commands if you don't intend to actually turn off your system, especially on a remote system.*

# **reboot**	*Reboot the computer*
# **halt -n**	*Don't run sync to sync hard drives before shutdown*
# **halt -p**	*The system will power down, if possible*
# **shutdown +10**	*Shutdown in ten minutes after warning the users*
# **shutdown -r 06:08**	*Reboot at 6:08 am*
# **shutdown +10 'Bye!'**	*Send custom message to users before shutdown*

Besides the reboot or init 6 commands, you can also use the old PC keystrokes Ctrl+Alt+Del to reboot your computer.

Straight to the Kernel

In general, when the kernel starts up on your BSD system, you shouldn't have to do too much with it. However, there are tools for checking the kernel that is in use and for seeing information about how the kernel started up. Also, if something goes wrong or if there is some extra support you need to add to the kernel, there are tools to do those things.

To find out **what version of BSD you are running,** type the following:

```
$ uname -r          Display name of current release
6.3-RELEASE
$ uname -a          Display all name and release information
FreeBSD myhost.localdomain 6.3-RELEASE FreeBSD 6.3-RELEASE #0: Wed Aug 16
    04:18:52 UTC 2008  root@dessler.cse.buffalo.edu:/usr/obj/usr/src/sys/GENERIC
    i386
```

When the kernel starts, messages about what occurs are placed in the system message buffer. You can **display the contents of the system message buffer** using the dmesg command:

```
$ dmesg |less
Copyright (c) 1992-2008 The FreeBSD Project.
Copyright (c) 1979, 1980, 1983, 1986, 1988, 1989, 1991, 1992, 1993, 1994
        The Regents of the University of California. All rights reserved.
FreeBSD is a registered trademark of The FreeBSD Foundation.
FreeBSD 6.3-RELEASE #0: Wed Jan 16 04:18:52 UTC 2008
    root@dessler.cse.buffalo.edu:/usr/obj/usr/src/sys/GENERIC
Timecounter "i8254" frequency 1193182 Hz quality 0
CPU: Intel Pentium III (648.03-MHz 686-class CPU)
  Origin = "GenuineIntel"  Id = 0x683  Stepping = 3

Features=0x387f9ff<FPU,VME,DE,PSE,TSC,MSR,PAE,MCE,CX8,SEP,MTRR,PGE,MCA,CMOV,PAT,
PSE36,PN,MMX,FXSR,SSE>
real memory  = 267124736 (254 MB)
avail memory = 251854848 (240 MB)
kbd1 at kbdmux0
ath_hal: 0.9.20.3 (AR5210, AR5211, AR5212, RF5111, RF5112, RF2413, RF5413)
hptrr: HPT RocketRAID controller driver v1.1 (Jan 16 2008 04:16:19)
acpi0: <CAYMAN 8C1A10UA> on motherboard
acpi0: Power Button (fixed)
Timecounter "ACPI-fast" frequency 3579545 Hz quality 1000
acpi_timer0: <24-bit timer at 3.579545MHz> port 0x408-0x40b on acpi0
  ...
```

If that buffer fills up, it may no longer contain the beginning of the recorded information. In that case, you can use less /var/log/dmesg.

Other information of interest about kernel processing can be found in the /var/log files, in particular, the messages file. You can page through those files as follows:

```
# less /var/log/messages*     Page through /var/log/messages
Aug 14 23:27:11 thompson newsyslog[557]: logfile first created
Aug 14 23:27:11 thompson syslogd: kernel boot file is /boot/kernel/kernel
  ...
Aug 14 23:27:11 thompson kernel: kbd1 at kbdmux0
```

```
Aug 14 23:27:11 thompson kernel: acpi0: <CAYMAN 8C1A100A> on motherboard
Aug 14 23:27:11 thompson kernel: acpi0: Power Button (fixed)
Aug 14 23:27:11 thompson kernel: Timecounter "ACPI-fast"
        frequency 3579545 Hz quality 1000
Aug 14 23:27:11 thompson kernel: cpu0: <ACPI CPU> on acpi0
Aug 14 23:27:11 thompson kernel: pcib0: <ACPI Host-PCI bridge> port 0xcf8-0xcff
on acpi0
Aug 14 23:27:11 thompson kernel: fxp0: <Intel 82559 Pro/100 Ethernet>
        port 0xde80-0xdebf mem 0xff8fd000-0 xff8fdfff,0xff700000-0xff7fffff
        irq 11 at device 1.0 on pci1
```

In the best circumstances, all the hardware connected to your computer should be detected and configured with the proper drivers. In some cases, however, either the wrong driver is detected or the necessary driver may not be available on your system. For those cases, FreeBSD offers ways of listing loadable modules and adding new ones to your system.

The kldstat command lets you view the names of the loaded modules, their address, size, and reference Id. Here is an example:

```
# kldstat
Id Refs Address     Size     Name
 1    7 0xc0400000  7a05b0   kernel
 2    1 0xc0ba1000  5c304    acpi.ko
 3    1 0xc0400000  7a05b0   linux.ko
```

If you want to find out more information about a particular module, you can use the kldstat command. Here's an example:

```
# kldstat -n acpi.ko        List status of a particular module
 2    1 0xc0ba1000 5c304    acpi.ko
# kldstat -v -n acpi.ko     Show more verbose information about module
Id Refs Address     Size     Name
 2    1 0xc0ba1000 5c304    acpi.ko
            Contains modules:
                    Id Name
                     1 nexus/acpi
                     2 acpi/acpi_button
                     3 acpi/acpi_isab
                     4 pcib/acpi_pci
                     5 acpi/acpi_pcib
                     6 pci/acpi_pcib
                     7 acpi/acpi_sysresource
    . . .
# kldstat -v -i 3           List status of a particular module by Id
Id Refs Address     Size     Name
 3    1 0xc0400000  7a05b0   linux.ko
Contains modules:
                    Id Name
                   391 linuxelf
                   392 linuxaout
```

If you decide that you need to **add a loadable module** to get some hardware item on your system working properly, you can use the `kldload` command.

```
# cd /boot/kernel          Change to directory containing modules
# kldload smbfs.ko         Load module for Samba filesystem
# kldload -v vesa.ko       Load vesa module and be more verbose
Loaded vesa.ko, id=7
```

To remove a loadable module that is currently loaded, you can use the `kldunload` command:

```
# kldunload smbfs.ko       Unload module for Samba filesystem
# kldunload -v vesa.ko     Unload vesa module and be more verbose
Unoaded vesa.ko, id=7
```

You can **control kernel parameters with the system running** using the `sysctl` command. You can also add parameters permanently to the `/etc/sysctl.conf` file, so they can load as a group or at each reboot. Here are some examples:

```
# sysctl -a | less         List all kernel parameters
kernel.ostype: FreeBSD
kernel.osrelease: 6.3-RELEASE
kern.osrevision: 199506
  ...
# sysctl kern.hostname     List value of particular parameter
kern.hostname: mycomputer.localdomain
# sysctl kern.geom.debugflags=16   Set value of kernel.geom.debugflags to 16
```

As noted earlier, if you want to change any of your kernel parameters permanently, you should add them to the `/etc/sysctl.conf` file. Parameter settings in that file are in the form *parameter = value*.

Poking at the Hardware

If you just generally want to find out more about your computer's hardware, there are a few commands you can try. First install pciutils (`pkg_add -r pciutils`). The `lspci` command from that package **lists information about PCI devices** on your computer:

```
# lspci                    List PCI hardware items
00:00.0 Host bridge: Intel Corporation 82810E DC-133 GMCH
  [Graphics Memory Controller Hub] (rev 03)
00:01.0 VGA compatible controller: Intel Corporation 82810E DC-133 CGC
  [Chipset Graphics Controller] (rev 03)
00:1e.0 PCI bridge: Intel Corporation 82801AA PCI Bridge (rev 02)
00:1f.0 ISA bridge: Intel Corporation 82801AA ISA Bridge (LPC) (rev 02)
00:1f.1 IDE interface: Intel Corporation 82801AA IDE Controller (rev 02)
00:1f.2 USB Controller: Intel Corporation 82801AA USB Controller (rev 02)
00:1f.3 SMBus: Intel Corporation 82801AA SMBus Controller (rev 02)
01:01.0 Ethernet controller: Intel Corporation 82557/8/9 [Ethernet Pro 100]
```

```
01:07.0 Multimedia audio controller: Ensoniq ES1371 [AudioPCI-97] (rev 06)
01:09.0 Network controller: Broadcom Corporation BCM4306 802.11b/g
   Wireless LAN Controller (rev 03)
   ...
# lspci -v              List PCI hardware items with more details
# lspci -vv             List PCI hardware items with even more details
```

Using the `dmidecode` command, you can **display information about your computer's hardware components**, including information about what features are supported in the BIOS (`pkg_add -r dmiencode`). Here is an example:

```
# dmidecode | less             List hardware components
# dmidecode 2.7
SMBIOS 2.3 present.
55 structures occupying 2021 bytes.
Table at 0x000F0EF0.

Handle 0x0000, DMI type 0, 20 bytes.
BIOS Information
 Vendor: Intel Corp.
 Version: CA8120A.86.0008.P04.0003290002
   ...
```

Summary

FreeBSD, OpenBSD, NetBSD, and other BSD systems make it easy for you to watch and modify many aspects of your running system to make sure it is operating at peak performance. Commands such as `top`, `vmstat`, and `iostat`, let you see how your system is using its memory, CPU, and storage devices. Using commands such as `date` and `cal`, as well as services such as NTP, you can watch and manage your system's date and time settings.

To manage the features that are set and services that come up when you boot your system, you can modify features associated with your `boot0` boot loader. Or you can change your boot loader to a different one, such as GRUB. Commands such as `reboot`, `halt`, and `shutdown` let you safely stop or reboot your computer.

When it comes to managing your computer's hardware, commands such as `kldstat`, `kldload`, and `kldunload` let you work with loadable modules. You can view information about your hardware with such commands as `lspci` and `dmidecode`.

11

Managing Network Connections

Connecting to a network from a BSD system is often as easy as attaching your computer's network interface card to your ISP's hardware (such as a DSL or cable modem) and rebooting. However, if your network interface doesn't come up or requires some manual intervention, there are many commands available for configuring network interfaces, checking network connections, and setting up special routing.

This chapter covers many useful commands for configuring and working with your network interface cards (NICs), such as sysinstall and ifconfig. In particular, it covers ways of configuring wired Ethernet, wireless Ethernet, and modem network hardware. The chapter describes commands such as netstat, dig, and ping for getting information about your network when your hardware is connected and network interfaces are in place.

IN THIS CHAPTER

Get network statistics

Starting network devices with ifconfig

Managing wireless cards

Checking DNS name resolution with dig, host, and hostname

Check connectivity with ping and arping

Trace connections with traceroute and route

Watch the network with netstat, tcpdump, and nmap

Configuring Network Interfaces Using sysinstall

When you first install your FreeBSD system, the installer lets you configure any wired Ethernet cards attached to your computer, with the use of a DHCP server detected on your network. Alternatively, you can set a static IP address, along with your hostname and IP addresses for your gateway machine and name servers. After installation, you can use the sysinstall utility to configure your network interfaces. Start it as root user by typing:

```
# sysinstall
```

From the FreeBSD Configuration menu that appears, select Networking ➪ Interfaces. At this point you have options of configuring your network interfaces based on the networking hardware connected to your computer. For example:

❑ **Ethernet Network Interface Card (fxp0, lnc0, or other)** — Wired connection to Ethernet network

❑ **Parallel Port IP (plip0)** — Direct connection to another computer between the parallel ports

❑ **Serial Line Internet Protocol (cuad0)** — Serial port connection to a modem or null modem to another computer

❑ **Point-to-Point Protocol (ppp0)** — Serial port connection to modem or null modem to another computer

Of the two serial interfaces, SLIP is older but PPP is more commonly used today. PLIP requires a special cable and, because Ethernet network cards are so inexpensive these days, PLIP is rarely used.

If your Ethernet NIC is supported, you should see the name of that card in the sysinstall display. To configure that interface, you can configure IPv6 networking. Then you have the option of either getting your computer's address information from DHCP, or configuring it manually. If you configure manually, you can enter the computer's hostname, domain name, gateway (IPv4), name server, IP address (IPv4) netmask, and any options to `ifconfig`.

In some cases, however, your network interfaces may not be working. Likewise, there may be ways you want to work with your network interfaces that are not supported from sysinstall. In those cases, the following sections describe how to work with your network interfaces from the command line.

> **NOTE** *The interface names for your Ethernet NICs are based on the driver used to support that NIC. If you are coming from a Linux environment you may expect Ethernet interfaces to be named eth0, eth1 and so on. In FreeBSD, the names might be fxp0, em0, lnc0 or something else. Examples in this chapter use fxp0 to represent a wired Ethernet NIC interface.*

Managing Network Interface Cards

If the network hardware on your computer didn't immediately come up and let you connect to the Internet, there are some steps you should go through to troubleshoot the problem:

❑ Check that your network interface card (NIC) is properly installed and that the cable is connected to your network (ISPs CPE, switch, and so on).

❑ After the cable is connected, make sure you have a link with no speed or duplex mismatches.

❑ If all else fails, consider replacing your NIC with a known-good spare to isolate a hardware failure.

To check your link from your BSD system and to set speed and duplex, the `ifconfig` command provides that and many other features.

NOTE *If you are used to tools such as* `ethtool` *and* `mii-tool`, *coming from Linux or other UNIX environments, the* `ifconfig` *command contains many of the same features you would get from those two commands.*

To **view the syntax of the ifconfig command**, type any invalid option:

```
# ifconfig -?          View options to the ifconfig command
ifconfig: illegal option -- ?
usage: ifconfig [-L] [-C] interface address_family [address [dest_address]]
                [parameters]
       ifconfig interface create
       ifconfig -a [-L] [-C] [-d] [-m] [-u] [-v] [address_family]
       ifconfig -l [-d] [-u] [address_family]
       ifconfig [-L] [-C] [-d] [-m] [-u] [-v]
```

To **display just the names of every available network interface,** use the -l option. The following example shows that there is a Ethernet NIC (fxp0), parallel port (plip0) and loopback (lo0):

```
# ifconfig -l          List names of network interfaces
fxp0 plip0 lo0
```

To **display settings for a specific Ethernet card,** add the interface name to the command. For example, to view card information for fxp0 (the first wired Ethernet NIC), type:

```
# ifconfig fxp0                See settings for NIC at fxp0
fxp0: flags=8843<UP,BROADCAST,RUNNING,SIMPLEX,MULTICAST> mtu 1500
       options=8<VLAN_MTU>
       inet 10.0.0.204 netmask 0xffffff00 broadcast 10.0.0.255
       ether 00:d0:b7:79:a5:35
       media: Ethernet autoselect (100baseTX <full-duplex>)
       status: active
```

To **display a capabilities list for a particular network card,** use the -m option:

```
# ifconfig -m fxp0       Display driver information for NIC
fxp0: flags=108843<UP,BROADCAST,RUNNING,SIMPLEX,NEEDSGIANT> mtu 1500
       options=8<VLAN_MTU>
       capabilities=8<VLAN_MTU>
```

187

```
inet 10.0.0.204 netmask 0xffffff00 broadcast 10.0.0.255
ether 00:d0:b7:79:a5:35
media: Ethernet autoselect (100baseTX <full-duplex>)
status: active
supported media:
        media autoselect
        media 100baseTX mediaopt full-duplex
        media 100baseTX
        media 10baseT/UTP mediaopt full-duplex
        media 10baseT/UTP
        media none
        media 100baseTX mediaopt hw-loopback
```

The ifconfig command can be used to **change NIC settings** as well as display them.

To hard-set the NIC to 100Mpbs with full duplex, type this:

```
# ifconfig fxp0 media 100baseTX mediaopt full-duplex    Change speed/duplex
# ifconfig fxp0                                          View new NIC settings
fxp0: flags=8843<UP,BROADCAST,RUNNING,SIMPLEX,MULTICAST> mtu 1500
        options=8<VLAN_MTU>
        inet 10.0.0.204 netmask 0xffffff00 broadcast 10.0.0.255
        ether 00:d0:b7:79:a5:35
        media: Ethernet 100baseTX <full-duplex>
        status: active
```

To hard-set the speed to 10Mpbs, type this:

```
# ifconfig fxp0 media 10baseT/UTP        Change speed
# ifconfig fxp0                           View new NIC settings
fxp0: flags=8843<UP,BROADCAST,RUNNING,SIMPLEX,MULTICAST> mtu 1500
        options=8<VLAN_MTU>
        inet 10.0.0.204 netmask 0xffffff00 broadcast 10.0.0.255
        ether 00:d0:b7:79:a5:35
        media: Ethernet 10baseT/UTP <full duplex>
        status: active
```

To **change the IP address and netmask,** type this:

```
# ifconfig fxp0 inet 10.0.0.208 netmask 255.0.0.0 Change IP and netmask
# ifconfig fxp0                                    View new NIC settings
fxp0: flags=8843<UP,BROADCAST,RUNNING,SIMPLEX,MULTICAST> mtu 1500
        options=8<VLAN_MTU>
        inet 10.0.0.208 netmask 0xff000000 broadcast 10.255.255.255
        ether 00:d0:b7:79:a5:35
        media: Ethernet 10baseT/UTP <full-duplex>
        status: active
```

The changes just made to your NIC settings are good for the current session. When you reboot, however, those settings will be lost. To **make these settings stick at the next reboot** or network restart, add the options to the ifconfig_fxp0 line in the /etc/rc.conf file (change fxp0 to the appropriate interface name if it's not the first Ethernet NIC interface). For example:

```
ifconfig_fxp0="inet 10.0.0.208 netmask 255.0.0.0 media 100baseTX"
```

The netstat command provides many ways to **get network interface statistics**. With no options, netstat **shows active network connections and active sockets** as follows:

```
$ netstat                   Show active connections and sockets
Active Internet connections
Proto Recv-Q Send-Q  Local Address           Foreign Address        (state)
tcp4      0      0  10.0.0.204.62963        10.0.0.204.ssh         TIME_WAIT
tcp4      0      0  10.0.0.204.ssh          einstein.47835         ESTABLISHED
Active UNIX domain sockets
Address  Type   Recv-Q Send-Q    Inode    Conn  Refs  Nextref Addr
c241aa64 stream      0      0        0 c241a9d8     0        0
c241a9d8 stream      0      0        0 c241aa64     0        0
c241a4ec stream      0      0 c2445bb0        0     0        0 /var/run/devd.pipe
  ...
```

To **show quick statistics on all network interfaces,** use netstat as follows:

```
$ netstat -i               Get network interface statistics for all interfaces
netstat -i
Name    Mtu Network      Address          Ipkts Ierrs   Opkts Oerrs  Coll
fxp0   1500 <Link#1>     00:d0:b7:79:a5:35  8019     0    2910     0     0
fxp0   1500 10           10.0.0.204          313     -     183     -     -
plip0  1500 <Link#2>                           0     0       0     0     0
lo0   16384 <Link#3>                          27     0      27     0     0
  ...
```

Use the -w option to get netstat to **refresh network interface statistics every second:**

```
$ netstat -w 2 -I fxp0               Refresh network statistics every 2 seconds
            input        (Total)           output
    packets  errs      bytes    packets  errs      bytes colls
         13     0        266         12     0        244     0
          2     0       5938          1     0      84282     0
         92     2       6676        116     0     115574     0
        183     3      16862        225     0     369602     0
        152     2      13642        191     0     264566     0
        137     4       6836        169     0     103890     0
        113     0      10276        139     0     144936     0
```

You can **check if there are active connections to your computer** from netstat with the -p option as follows:

```
$ netstat -p tcp               Display active TCP connections
Active Internet connections
```

189

```
Proto Recv-Q Send-Q  Local Address        Foreign Address       (state)
tcp4    0      0  10.0.0.204.ssh       thompson.62963        ESTABLISHED
tcp4    0      0  10.0.0.204.ssh       einstein.47835        ESTABLISHED
```

As the output indicates, the netstat shows two connections from remote computers that have active ssh sessions to the local computer. Here are some other quick examples of the netstat command:

$ **netstat -r**	*Display kernel routing tables for IPv4 and IPv6*
$ **netstat -rs**	*Display routing stats (bad routes, dynamic routes)*
$ **netstat -s -p tcp | less**	*Display detailed statistics for TCP interfaces*
$ **netstat -n**	*Display output with IP addresses, not hostnames*
$ **netstat -m**	*Display information on network memory buffers*

Managing Network Connections

Starting and stopping the network interfaces for your wired Ethernet connections to your LAN or the Internet are usually handled automatically at the time you boot and shut down your BSD system. However, you can run scripts from the /etc/rc.d directory to start and stop your network interfaces any time you want or edit the /etc/rc.conf file to set whether or not your network services start automatically.

The ifconfig command can also be used to configure, activate, and deactivate interfaces.

Starting and Stopping Ethernet Connections

The reason that your wired Ethernet interfaces just come up in many cases when you boot your BSD system is that the netif service is set to be on when the system boots up. After the system is booted, you can use the netif script to stop, start, and restart your network interfaces.

The script that starts your network interfaces in FreeBSD is /etc/rc.d/netif. As with other BSD services, you can start and stop the netif service by running the script with options such as start, stop, and restart.

To **take all network interfaces offline then bring them back online**, type the following as root user:

```
# /etc/rc.d/netif restart      Shutdown and bring up network interfaces
Stopping network: lo0 fxp0 plip0.
DHCPREQUEST on fxp0 to 255.255.255.255 port 67
DHCPACK from 10.0.0.1
bound to 10.0.0.204 -- renewal in 7200 seconds.
lo0: flags=8049<UP,LOOPBACK,RUNNING,MULTICAST> mtu 16384
        inet6 fe80::1%lo0 prefixlen 64 scopeid 0x3
        inet6 ::1 prefixlen 128
        inet 127.0.0.1 netmask 0xff000000
fxp0: flags=8843<UP,BROADCAST,RUNNING,SIMPLEX,MULTICAST> mtu 1500
```

```
options=8<VLAN_MTU>
inet 10.0.0.204 netmask 0xffffff00 broadcast 10.0.0.255
ether 00:d0:b7:79:a5:35
media: Ethernet 10baseT/UTP <full-duplex>
status: active
```

Use the start and stop options to **start and stop your network interfaces**, respectively:

```
# /etc/rc.d/netif stop      Shutdown network interfaces
# /etc/rc.d/netif start     Bring up network interfaces
```

You can also use the ifconfig command to bring network interfaces up and down. For example:

```
# ifconfig fxp0 down        Turn off network interface for Ethernet card (fxp0)
# ifconfig fxp0 -d          List network interfaces that are down
fxp0: flags=8802<BROADCAST,SIMPLEX,MULTICAST> mtu 1500
  ...
# ifconfig fxp0 up          Turn on network interface for Ethernet card (fxp0)
# ifconfig fxp0 -u          List network interfaces that are up
fxp0: flags=8843<UP,BROADCAST,RUNNING,SIMPLEX,MULTICAST> mtu
  ...
```

Note that the network interfaces will appear as active after running ifconfig with the down option. However, the words UP and RUNNING will no longer appear when you list the interface and no data will be able to go in either direction across that interface.

When your network interfaces are up, there are tools you can use to view information about those interfaces and associated NICs.

Starting and Stopping Network Services

You can start and stop services associated with your network interfaces in much the same way that you used the netif script to start and stop the interfaces. Services such as the Secure Shell (sshd) and Network File System (nfsd) can be set to start automatically when the system boots based on settings in the /etc/rc.conf file.

Information on how to configure and start network services is contained in Chapter 10. To find out the options available when you run network service scripts, just type the path to the script with no options. For example:

```
# /etc/rc.d/sendmail        Check options available with start-up script
Usage: /etc/rc.d/sendmail [fast|force|one](start|stop|restart|rcvar|status|poll)
```

Here are some examples of starting and using network services that have already been configured:

```
# /etc/rc.d/sshd restart    Stop and start the SSH service
# /etc/rc.d/sshd reload     Reload config files from /etc/ssh directory
```

```
# /etc/rc.d/sshd keygen      Generate host keys, if you need them (/etc/ssh)

# /etc/rc.d/nfsd status      Check status of NFS service
nfsd is not running
# /etc/rc.d/nfsd start       Start the NFS service
Starting nfsd
# /etc/rc.d/nfsd start       Show process IDS of NFS server processes
Waiting for PIDS: 8394 8395 8396 8397 8398
```

Using Wireless Connections

Setting up wireless connections in FreeBSD has been tricky in the past, primarily due to the fact that open source drivers have not been available for the vast majority of wireless LAN cards on the market. So the first thing you need to do is choose a wireless card that is supported by BSD. The next thing is to configure your wireless network interface using the ifconfig command.

Getting Wireless Driver

If you have any choice in the matter, you should purchase a wireless LAN card that has open source drivers available that are packaged with your BSD system. If you are not sure of the manufacturer and model of your wireless card, if you have a PCI card you can **determine exactly what wireless card you have**, using the lspci command (pkg_add -r pciutils):

```
# lspci | grep -i wireless      Search for wireless PCI cards
01:09.0 Network controller: Broadcom Corporation BCM4306 802.11b/g
   Wireless LAN Controller (rev 03)
```

The wireless card shown is not one of the supported cards. If that is the case with your card, you might be able to use the ndis miniport driver wrapper (type **man ndis**). With the ndis driver you can use Windows drivers to get your wireless LAN cards to work.

Wireless LAN cards for which there are drivers in FreeBSD are shown in Table 11-1

Table 11-1: Wireless LAN Cards for FreeBSD

Driver name	Supported Wireless Cards	Line to add to /boot/loader.conf
an	Aironet Communications 4500/4800 Cisco Aironet 340 and 350 series Xircom Wireless Ethernet Adapter	if_an_load="YES"
ath	Atheros 802.11 Wireless Adapter Supports all Atheros Cardbus/PCI (except AR5005VL)	if_ath_load="YES"

Table 11-1: Wireless LAN Cards for FreeBSD (*continued*)

Driver name	Supported Wireless Cards	Line to add to /boot/loader.conf
awi	AMD PCnetMobile IEEE802.11 BayStack 650/660 Icom SL-200 Melco WLI-PCM NEL SSMagic Netwave AirSurfer Plus/Pro Nokia C020 WLAN Farallon SkyLINE	if_awi_load="YES"
cnw	Netwave AirSurfer Wireless LAN Xircon CreditCard Netwave	if_cnw_load="YES"
ipw	Intel PRO/Wireless 2100 MiniPCI	if_ipw_load="YES"
iwi	Intel PRO/Wireless 2200BG/ 2225BG MiniPCI/ 2915ABG 802.11 Adapters	if_iwi_load="YES"
ral	Ralink Technology RT2500	if_ral_load="YES"
ural	Ralink Technology RT2500USB	if_ural_load="YES"
wi	Dozens of cards that include the following wireless chipsets: Lucent Hermes, Intersil PRISM-II, Intersil PRISM-2.5 and Symbol Spectrun24	if_wi_load="YES"

As indicated in the third column, if the wireless driver isn't already built into your kernel, you can configure it to load as a module when you boot your computer. Just add the line shown to the /boot/loader.conf file. Along with the specific driver for your card, you also need the wlan 802.11 generic driver:

```
wlan_load="YES"
```

Configuring Wireless Interfaces

Here are some ifconfig command lines to configure network interfaces for the supported cards shown in Table 11-1 (once the drivers have been loaded). To give you an idea of the available options, different options are shown with each wireless interface command line:

```
# ifconfig an0 inet 10.0.1.1 netmask 0xffffff00     Add Aironet card interface
# ifconfig ath0 inet 10.0.1.1 \        Connect Atheros card to existing network
    netmask 0xffffff00 ssid "net01"     named net01
# ifconfig awi0 inet 10.0.1.1 \        Connect PCnetMobile card (64-bit WEP)
    netmask 0xffffff00 ssid "net01"
    wepmode on wepkey 0x45320185622
```

193

```
# ifconfig cnw0 inet 10.0.1.1 \        Connect Netwave Airsurfer access point
    netmask 0xffffff00 ssid "net01" \
    mode 11g mediaopt hostap
# ifconfig ipw0 inet 10.0.1.1 \        Connect Intel PRO 2100 (104-bit WEP)
    netmask 0xffffff00 ssid "net01" \
    wepmode on wepkey 0x0100294853522415091012431 2
# ifconfig iwi0 inet 10.0.1.1 \        Connect Intel PRO 2200BG (128-bit WEP)
    netmask 0xffffff00 ssid "net01" \
    wepmode on wepkey 0x010203040506070809101112 13 weptxkey 1
```

After the wireless card interface is configured, you can check it or bring it up and down as you would any network interface. You can also do a few other things to check on the wireless network. For example:

```
# ifconfig iwi0              Check the status of wireless connection
# ifconfig ath0 down         Turn off wireless network
# ifconfig ipw0 up           Bring up wireless network
# ifconfig cnw0 scan         Scan for and display any stations found
```

There are other commands for working with wireless cards after they have been configured. For example, you can use the wicontrol (Aironet cards), ancontrol (Aironet cards) and raycontrol (Raylink cards) commands to view and work with settings on your wireless cards. Here are some commands for working with Atheros, Intersil, or Lucent wireless cards:

```
# wicontrol -i wi0 -o     Display statistics associated with wireless card
# wicontrol -i wi0 -C     Display cached signal strength information
# wicontrol -i wi0 -X     Erase cached signal strength information
# raycontrol -i ray0 -o   Display current statistics from driver
# raycontrol -i ray0 -t 3     Set transmission rate to medium
# raycontrol -i ray0 -n net02  Set network name to net0
# ancontrol -i an0 -A     Display access point that is preferred
# ancontrol -i an0 -S     Display list of SSIDs
```

Checking Name Resolution

Because IP addresses are numbers, and people prefer to address things by name, TCP/IP networks (such as the Internet) rely on DNS to resolve hostnames into IP addresses. FreeBSD provides several tools for looking up information related to DNS name resolution.

When you first installed FreeBSD, you either identified Domain Name System (DNS) servers to do name resolution or had them assigned automatically from a DHCP server. That information is then stored in the /etc/resolv.conf file, looking something like the following:

```
nameserver 11.22.33.44
nameserver 22.33.44.55
```

The numbers shown above are replaced by real IP addresses of computers that serve as DNS name servers. When you can connect to working DNS servers, you can use commands to query those servers and look up host computers.

You can use the `dig` command (which should be used instead of the deprecated `nslookup` command) to look up information from a DNS server. The `host` command can be used to look up address information for a hostname or domain name.

To **search your DNS servers for a particular hostname** (in the following examples www.turbosphere.com), use the `dig` command as follows:

```
$ dig www.turbosphere.com      Search DNS servers set in /etc/resolv.conf
; <<>> DiG 9.3.3 <<>> www.turbosphere.com
;; global options:  printcmd
;; Got answer:
;; ->>HEADER<<- opcode: QUERY, status: NOERROR, id: 45
;; flags: qr rd ra; QUERY: 1, ANSWER: 2, AUTHORITY: 2, ADDITIONAL: 2

;; QUESTION SECTION:
;www.turbosphere.com.           IN      A
...
```

Instead of using your assigned name server, you can **query a specific name server**. This is useful if you believe that your name server is not resolving the address of a particular host properly. So you can check different servers to see how the name resolves. The following example queries the DNS server at `4.2.2.1`:

```
$ dig www.turbosphere.com @4.2.2.1
```

Using `dig`, you can also **query for a specific record type**:

```
$ dig turbosphere.com mx   Queries for the mail exchanger
$ dig turbosphere.com ns   Queries for the authoritative name servers
```

Use the `+trace` option to **trace a recursive query** from the top-level DNS servers down to the authoritative servers:

```
$ dig +trace www.turbosphere.com   Recursively trace DNS servers
```

If you just want to **see the IP address of a host computer,** use the `+short` option:

```
$ dig +short www.turbosphere.com   Display only name/IP address pair
turbosphere.com.
66.113.99.70
```

You can use `dig` **to do a reverse lookup to find DNS information based on IP address:**

```
$ dig -x 66.113.99.70            Get DNS information based on IP address
```

You can use `host` to **do a reverse DNS lookup** as well:

```
$ host 66.113.99.70
70.99.133.66.in-addr.arpa domain name pointer boost.turbosphere.com.
```

To **get hostname information for the local machine,** use the `hostname` and `dnsdomainname` commands:

```
$ hostname               View the local computer's full DNS hostname
boost.turbosphere.com
$ hostname -s            View the local computer's short hostname
boost
```

You can also use `hostname` to **set the local hostname temporarily** (until the next reboot). Here's an example:

```
# hostname server1.example.com    Set local hostname
```

Changing the hostname of a running machine may adversely affect some running daemons. Instead, we recommend you **set the local hostname so it is set each time the system starts up.** One way to do that is to set the hostname option in the `/etc/rc.conf` file. For the previous example, the hostname line would appear as follows:

```
hostname="server1.example.com"
```

Troubleshooting Network Problems

Troubleshooting networks is generally done from the bottom layer up. As discussed in the beginning of this chapter, the first step is to make sure that the physical network layer components (cables, NICs, and so on) are connected and working. Next, check that the links between physical nodes are working. After that, there are lots of tools for checking the connectivity to a particular host.

Checking Connectivity to a Host

When you know you have a link and no duplex mismatch, the next step is to `ping` your default gateway. You should have configured the default gateway (gw), whether you did that manually or had it set automatically by DHCP when the network started. To **check your default gateway in the actual routing table,** use the `route` command to find a host on the other side of that gateway as follows:

```
# route get example.com
   route to: www.example.com
destination: default
      mask: default
   gateway: 10.0.0.1
 interface: fxp0
```

```
    flags: <UP,GATEWAY,DONE,STATIC>
recvpipe   sendpipe   ssthresh   rtt,msec    rttvar   hopcount        mtu      expire
       0          0          0          0          0          0       1500           0
```

The gateway for the default route is 10.0.0.1. To make sure there is IP connectivity to that gateway, use the ping command as follows:

```
$ ping 10.0.0.1
PING 10.0.0.1 (10.0.0.1) 56 data bytes
64 bytes from 10.0.0.1: icmp_seq=0 ttl=64 time=1.43 ms
64 bytes from 10.0.0.1: icmp_seq=1 ttl=64 time=0.382 ms
64 bytes from 10.0.0.1: icmp_seq=2 ttl=64 time=0.313 ms
64 bytes from 10.0.0.1: icmp_seq=3 ttl=64 time=0.360 ms

--- 10.0.0.1 ping statistics ---
4 packets transmitted, 4 received, 0% packet loss
round-trip min/avg/max/stddev = 0.313/0.621/1.432/0.469 ms
```

> **NOTE**   *Some hosts are configured to ignore ping requests. So not getting a reply doesn't indicate that the host or gateway is down.*

By default, ping continues until you press Ctrl+C. Other ping options include the following:

```
$ ping -a 10.0.0.1          Add an audible ping as ping progresses
$ ping -c 4 10.0.0.1        Ping 4 times and exit (default in Windows)
$ ping -q -c 5 10.0.0.1     Show summary of pings (works best with -c)
# ping -f 10.0.0.1          Send a flood of pings (must be root)
$ ping -i 3 10.0.0.1        Send packets in 3-second intervals
# ping -s 1500 10.0.0.1     Set packet size to 1500 bytes (must be root)
PING 10.0.0.1 (10.0.0.1) 1500 data bytes
```

Use the ping flood option with caution. By default, ping sends small packets (56 bytes). Large packets (such as the 1500-byte setting just shown) are good to make faulty NICs or connections stand out. Only the root user can send a flood of pings or pings with byte sized over the default 56 bytes.

Checking Address Resolution Protocol (ARP)

If you're not able to ping your gateway, you may have an issue at the Ethernet MAC layer. The Address Resolution Protocol (ARP) can be used to find information at the MAC layer. To view and configure ARP entries, use the arp command. This example shows arp listing computers in the ARP cache by hostname:

```
# arp -a          List all current ARP entries
ritchie  (10.0.0.1) at 00:10:5a:ab:f6:a7 on fxp0 [ethernet]
einstein (10.0.0.50) at 00:0b:6a:02:ec:98 on fxp0 [ethernet]
thompson (10.0.0.204) at 00:d0:b7:79:a5:35 on fxp0 permanent [ethernet]
```

In this example, you can see the names of other computers that the local computer's ARP cache knows about and the associated hardware address (MAC address) of each computer's NIC. To **delete an entry from the ARP cache,** use the -d option:

```
# arp -d 10.0.0.50            Delete address 10.0.0.50 from ARP cache
```

Instead of just letting ARP dynamically learn about other systems, you can **add static ARP entries to the cache** using the -s option:

```
# arp -s 10.0.0.51 00:0B:6A:02:EC:95    Add IP and MAC addresses to ARP
```

To **query a subnet to see if an IP is already in use,** and to find the MAC address of the device using it, use the arping command (pkg_add -r arping). The arping command can be used to check for IP conflicts before bringing an Ethernet NIC up. Here are examples:

```
# arping 10.0.0.50            Query subnet to see if 10.0.0.50 is in use
ARPING 10.0.0.50
60 bytes from 00:0b:6a:02:ec:98 (10.0.0.50): index=0 time=9.966 msec
60 bytes from 00:0b:6a:02:ec:98 (10.0.0.50): index=1 time=9.930 msec
60 bytes from 00:0b:6a:02:ec:98 (10.0.0.50): index=2 time=9.930 msec
60 bytes from 00:0b:6a:02:ec:98 (10.0.0.50): index=3 time=9.931 msec
^C
--- 10.0.0.50 statistics ---
4 packets transmitted, 4 packets received,   0% unanswered
# arping -I fxp0 10.0.0.50    Specify interface to query from
```

Like the ping command, the arping command continuously queries for the address until the command is ended by typing Ctrl+C. Typically, you just want to know if the target is alive, so you can run the following command:

```
# arping -c 1 10.0.0.51    Query 10.0.0.50 and stop after 2 counts
```

Tracing Routes to Hosts

After you make sure that you can ping your gateway and even reach machines that are outside your network, you may still have issues reaching a specific host or network. If that's true, you can **use traceroute to find the bottleneck or point of failure:**

```
$ traceroute boost.turbosphere.com   Follow the route taken to a host
traceroute to boost.turbosphere.com (66.113.99.70),64 hops max,40 byte packets
 1  10.0.0.1 (10.0.0.1)  0.281 ms  0.289 ms  0.237 ms
 2  t1-03.hbci.com (51.55.11.1)  6.213 ms  6.189 ms  6.083 ms
 3  172.17.2.153 (172.17.2.153)  14.070 ms  14.025 ms  13.974 ms
 4  so-0-3-2.ar2.MIN1.gblx.net (208.48.1.117)  19.076 ms  19.053 ms 19.004 ms
 5  so1-0-0-2488M.ar4.SEA1.gblx.net(67.17.71.210)94.697 ms 94.668 ms 94.612ms
 6  64.215.31.114 (64.215.31.114)  99.643 ms  101.647 ms  101.577 ms
 7  dr02-v109.tac.opticfusion.net(209.147.112.50)262.301ms 233.316ms 233.153 ms
 8  dr01-v100.tac.opticfusion.net (66.113.96.1)  99.313 ms 99.401 ms 99.353 ms
 9  boost.turbosphere.com (66.113.99.70)  99.251 ms  96.215 ms  100.220 ms
```

As you can see, the longest hop is between 4 (Global Crossing probably in Minneapolis) and 5 (GC in Seattle). That gap is not really a bottleneck; it just reflects the distance between those hops. Sometimes, the last hops look like this:

```
28  * * *
29  * * *
30  * * *
```

The lines of asterisks (*) at the end of the trace can be caused by firewalls that block traffic to the target. However, if you see several asterisks before the destination, those can indicate heavy congestion or equipment failures and point to a bottleneck.

By default, traceroute uses UDP packets, which provide a more realistic performance picture than ICMP. That's because some Internet hops will give lower priority to ICMP traffic. If you'd still like to trace using ICMP packets, try this command:

```
# traceroute -I boost.turbosphere.com   Use ICMP packets to trace a route
```

To **trace a route to a remote host using TCP packets,** use the -T option to traceroute:

```
# traceroute -P TCP boost.turbosphere.com   Use TCP packets to trace a route
```

By default, traceroute connects to port 80. You can **set a different port** using the -p option:

```
# traceroute -P TCP -p 25 boost.turbosphere.com   Connect to port 25 in trace
```

You can **view IP addresses instead of hostnames** by disabling name resolution of hops:

```
$ traceroute -n boost.turbosphere.com   Disable name resolution in trace
```

To view and manipulate the kernel's routing table, the route command used to be the tool of choice. This is slowly being replaced by the ip route command in some Linux distributions, but is still commonly used in BSD distributions.

You can use the route command to **display your local routing table.** Here are two examples of the route command, with and without DNS name resolution:

```
# route get freebsd.org          Display local routing table information
   route to: freebsd.org
destination: default
      mask: default
   gateway: 10.0.0.1
 interface: fxp0
     flags: <UP,GATEWAY,DONE,STATIC>
 recvpipe  sendpipe  ssthresh  rtt,msec  rttvar  hopcount    mtu    expire
        0         0         0         0        0         0   1500         0
# route -n get freebsd.org       Display routing table without DNS lookup
route to: 69.147.83.40
destination: default
```

199

```
       mask: default
    gateway: 10.0.0.1
  interface: fxp0
      flags: <UP,GATEWAY,DONE,STATIC>
recvpipe  sendpipe  ssthresh  rtt,msec   rttvar  hopcount     mtu    expire
     0         0         0         0        0         0      1500         0
```

You can **change the default route on your system** using the add default options as follows:

```
# route add default 10.0.0.2        Change the default route
```

You can **add a new route to your network** by specifying the destination and the IP address of the gateway (such as, 10.0.0.100):

```
# route add -net 192.168.0.0 netmask 255.255.255.0 gw 10.0.0.100
```

You can **delete a route** using the delete option:

```
# route delete -net 192.168.0.0 Delete a route
```

To **make a new route permanent,** create a defaultrouter entry in the /etc/rc.conf file. For example, to make the default route be set to 10.0.0.2 at each system reboot, you could add the following entry to the file /etc/rc.conf:

```
defaultrouter="10.0.0.2"
```

Displaying netstat Connections and Statistics

Another command that can display information about the routing table is the netstat command. However, netstat can also **display information about packets sent between transport-layer protocols** (TCP and UDP), and ICMP.

To use netstat to **display the routing table,** type the following:

```
# netstat -rn          Display the routing table
Routing tables
Internet:
```

Destination	Gateway	Flags	Refs	Use	Netif	Expire
default	10.0.0.1	UGS	0	681	fxp0	
10.0.0.1	00:10:5a:ab:f6:a7	UHLW	2	0	fxp0	268
10.0.0.50	00:0b:6a:02:ec:98	UHLW	2	980	fxp0	690
127.0.0.1	127.0.0.1	UH	0	32	lo0	

```
  ...
```

To use `netstat` to display detailed summaries of activities for TCP, ICMP, UDP and protocols, type the following:

```
$ netstat -s | less        Show summary of TCP, ICMP, UDP activities
tcp:
        21156 packets sent
                19743 data packets (1184618 bytes)
                207 data packets (44928 bytes) retransmitted
                62 data packets unnecessarily retransmitted
                0 resends initiated by MTU discovery
                964 ack-only packets (149 delayed)
                0 URG only packets
                0 window probe packets
    ...
```

You can see a **list of TCP statistics for each interface,** by typing the following:

```
# netstat -i -p tcp           View TCP activities
```

Name	Mtu	Network	Address	Ipkts	Ierrs	Opkts	Oerrs	Coll
fxp0	1500	\<Link#1\>	00:d0:b7:79:a5:35	38600	0	36776	0	0
plip0	1500	\<Link#2\>		0	0	0	0	0
lo0	16384	\<Link#3\>		40	0	40	0	0
lo0	16384	fe80:3::1	fe80:3::1	0	-	0	-	-
lo0	16384	localhost.loc	::1	4	-	4	-	-

```
    ...
```

You can **view information about active sockets.** This includes information on server processes listening for requests from the network:

```
# netstat -AanW -p tcp
Active Internet connections (including servers)
```

Socket	Proto	Recv-Q	Send-Q	Local Address	Foreign Address	(state)
c24e0000	tcp4	0	0	127.0.0.1.6010	*.*	LISTEN
c24c6910	tcp4	0	0	10.0.0.204.22	10.0.0.50.45664	ESTABLISHED
c24c6570	tcp4	0	0	127.0.0.1.25	*.*	LISTEN
c24c6ae0	tcp4	0	0	*.22	*.*	LISTEN
c24c5000	tcp4	0	0	*.949	*.*	LISTEN
c24c51d0	tcp4	0	0	*.897	*.*	LISTEN
c24c5740	tcp4	0	0	*.2049	*.*	LISTEN
c24c5ae0	tcp4	0	0	*.649	*.*	LISTEN
c24c5cb0	tcp4	0	0	*.111	*.*	LISTEN

From the example above, you can see that there is one established connection (a remote login via `ssh` on port 22 from the host at address 10.0.0.50). Other sockets represent processes listening for a variety of service requests.

To display how much data has been transferred over a particular interface (in bytes), use the -I and -b options. For example:

```
# netstat -I fxp0 -b
Name Mtu Network  Address         Ipkts Ierrs  Ibytes Opkts Oerrs  Obytes
fxp0 1500 <Link#1> 00:d0:b7:79:a5:35 39753     0 5213277 37430     0 4322243
fxp0 1500 10/24    thompson        39662     - 4651787 37388     - 3797160
```

Other Useful Network Tools

If you'd like to see header information about packets as they are sent and received by your system, use tcpdump. The tcpdump command has a lot of advanced features, most of which revolve around filtering and finding a needle in a haystack of packets. If you run tcpdump on a remote machine, your screen will be flooded with all the ssh traffic between your client and the remote machine. To get started without having to learn too much about how tcpdump filtering works, run the following command:

```
# tcpdump not port ssh      Find all TCP packets EXCEPT those associated with ssh
```

If you'd like to dig deeper into packet-level traffic, use wireshark (formerly known as ethereal). A graphical version of wireshark is available for the GNOME desktop environment (pkg_add -r wireshark). You can run wireshark with X over ssh on a remote machine. Wireshark is a very powerful packet sniffer that rivals the best commercial tools.

To explore networks and remote machines and see what services they offer, use nmap (pkg_add -r nmap). The nmap command is the most common port scanner. It was even featured in the movie *The Matrix Reloaded*. Make sure that you are authorized to scan the systems or networks you are scanning. The nmap command is part of the nmap package and can be run as a user, but several scan types require root privilege.

Here's how to do a basic host scan with nmap:

```
# nmap 127.0.0.1      Scan your localhost, to see how nmap works
# nmap 10.0.0.1       Scan ports on computer at 10.0.0.1
```

To get maximum verbosity from nmap, use the -vv option:

```
# nmap -vv 10.0.0.1      Show maximum verbosity from nmap output
```

To use nmap to scan an entire network, use the network address as an argument. In the following example, we add the -sP option to tell nmap to perform a simple ping sweep:

```
# nmap -vv -sP 10.0.0.0/24    Scan hosts on an entire network
```

You can be very specific about the information that nmap gathers for you. In the following example, the -P0 option tells nmap not to use ping (this is good for scanning machines that don't respond to ping). The -O option displays OS fingerprinting for the machine you are scanning. The -p 100-200 tells nmap to scan only ports 100 through 200:

```
# nmap -vv -P0 -O -p 100-200 10.0.0.1    No ping, OS fingerprint, ports 100-200
```

The nmap command has a lot more options for advanced usage. Refer to the nmap man page (man nmap) for further information.

Summary

Nearly every aspect of the network connections from your BSD system can be configured, checked, and monitored using command line tools. You can view and change settings of your NICs using the ifconfig command. You can view network statistics with netstat.

To start and stop your network, commands such as netif and ifconfig are easy to manage. When a connection is established, you can see statistics about that connection using netstat and route commands.

To check DNS name resolution, use the dig, host, and hostname commands. Commands for checking connectivity and routes to a host include ping, arp, traceroute, and arping.

12

Accessing Network Resources

In the time it takes to fire up a graphical FTP client, you could already have downloaded a few dozen files from a remote server using command line tools. Even when a GUI is available, commands for transferring files, web browsing, sharing directories, and reading mail can be quick and efficient to use. When no GUI is available, they can be lifesavers.

This chapter covers commands for accessing resources (files, e-mail, shared directories, and online chats) over the network.

IN THIS CHAPTER

Web browsing with elinks

Wget, curl, lftp, and scp for file transfers

Sharing directories with NFS, Samba, and SSHFS

IRC chats with irssi

Mail and mutt e-mail clients

Running Commands to Browse the Web

Text-mode web browsers provide a quick way to check that a web server is working or to get information from a web server when a useable GUI isn't available. The once-popular lynx text-based browser was supplanted in most UNIX-like systems by the links browser, which was later replaced by elinks.

The elinks browser runs in a terminal window. Aside from not displaying images in the terminal, elinks can handle most basic HTML content and features: tables, frames, tabbed browsing, cookies, history, mime types, and simple cascading style sheets (CSS). You can even use your mouse to follow links and select menu items.

Because elinks supports multiple colors, as long as the terminal you are using supports multiple colors, it's easy to spot links and headings in the text. (Colors may not work within a screen session.) Here are some examples of elinks command lines:

```
$ elinks                         Prompts for file name or URL
$ elinks www.handsonhistory.com  Opens file name or URL you request
```

If you have a mouse, click near the top of the terminal window to see the menu. Select the menu name or item you want. Select a link to go to that link. Table 12-1 shows elinks keyboard navigation keys.

Table 12-1: Control Keys for Using elinks

Keys	Description	Keys	Description
Esc (or F9)	Toggle menu on and off (then arrow keys or mouse to navigate menus).	=	View page information.
Down arrow	Go to next link or editable field on page.	Ctrl+R	Reload page.
Up arrow	Go to previous link or editable field on the page.	a	Bookmark current page.
Right arrow or Enter	Go forward to highlighted link. Enter text in highlighted form field.	t	Open new browser tab.
Left arrow	Go back to previous page.	>	Go to next tab.
/	Search forward.	<	Go to previous tab.
?	Search backwards.	c	Close current tab.
n	Find next.	d	Download current link.
N	Find previous.	D	View downloads.
PageUp	Scroll one page up.	A	Add current link to bookmarks.
PageDown	Scroll one page down.	s	View bookmarks.
g	Go to a URL.	v	View current image.
q or Ctrl+C	Exit elinks.	h	View global history manager.

You can add global settings for elinks to /etc/elinks.conf. Per-user settings are stored in each user's $HOME/.elinks directory. Type man elinkskeys to see available settings.

Transferring Files

Commands available with FreeBSD for downloading files from remote servers (HTTP, HTTPS, FTP, or SSH) are plentiful and powerful. You might choose one command over another because of the specific options you need. For example, you may want to perform a download over an encrypted connection, resume an aborted download, or do recursive downloads. This section describes how to use wget, ftp, lftp, scp, and sftp.

Downloading Files with wget

Sometimes you need to **download a file from a remote server** using the command line. For example, you find a link to a software package, but the link goes through several HTTP redirects that prevent pkg_add from installing straight from HTTP. Or you may want to script the automated download of a file, such as a log file, every night.

The wget command can download files from web servers (HTTP and HTTPS) and FTP servers (pkg_add -r wget). With a server that doesn't require authentication, a wget command can be as simple as the wget command and the location of the download file:

```
$ wget http://upload.wikimedia.org/wikipedia/commons/2/2c/Chokladbollar.jpg
```

If, for example, an **FTP server requires a login and password**, you can enter that information on the wget command line in the following forms:

```
$ wget ftp://user:password@ftp.example.com/path/to/file
$ wget --user=user --password=password ftp://ftp.example.com/path/to/file
```

For example:

```
$ wget ftp://chris:mykuulpwd@ftp.linuxtoys.net/home/chris/image.jpg
$ wget --user=chris --password=mykuulpwd \
        ftp://ftp.linuxtoys.net/home/chris/image.jpg
```

You can **use wget to download a single web page** as follows:

```
$ wget http://www.google.com        Download only the web page
```

If you open the resulting index.html, you'll have all sorts of broken links. To download all the images and other elements required to render the page properly, use the -p option:

```
$ wget -p http://www.google.com        Download web page and other elements
```

When you open the resulting index.html in your browser, chances are you will still have all the broken links even though all the images were downloaded. That's because the links need to be translated to point to your local files. So instead, do this:

```
$ wget -pk http://www.google.com        Download pages and use local file names
```

And if you'd like `wget` to keep the original file and also do the translation, type this:

```
$ wget -pkK http://www.google.com     Rename to local names, keep original
```

Sometimes an HTML file you download does not have a `.html` extension, but ends in `.asp` or `.cgi` instead. That may result in your browser not knowing how to open your local copy of the file. You can have `wget` append `.html` to those files using the `-E` option:

```
$ wget -E http://www.aspexamples.com     Append .html to downloaded files
```

With the `wget` command, you can **recursively mirror an entire web site**. While copying files and directories for the entire depth of the server's file structure, the `-m` option adds timestamping and keeps FTP directory listings. (Use this with caution, because it can take a lot of time and space):

```
$ wget -m http://www.linuxtoys.net
```

Using some of the options just described, the following command line results in the most **usable local copy of a web site**:

```
$ wget -mEkK http://www.linuxtoys.net
```

If you have ever had a large file download (such as a CD or DVD image file) disconnect before it completed, you may find the `-c` option to `wget` to be a lifesaver. Using `-c`, `wget` resumes where it left off, **continuing an interrupted file download**. For example:

```
$ wget http://example.com/DVD.iso     Begin downloading large file
  . . .
95%[==========  ] 685,251,583 55K/s   Download killed before completion
$ wget -c http://example.com/DVD.iso  Resume download where stopped
  . . .
HTTP request sent, awaiting response... 206 Partial Content
Length: 699,389,952 (667), 691,513 (66M) remaining [text/plain]
```

Because of the continue feature (`-c`), `wget` can be particularly useful for those with slow Internet connections who need to download large files. If you have ever had a several hour download get killed just before it finished, you'll know what we mean. (Note that if you don't use `-c` when you mean to resume a file download, the file will be saved to a different file: the original name with a `.1` appended to it.)

Transferring Files with cURL

The client for URLs application (`curl` command) provides similar features to `wget` for transferring files using web and FTP protocols. However, the `curl` command can also transfer files using other popular protocols, including SSH protocols (SCP and SFTP), LDAP, DICT, Telnet, and File.

Instead of supporting large, recursive downloads (as wget does), curl is designed for *single-shot file transfers*. It does, however, support more protocols (as noted) and some neat advanced features. Here are a few interesting examples of **file transfers with curl** for downloading a three-disc set of ISO images for FreeBSD:

```
$ curl -O \
ftp.freebsd.org/pub/FreeBSD/ISO-IMAGES-i386/6.3/6.3-RELEASE-i386-disc[1-3].iso
$ curl -OO \
ftp.freebsd.org/pub/FreeBSD/ISO-IMAGES-i386/6.3/6.3-RELEASE-i386-disc{1,2,3}.iso
```

The commands just shown illustrate how to use square brackets to indicate a range [1-3] and curly brackets for a list {1,2,3} of characters or numbers to match files.

The following set of curl commands illustrates how to download, upload, and delete files from password-protected servers.

```
$ curl -O ftp://chris:MyPasswd@ftp.example.com/home/chris/fileA \
   -Q '-DELE fileA'
$ curl -T install.log ftp://chris:MyPasswd@ftp.example.com/tmp/ \
   -Q "-RNFR install.log" -Q "-RNTO Xinstall.log
$ curl ftp://ftp.freebsd.org/pub/FreeBSD/doc/en/books/     List books contents
```

The first command line adds a user name and password (chris:MyPasswd), downloads a file (fileA) from the server, and then deletes the file on the server once the download is done (-Q '-DELE fileA'). The next example uploads (-T) the file install.log to an FTP server. Then it renames the remote file to Xinstall.log. The last example tells curl to list the contents of the /pub/FreeBSD/doc/en/books/ directory at ftp.freebsd.org.

Transferring Files with FTP Commands

Most BSD systems come with the standard FTP client (ftp command), that works the same way it does on most UNIX and Windows systems. We recommend you use the full-featured user-friendly lftp instead (as root, type pkg_add -r lftp).

With these FTP clients, you open a session to the FTP server (as opposed to just grabbing a file, as you do with wget and curl). Then you navigate the server much as you would a local file system, getting and putting documents across the network connection. Here are examples of how to **connect to an FTP server with lftp**:

```
$ lftp ftp.freebsd.org          Anonymous connection
lftp ftp.freebsd.org:~>
$ lftp francois@example.com      Authenticated connection
lftp example.com:~>
$ lftp -u francois example.com   Authenticated connection
Password: ******
lftp example.com:~>
$ lftp -u francois,Mypwd example.com   Authentication with password
lftp example.com:~>
```

209

```
$ lftp                                   Start lftp with no connection
lftp :~> open ftp.freebsd.org            Start connection in lftp session
lftp ftp.freebsd.org:~>
```

> **WARNING!**   *The fourth example should be avoided in real life. Passwords that are entered in a command line end up stored in clear text in your ~/*.bash_history, *if you use the* bash *shell. They may also be visible to other users in the output of* ps auwx.

When a connection is established to an FTP server, you can use a set of commands during the FTP session. FTP commands are similar to shell commands. Just as in a bash shell, you can press Tab to autocomplete file names. In a session, lftp also supports sending multiple jobs to the background (Ctrl+Z) and returning them to foreground (wait or fg). These are useful if you want to continue traversing the FTP site while files are downloading or uploading. Background jobs run in parallel. Type jobs to see a list of running background jobs. Type help to see a list of lftp commands.

The following sample lftp session illustrates **useful commands when downloading**:

```
$ lftp ftp.freebsd.org
lftp ftp.freebsd.org:~> pwd                              Check current directory
ftp://ftp.freebsd.org
lftp ftp.freebsd.org:~> ls                               List current directory
drwxr-xr-x   3 ftpuser  ftpuser     512 Jun  5  2007 pub
drwxr-xr-x   3 ftpuser  ftpuser     512 Jun  5  2007 sup
lftp ftp.freebsd.org:~> cd /pub/FreeBSD/doc/en/books/faq  Change directory
lftp ftp.freebsd.org:...> get book.pdf.bz2                Download a file
book.pdf.bz2 at 776398 (1%) 467.2K/s eta:26m {Receiving data]
lftp ftp.freebsd.org:...> <Ctrl+z>                    Send download to background
lftp ftp.freebsd.org:...> cd /pub/FreeBSD/doc/en/articles/explaining-bsd
lftp ftp.freebsd.org:...> mget *                      Get all from explaining-bsd
lftp ftp.freebsd.org:...> !ls                            Run local ls
lftp ftp.freebsd.org:...> bookmark add article           Bookmark location
lftp ftp.freebsd.org:...> quit                           Close lftp
```

This session logs in as the anonymous user at ftp.freebsd.org. After changing to the directory containing the document I was looking for, I downloaded it using the get command. By typing Ctrl+Z, the download could continue while I did other activities. Next, the mget command (which allows wildcards such as *) downloaded all files from the explaining-bsd directory.

Any command preceded by an exclamation mark (such as !ls) is executed by the local shell. The bookmark command saves the current location (in this case, the directory /pub/FreeBSD/doc/en/articles/explaining-bsd on the freebsd.org FTP site) under the name article, so next time I can run lftp article to return to the same location. The quit command ends the session.

Here are some useful commands during an authenticated lftp upload session. This assumes you have the necessary file permissions on the server:

```
$ lftp chris@example.com
Password: ******
lftp example.com:~> lcd /home/chris/songs    Change to a local directory
lftp example.com:~> cd pub/uploads           Change to server directory
lftp example.com:~> mkdir songs              Create directory on server
lftp example.com:~> chmod 700 songs          Change remote directory perms
lftp example.com:~> cd songs                 Change to the new directory
lftp example.com:~> put song.ogg tune.ogg    Upload files to server
3039267 bytes transferred
lftp example.com:~> mput /var/songs/*        Upload matched files
lftp example.com:~> quit                     Close lftp
```

The lftp session illustrates how you can use shell command names to operate on remote directories (provided you have permission). The mkdir and chmod commands create a directory and leave permissions open only to your user account. The put command uploads one or more files to the remote server. The mput command can use wildcards to match multiple files for download. Other commands include mirror (to download a directory tree) and mirror -R (to upload a directory tree).

lftp also provides a shell script for non-interactive download sessions: lftpget. The syntax of lftpget is similar to that of the wget command:

```
$ lftpget ftp://ftp.freebsd.org:/pub/FreeBSD/doc/en/books/handbook/book.pdf.bz2
```

Keep in mind that standard FTP clients are insecure because they do all their work in clear text. So your alternative, especially when security is a major issue, is to use SSH tools to transfer files.

Using SSH Tools to Transfer Files

Because SSH utilities are among the most important tools in a system administrator's arsenal of communications commands, some of the more complex uses of configuring and using SSH utilities are covered in Chapter 13. However, in their most basic form, SSH utilities are the tools you should use most often for basic file transfer.

In particular, the scp command will do most of what you need to get a file from one computer to another, while making that communication safe by encrypting both the password stage and data transfer stage of the process. The scp command replaces the rcp command as the most popular tool for host-to-host file copies.

> **WARNING!** *You do not get a warning before overwriting existing files with* scp, *so be sure that the target host doesn't contain any files or directories you want that are in the path of your* scp *file copies.*

Copying Remote Files with scp

To use scp to transfer files, the SSH service (usually the sshd server daemon) must be running on the remote system. Here are some examples of useful scp commands:

```
$ scp myfile francois@server1:/tmp/        Copy myfile to server1
Password: ******
$ scp server1:/tmp/myfile .                Copy remote myfile to local working dir
Password: ******
```

Use the -p option to preserve permissions and timestamps on the copied files:

```
$ scp -p myfile server1:/tmp/
```

If the SSH service is configured to listen on a port other than the default port 22, use -P to indicate that port on the scp command line:

```
$ scp -P 12345 myfile server1:/tmp/        Connect to a particular port
```

To do recursive copies, from a particular point in the remote file system, use the -r option:

```
$ scp -r mydir francois@server1:/tmp/      Copies all mydir to remote /tmp
```

Although scp is most useful when you know the exact locations of the file(s) you need to copy, sometimes it's more helpful to browse and transfer files interactively.

Copying Remote Files in sftp and lftp Sessions

The sftp command lets you use an ftp-like interface to find and copy files over SSH protocols. Here's an example of how to start an sftp session:

```
$ sftp chris@server1
chris@server1's password: *****
sftp>
```

Use sftp in the same manner as you use regular ftp clients. Type ? for a list of commands. You can change remote directories (cd), change local directories (lcd), check current remote and local directories (pwd and lpwd), and list remote and local contents (ls and lls). Depending on the permission of the user you logged in as, you may be able to create and remove directories (mkdir and rmdir), and change permissions (chmod) and ownership/group (chown and chgrp) of files and directories.

You can also use lftp (discussed earlier in this chapter) as an sftp client. Using lftp adds some user-friendly features such as path completion using the Tab key:

```
$ lftp sftp://chris@server1
Password: ********
lftp chris@server1:~>
```

Using Windows File Transfer Tools

In many cases, people need to get files from BSD servers using Windows clients. If your client operating system is Windows, you can use one of the following open source tools to get files from BSD servers:

❑ **WinSCP** (`http://winscp.net`): Graphical `scp`, `sftp`, and FTP client for Windows over SSH1 and SSH2 protocols.

❑ **FileZilla** (`http://filezilla.sourceforge.net`): Provides graphical client FTP and SFTP services in Windows, as well as offering FTP server features.

❑ **PSCP** (`www.chiark.greenend.org.uk/~sgtatham/putty/`): Command line `scp` client that is part of the PuTTY suite.

❑ **PSFTP** (`www.chiark.greenend.org.uk/~sgtatham/putty/`): Command line `sftp` client that is part of the PuTTY suite.

Sharing Remote Directories

Tools described to this point in the chapter provide atomic file access, where a connection is set up and files are transferred in one shot. In times where more persistent, on-going access to a remote directory of files is needed, services for sharing and mounting remote file systems can be most useful. Such services include Network File System (NFS), Samba, and SSHFS.

Sharing Remote Directories with NFS

Before sharing directories from your BSD system with NFS, you must start the NFS service. To do this in FreeBSD, copy NFS lines from the `/etc/defaults/rc.conf` file to the `/etc/rc.conf` file and enable them. Here is what we added to the file `/etc/rc.conf`:

```
nfs_server_enable="YES"       # This host is an NFS server (or NO).
rpc_lockd_enable="YES"        # Run NFS rpc.lockd needed for client/server.
rpc_statd_enable="YES"        # Run NFS rpc.statd needed for client/server.
nfs_server_flags="-u -t -n 4" # Flags to nfsd (if enabled)
```

The NFS service will start the next time you reboot BSD. Or you can start it immediately by typing this as root user:

```
# nfsd -u -t -n 4          Start the NFS service manually
```

When your BSD system is running the NFS service, you can add entries to the `/etc/exports` file on the server to share directories with remote clients and `showmount` commands to see available and mounted shared directories. Mounting a shared directory is done with special options to the standard `mount` command.

Sharing Directories from an NFS Server

With the NFS server running as just described, directories can be shared from that server by adding entries to the /etc/exports file. Here are examples of entries to that file:

```
/usr/ports /usr/ports/Tools dt001     Let dt01 mount /usr/ports, /usr/ports/Tools
/usr/ports -rw mapall=jake            Share read/write, all users map to jake
/usr/ports -alldirs -network 10.0.0   All on 10.0.0 can mount all /usr/ports dirs
```

The examples just shown illustrate how an NFS server can share a specific directory (/usr/ports), several specific directories (/usr/ports/Tools), or any directory beneath the named directory (-alldirs). Client permission can be mapped into specific users on the server (mapall=) and host access can be granted to machines on select subnets (-network).

Viewing and Exporting NFS Shares

From the BSD server system, you can use the showmount command to see what shared directories are available from the local system. For example:

```
# /usr/sbin/showmount -e
Export list for server.example.com
/export/myshare  client.example.com
/mnt/public     *
```

From a client BSD system, you can use the showmount command to see what shared directories are available from a selected computer. For example:

```
# /usr/sbin/showmount -e server2.example.com
Exports list on server2.example.com
/export/myshare client.example.com
/mnt/public     *
```

Mounting NFS Shares

Use the mount command to mount a remote NFS share on the local computer. Here is an example:

```
# mkdir /mnt/server-share
# mount server.example.com:/export/myshare /mnt/server-share
```

This example notes the NFS server (server.example.com) and the shared directory from that server (/export/myshare). The local mount point, which must exist before mounting the share, appears at the end of the command (/mnt/server-share).

Pass NFS-specific options to the mount command by adding them after the -o option:

```
# mount -o rw,hard,intr server.example.com:/export/myshare /mnt/server-share
```

The rw option mounts the remote directory with read-write permissions, assuming that permission is available. With hard set, someone using the share will see a server not responding message when a read or write operation times out. If that happens, having set the intr option lets you **interrupt a hung request to a remote server** (type Ctrl+C).

Sharing Remote Directories with Samba

Samba is the open source implementation of the Windows file and print sharing protocol originally known as Server Message Block (SMB) and now called Common Internet File System (CIFS). There is an implementation of Samba in BSD, as well as in many other operating systems. You can install the basic Samba package by typing this as root user:

```
$ pkg_add -r samba3
```

Graphical tools for sharing, querying, and mounting shared SMB directories from Windows include the Samba SWAT web-based administration tool. To **use the SWAT tool** in FreeBSD, enable the inetd service (add inetd_enable="YES" to /etc/rc.conf) and turn on SWAT (remove the comment character from the swat line in /etc/inetd.conf). Reboot (or run /usr/sbin/inetd -wW -C 60) and open SWAT by pointing your browser at the SWAT service (http://localhost:901) and typing the root user name and password.

You can create an initial /usr/local/etc/smb.conf file from the Samba SWAT screen or create it directly using any text editor. Commands for working with Samba shares can be used to query SMB servers, mount directories, and share directories.

To start a Samba server, you can run the smbd and nmbd servers manually. However, if you have SWAT running as described above, you can start the entire service (with the proper options), add shares, and view your configuration from the SWAT screen. From the Samba SWAT screen, select STATUS, then choose Start All to start the service.

Viewing and Accessing Samba Shares

To **scan your network for SMB hosts**, type the following:

```
$ findsmb
                          *=DMB
                          +=LMB
IP ADDR          NETBIOS NAME  WORKGROUP/OS/VERSION
---------------------------------------------------------------------
192.168.1.1      SERVER1       +[MYWORKGROUP] [Unix] [Samba 3.0.25a-3.fc7]
```

To **view a text representation of your network neighborhood** (shared directories and printers), use smbtree:

```
# smbtree
Password: ******
MYGROUP
    \\THOMPSON             Samba Server Version 3.0.25a-3.fc7
```

```
    \\THOMPSON\hp2100    HP LaserJet 2100M Printer
    \\THOMPSON\IPC$      IPC Service (Samba Server Version 3.0.25a-3.fc7)
  \\EINSTEIN             Samba Server
    \\EINSTEIN\hp5550    HP DeskJet 5550 Printer
    \\EINSTEIN\IPC$      IPC Service (Samba Server)
```

To add an existing BSD user as a Samba user, use the smbpasswd command:

```
# smbpasswd -a francois
New SMB password: ******
Retype new SMB password: ******
Added user francois
```

To list services offered by a server to an anonymous user, type the following:

```
$ smbclient -L server
Password: ******
Anynymous login successful
Domain=[MYGROUP] OS=[Unix] Server=Samba 3.0.23c
tree connect failed: NT_STSTUS_LOGON_FAILURE
```

Here's the output from smbclient for a specific user named francois:

```
$ smbclient -L server -U francois
Password: ******
Domain=[MYGROUP] OS=[Unix] Server=[Samba 3.0.23c]

    Sharename    Type    Comment
    ---------    ----    -------
    IPC$         IPC     IPC Service (Samba Server Version 3.0.23c)
    hp5550       Printer HP DeskJet 5550 Printer

        Server              Comment
        ---------           -------
        THOMPSON            Samba Server Version 3.0.23c

        Workgroup           Master
        ---------           -------
        MYGROUP             THOMPSON
```

To connect to a Samba share ftp-style, type the following:

```
$ smbclient //192.168.1.1/myshare -U francois
Password:
Domain=[MYWORKGROUP] OS=[Unix] Server=[Samba 3.0.23c]
smb: \>
```

As with most FTP clients, type **help** or **?** to see a list of available commands. Likewise, you can use common shell-type commands, such as cd, ls, get, put, and quit, to **get around on the SMB host.**

Mounting Samba Shares

You can **mount remote Samba shares on your local file system** much as you would a local file system or remote NFS file system. To mount the share:

```
# mount -t smbfs //francois@192.168.1.1/myshare /mnt/mymount/
```

> **NOTE** *The Samba file system (smbfs), while still available on FreeBSD, is deprecated on some Linux systems. If you are mounting a Samba share from a BSD system to a Linux system, indicate CIFS (-t cifs) as the file system type when you mount that remote Samba share.*

You can **see the current connections and file locks** on a server using the smbstatus command. This will tell you if someone has mounted your shared directories or is currently using an smbclient connection to your server:

```
# smbstatus
Samba version 3.0.23c
PID     Username     Group     Machine
---------------------------------------------
 5466   francois     francois 10.0.0.55   (10.0.0.55)

Service    pid   machine    Connected at
---------------------------------------------
myshare    5644  10.0.0.55  Tue Jun  3 15:08:29 2008

No locked files
```

To see a more **brief output,** use the -b option:

```
$ smbstatus -b
```

Looking Up Samba Hosts

NetBIOS names are used to identify hosts in Samba. You can **determine the IP address of a computer** using the nmblookup command to broadcast for a particular NetBIOS name on the local subnet as follows:

```
$ nmblookup thompson
querying thompson on 192.168.1.255
192.168.1.1 server1<00>
```

To **find the IP address for a server on a specific subnet,** use the -U option:

```
$ nmblookup -U 192.168.1.0 server1
querying server1 on 192.168.1.255
192.168.1.1 server1<00>
```

Checking Samba Configuration

If you are unable to use a Samba share or if you have other problems communicating with your Samba server, you can test the Samba configuration on the server. The testparm command can be used to **check your main Samba configuration file** (smb.conf):

```
$ testparm
Load smb config files from /usr/local/etc/smb.conf
Processing section "[homes]"
Processing section "[printers]"
Processing section "[myshare]"
Loaded services file OK.
Server role: ROLE_STANDALONE
Press Enter to see a dump of your service definitions
```

After pressing Enter as instructed, you can see the settings from your smb.conf file. Here's how an entry for the myshare shared directory, used earlier in an example, might appear in the smb.conf file:

```
[myshare]
          path = /home/francois
          username = francois
          valid users = francois
          hosts allow = einstein
          available = yes
```

This entry allows the Samba user francois to access the /home/francois directory (represented by the myshare share name) from the host computer named einstein. The share is shown as being currently available.

The previous example of testparm showed the entries you set in the smb.conf file. However, it doesn't **show all the default entries you didn't set.** You can view those using the -v option. Pipe it to the less command to page through the settings:

```
$ testparm -v | less
```

If you want to **test a configuration file before it goes live,** you can tell testparm to use a file other than /etc/samba/smb.conf:

```
$ testparm /etc/samba/test-smb.conf
```

Sharing Remote Directories with SSHFS

Another magical trick you can do over the SSH protocol is mount remote file systems. Using the SSH file system (sshfs), you can mount any directory from an SSH server that your user account can access from your local BSD system. sshfs provides encryption of the mount operation as well as of all the data being transferred. Another cool aspect of sshfs is that it requires no setup on the server side (other than having SSH service running).

Here is a quick procedure for **mounting a directory of documents from a remote server to a local directory**. Doing this only requires that the remote server is running SSH, is accessible, and that the directory you want is accessible to your user account on the server. Here we are mounting a directory named /var/docs from the host at 10.0.0.50 to a mount point called /mnt/docs on the local system:

```
# pkg_add -r fusefs-sshfs              Install fuse-sshfs software
# kldload /usr/local/modules/fuse.ko   Install fuse.ko module
# sysctl vfs.usermount=1               Allow regular users to mount
# mkdir /mnt/docs                      Create mount point
# sshfs chris@10.0.0.50:/var/docs /mnt/docs  Mount remote directory
```

When you are done using the remote directory, you can **unmount** it with the umount command:

```
# umount /var/docs              Unmount remote directory
```

Chatting with Friends in IRC

Despite the emergence of instant messaging, Internet Relay Chat (IRC) is still used by a lot of people today. Freenode.net has tons of chat rooms dedicated to supporting major open source software projects. In fact, many people stay logged into them all day and just watch the discussions of their favorite BSD projects scroll by. This is known as *lurking*.

The xchat utility is a good graphical, multi-operating system IRC client (to install, type pkg_add -r xchat). Once the xchat package is installed, from the GNOME desktop in FreeBSD you can select Applications ⇨ Internet ⇨ XChat IRC. But the elite way to do IRC is to run a text-mode client in screen on an always-on machine, such as an old server. Another similar option is to use an IRC proxy client, also known as a *bouncer*, such as dircproxy.

The original IRC client was ircII. It allowed the addition of scripts — in some ways similar to macros found in productivity suites — that automated some of the commands and increased usability. The most popular was PhoEniX by Vassago. Then came BitchX, which started as an ircII script and then became a full-blown client. Today, most people use irssi. To **install and launch irssi** from FreeBSD, type:

```
# pkg_add -r irssi
$ irssi -n JayJoe200x
```

In this example, the user name (nick) is set to JayJoe199x (you should choose your own). You should see a blue status bar at the bottom of the screen indicating that you are in Window 1, the status window. IRC commands are preceded with a / character. For example, to **connect to the freenode server**, type:

```
/connect chat.freenode.net
```

219

If you don't add your user name on the command line, you are connected to chat .freenode.net under the user name you are logged in under. On IRC, a chat room is called a *channel* and has a pound sign (#) in front of the name. Next, try joining the #freebsd IRC channel:

```
/join #freebsd
```

Your screen should look similar to Figure 12-1.

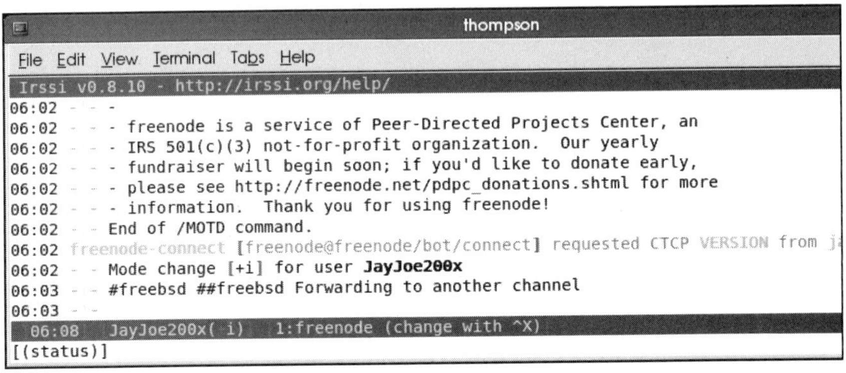

Figure 12-1: irssi connected to #freebsd on Freenode

You are now in the channel in Window 2, as indicated in the status bar. Switch among the irssi windows by typing Alt+1, Alt+2, and so on (or Ctrl+N and Ctrl+P). To get help at any time, type /help. To get help for a command, type /help *command*, where *command* is the name of the command you want more information on. Help text will output in the status window, not necessarily the current window.

To add to the IRC chat, simply type a message and press Enter to send the message to those in the channel. Type /part to leave a channel. Type /quit to exit the program.

There is a lot more to irssi. You can customize it and improve your experience significantly. Refer to the irssi documentation (www.irssi.org/documentation) for more information about how to use irssi.

Using Text-Based e-mail Clients

Most Mail User Agents (MUAs) are GUI-based these days. So if you began using e-mail in the past decade or so, you probably think of Evolution, Kmail, Thunderbird, or (on Windows systems) Outlook when it comes to e-mail clients. On the first UNIX and BSD systems, however, e-mail was handled by text-based applications.

If you find yourself needing to check e-mail on a remote server or other text-based environment, venerable text-based mail clients are available and still quite useful. In fact, some hard-core geeks still use text-based mail clients exclusively, touting their efficiency and scoffing at HTML-based messages.

The mail clients described in this chapter expect your messages to be stored in standard MBOX format on the local system. That means that you are either logged into the mail server or you have already downloaded the messages locally (for example, by using POP3 or similar).

> **NOTE** *Text-based mail clients can be used to read mail already downloaded by other mail clients. For example, you could open your Evolution mail Inbox file by typing* mail -f $HOME/.evolution/mail/local/Inbox.

Managing e-mail with mail

The oldest, and easiest to use when you just want a quick check for messages in the root user's mailbox on a remote server, is the mail command (/bin/mail). If your $MAIL variable is set, just login as root and type mail. Otherwise, use the -f option, as noted earlier, to identify the mailbox file directly (mail -f /var/mail/root).

Although mail can be used interactively, it is often used for **sending script-based e-mails**. Here are some examples:

```
$ uname -a | mail -s 'My BSD version' chris@example.com
$ ps auwx | mail -s 'My Process List' chris@example.com
```

The two mail examples just shown provide quick ways to mail off some text without having to open a GUI mail application. The first example sends the output from the uname -a command to the user chris@example.com. The subject (-s) is set to 'My BSD Version'. In the second example, a list of currently running processes (ps auwx) is sent to the same user with a subject of 'My Process List'.

Used interactively, by default the mail command opens the mailbox set by your current shell's $MAIL value. For example:

```
# echo $MAIL
/var/mail/root
# mail
Mail version 8.1 6/6/93.  Type ? for help.
"/var/mail/root": 25 messages 25 new
>N  1 root@thompson.locald  Tue Jan  8 03:02  41/1193  "X5 security run output"
 N  2 root@thompson.locald  Tue Jan  8 03:02  73/2504  "X5 daily run output"
 N  3 root@thompson.locald  Sat Jan 19 03:02  35/1119  "X5 security run output"
 N  4 root@thompson.locald  Sat Jan 19 03:02  70/2419  "X5 daily run output"
 &
```

The current message has a greater-than sign (>) next to it. New messages have an N at the beginning, unread (but not new) have a U, and if there is no letter, the message has been read. The prompt at the bottom (&) is ready to accept commands.

At this point, you are in command mode. You can use simple commands to **move around** and **perform basic mail functions** in `mail`. Type **?** to see a list of commands, or type the number of the message you want to see. Type **v3** to open the third message in the `vi` editor. Type **h18** to see a list of message headers that begins with message 18. To reply to message 7, type **r7** (type your message, then put a dot on a line by itself to send the message). Type **d4** to delete the fourth message (or **d4-9** to delete messages four through nine). Type **!bash** to escape to the shell (then exit to return to `mail`).

Before you exit `mail`, know that any messages you view will be copied from your mailbox file to your `$HOME/mbox` file when you exit, unless you preserve them (`pre*`). To have all messages stay in your mailbox, exit by typing **x**. To save your changes to the mailbox, type **q** to exit.

You can open any file that is in MBOX format when you use mail. For example, if you are logged in as root user, but want to open the mailbox for the user `chris`, type this:

```
# mail -f /var/mail/chris
```

Managing e-mail with mutt

If you want to use a command-line mail client on an on-going basis, we recommend you use `mutt` instead of `mail`. The `mail` command has many limitations, such as not being able to send attachments without encoding them in advance (such as with the `uuencode` command), while `mutt` has many features for handling modern e-mail needs. The `mutt` command is part of the mutt package (`pkg_add -r mutt`).

Like `mail`, `mutt` can also be used to pop off a message from a script. `mutt` also adds the capability to **send attachments**. For example:

```
$ mutt -s "My BSD Version" -a /tmp/version.txt \
     chris@example.com < email-body.txt
$ mutt -s "My BSD Version" -a /tmp/version.txt \
     chris@example.com < /dev/null
```

The first example just shown includes the file `email-body.txt` as the body of the message and attaches the file `/tmp/version.txt` as an attachment. The second example sends the attachment, but has a blank message body (`< /dev/null`).

You can **begin your mutt mail session** (assuming your default $MAIL mailbox) by simply typing:

```
$ mutt
```

```
/home/chris/Mail does not exist. Create it? ([yes]/no): y

q:Quit  d:Del  u:Undel  s:Save  m:Mail  r:Reply  g:Group  ?:Help

   1 O   Jun 16 Jason Buckman    (  69) Try out tripwire
   2 O   Jun 18 Billy Bob        ( 171) Visit the place

--Mutt: /var/mail/root [Msgs:22 New:2 Old:20 63K]--(date/date)--(all)--
```

Because mutt is screen-oriented, it is easier to use than mail. As with mail, you use key commands to move around in mutt. As usual, type ? to get help. Hints appear across the top bar to help you with your mail. Use the up and down arrow keys to highlight the messages you want to read. Press Enter to view the highlighted message. Use PageUp and PageDown to page through each message or advance to the next message. Press i to return to the message headers.

Search forward for text using slash (/) or backwards using Escape slash (Esc-/). Type n to search again. Press Tab to jump to the next new or unread message. Or go to the previous one using Esc-Tab. Type s to save the current message to a file. Type d to delete a message. To undelete a message, type the message number to go to it, then press u to undelete it.

To send a new mail message, type m. After adding the recipient and subject, a blank message opens in vi (or whatever you have your $EDITOR set to). After exiting the message body, type a to add an attachment, if you like. Type ? to see other ways of manipulating your message, headers or attachments. Press y to send the message or q to abort the send.

When you are done, type x to exit without changing your mailbox; type q to exit and incorporate the changes you made (messages read, deleted, and so on).

Summary

Network access commands provide quick and efficient ways to get content you need over a network. The elinks web browser is a popular screen-oriented command for browsing the Web or taking a quick look at any HTML file. Dozens of commands are available to download files over FTP, HTTP, SSH, or other protocols, including wget, curl, lftp, and scp.

For more on-going access to remote directories of files, this chapter covers how to use NFS, Samba, and SSHFS command tools. You can do IRC chats, which are popular among open source projects, using the irssi command. For text-based e-mail clients, you have choices such as the mail and mutt commands.

13

Doing Remote System Administration

Most professional BSD administrators do not run a graphical interface on their Internet servers. As a result, when you need to access other computers for remote administration, you will almost surely need to work from the command line at some time. Luckily, there are many feature-rich BSD commands to help you do so.

Tools associated with the Secure Shell (SSH) service not only allow remote login and file transfer, but they also offer encrypted communication to keep your remote administration work secure. With tools such as Virtual Network Computing (VNC), you can have a server's remote desktop appear on your local client computer. These and other features for doing remote systems administration are described in this chapter.

Doing Remote Login and Tunneling with SSH

IN THIS CHAPTER

Configuring SSH

Using SSH for remote login

Using SSH to do tunneling

Using SSH to provide proxy service

Using SSH with private keys

Using screen remote multiplexing terminal

Accessing remote Windows desktops

Sharing remote desktops with VNC

BSD systems, like their big brother UNIX, grew up on university networks. At a time when the only users of these networks were students and professors, and with networks mostly isolated from each other, there was little need for security.

Applications and protocols that were designed in those times (the 1970s and 1980s) reflect that lack of concern for encryption and authentication. SMTP is a perfect example of that. This is also true of the first generation of UNIX remote tools: telnet, ftp (file transfer protocol), rsh (remote shell), rcp (remote copy), rexec (remote execution) and rlogin (remote login). These tools send user credentials and traffic in clear text. For that reason, they are very dangerous to use on the public, untrusted Internet, and have become mostly deprecated and replaced with the Secure Shell (SSH) commands (ssh, scp, sftp commands, and related services).

Although there are still some uses for the legacy remote commands (see the "Using Legacy Communications Tools" sidebar), most of this section describes how to use SSH commands to handle most of your needs for remote communications commands.

Using Legacy Communications Tools

Despite the fact that SSH provides better tools for remote communications, legacy communications commands, sometimes referred to as r commands, are still included with most major BSD distributions. Some of these tools will perform faster than equivalent SSH commands because they don't need to do encryption. So some old-school UNIX administrators may use them occasionally on private networks or still include them in old scripts. Although, for the most part, you should ignore these legacy remote commands, one of these commands in particular can be useful in some cases: telnet.

The telnet command is still used to communicate with some network appliances (routers, switches, UPSes, and so on) that do not have the horsepower to run an ssh daemon. Even though it poses a security risk, some appliance manufactures include telnet support anyway.

One good way to use the telnet command, however, is for troubleshooting many Internet protocols such as POP3, SMTP, HTTP, and others. Under the hood, these plain-text protocols are simply automated telnet sessions during which a client (such as a browser or mail user agent) exchanges text with a server. The only difference is the TCP port in use. Here is an example of how you could telnet to the HTTP port (80) of a web server:

```
$ telnet www.example.com 80
Trying 208.77.188.166...
Connected to www.example.com.
Escape character is '^]'.
GET /index.html
<!DOCTYPE html PUBLIC "-//W3C//DTD XHTML 1.1//EN"
 "http://www.w3.org/TR/xhtml11/DTD/xhtml11.dtd">
<html xmlns="http://www.w3.org/1999/xhtml" xml:lang="en">
        <head>
                <title>My Web server...
```

Similarly, you can telnet to a mail server on port 25 (SMTP) and 110 (POP3) and issue the proper commands to troubleshoot e-mail problems. For more complete descriptions of using the telnet command to troubleshoot network protocols, refer to *Linux Troubleshooting Bible* (ISBN 076456997X, Wiley Publishing, 2004), pages 505 and 508.

If you need to forcefully exit your telnet session, type the escape sequence (Ctrl+] by default). This will stop sending your keyboard input to the remote end and bring you to the telnet command prompt where can type quit or ? for more options.

Configuring SSH

Nowadays, the all-purpose tool of remote system administration is Secure Shell (SSH). SSH commands and services replace all the old remote tools, add strong encryption, public keys, and many other features. The most common implementation of SSH in the free and open source software world is OpenSSH (www.openssh.com), maintained by the OpenBSD project. OpenSSH provides both client and server components. Here are a few facts about SSH:

❑ For Windows, you can use the SSH tools within Cygwin (www.cygwin.com). But unless you're already using Cygwin (a UNIX-like environment for Windows), we recommend PuTTY (www.chiark.greenend.org/uk/sgatatham/putty). PuTTY is a powerful open source Telnet/SSH client.

❑ Use SSH version 2 whenever possible, because it is the most secure. Some SSH-enabled network appliances may only support older, less secure versions. OpenSSH supports all versions. Some older BSD systems accepted SSH v1 and v2 connections. Newer releases accept version 2 by default.

❑ In FreeBSD, to enable the SSH service, check that the following line is contained in the /etc/rc.conf file (which it should be by default):

        sshd_enable="YES"

To configure the service, edit the /etc/ssh/sshd_config file.

❑ To configure the ssh client, edit the /etc/ssh/ssh_config file.

If you prefer to use graphical tools to administer your remote BSD system, you can enable *X11 Tunneling* (also called *X11 Port Forwarding*). With X11 Tunneling enabled (on both the SSH client and server), you can start an X application on the server and have it displayed on the client. All communication across that connection is encrypted.

FreeBSD comes with X11 forwarding turned on (X11Forwarding yes) for the server (sshd daemon). You still need to enable it on the client side. To enable X11 forwarding on the client for a one-time session, connect with the following command:

```
$ ssh -X francois@myserver
```

To enable X11 forwarding permanently for all users, add ForwardX11 yes to /etc/ssh/ssh_config. To enable it permanently for a specific user only, add the lines to that user's ~/.ssh/config. After those settings have been added, the –X option is no longer required to use X11 Tunneling. Run ssh to connect to the remote system as you would normally. To test that the tunneling is working, run xclock after ssh'ing into the remote machine, and it should appear on your client desktop.

SSH Tunneling is an excellent way to securely use remote graphical tools!

Logging in Remotely with ssh

To **securely log in to a remote host**, you can use either of two different syntaxes to specify the user name:

```
$ ssh -l francois myserver
$ ssh francois@myserver
```

However, `scp` and `sftp` commands (discussed in Chapter 12) only support the *user@server* syntax, so we recommend you get used to that one. If you don't specify the user name, `ssh` will attempt to log in using the same user you are logged in as locally. When connected, if you need to **forcefully exit your ssh session**, type the escape sequence of a tilde followed by a period (~ .).

Accessing SSH on a Different Port

For security purposes, a remote host may have its **SSH service listening to a different port** than the default port number 22. If that's the case, use the -p option to `ssh` to contact that service:

```
$ ssh -p 12345 francois@turbosphere.com    Connect to SSH on port 12345
```

Using SSH to Do Tunneling (X11 Port Forwarding)

With SSH tunneling configured as described earlier, the SSH service forwards X Window System clients to your local display. However, tunneling can be used with other TCP-based protocols as well.

Tunneling for X11 Clients

The following sequence of commands illustrates **starting an SSH session, then starting a few X applications so they appear on the local desktop:**

```
$ ssh -X francois@myserver               Start ssh connection to myserver
francois@myserver's password: *******
[francois@myserver ~}$ echo $DISPLAY     Show the current X display entry
localhost:10.0                           SSH sets display to localhost:10.0
[francois@myserver ~}$ xeyes&                 Show moving desktop eyes
[francois@myserver ~}$ gnome-system-monitor&  Monitor system activities
[francois@myserver ~}$ xcalc&                 Use a calculator
```

As more connections are requested, the $DISPLAY will be set to 11.0, 12.0, and so on.

Tunneling for CUPS Printing Remote Administration

X11 is not the only protocol that can be tunneled over SSH. You can **forward any TCP port** with SSH. This is a great way to configure secure tunnels quickly and easily. No configuration is required on the server side.

For example, `myserver` is a print server with the CUPS printing service's web-based user interface enabled (running on port `631`). That GUI is only accessible from the local machine. On my client PC, I tunnel to that service using `ssh` with the following options:

```
$ ssh -L 1234:localhost:631 myserver
```

This example forwards port `1234` on my client PC to localhost port `631` on the server. I can now browse to `http://localhost:1234` on my client PC. This will be redirected to `cupsd` listening on port `631` on the server. Note that you need root privilege to forward ports with numbers less than 1024.

Tunneling to an Internet Service

Another example of using SSH tunneling is when your local machine is blocked from connecting to the Internet, but you can get to another machine (`myserver`) that has an Internet connection. The following example enables you to visit the Google.com web site (HTTP, TCP port 80) across an SSH connection to a computer named `myserver` that has a connection to the Internet:

```
$ ssh -L 12345:google.com:80 myserver
```

With this example, any connection to the local port `12345` is directed across an SSH tunnel to `myserver`, which in turn opens a connection to `Google.com` port 80. You can now browse to `http://localhost:12345` and use `myserver` as a relay to the Google.com web site. Since you only intend to use `ssh` to forward a port, and not to obtain a shell on the server, you can add the `-N` option to prevent the execution of remote commands:

```
$ ssh -L 12345:google.com:80 -N myserver
```

Using SSH as a SOCKS Proxy

The previous example demonstrates that you can forward a port from the client to a machine other than the server. In the real world, the best way to get your browser traffic out of your local network via an encrypted tunnel is using SSH's built-in SOCKS proxy feature. For example:

```
$ ssh -D 12345 myserver
```

The dynamic (`-D`) option of `ssh` enables you to log in to `myserver` (as usual). As long as the connection is open, all requests directed to port `12345` are then forwarded to `myserver`. Next, set your browser of choice to use `localhost` port `12345` as a SOCKS v4 proxy and you're good to go.

For example, to get to the Connection Settings window in your Firefox browser select Edit ➪ Preferences. Then either choose General ➪ Connection Settings (Firefox 1.5) or

Advanced ➪ Network ➪ Settings (Firefox 2). Select Manual proxy configuration, but do not enter anything on the fields for HTTP and other protocols. They all work over SOCKS v4. See the Firefox Connections Settings window in Figure 13-1.

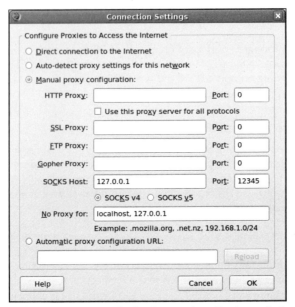

Figure 13-1: Use the Firefox Connections Settings window for proxy configuration.

To test your setup, try disconnecting your ssh session and browsing to any web site. Your browser should give you a proxy error.

From a Windows client, the same port forwarding can be accomplished in Putty by selecting Connection ➪ SSH ➪ Tunnels.

Using ssh with Public Key Authentication

Up to this point, we've only used ssh with the default password authentication. The ssh command also supports public key authentication. This offers several benefits:

❑ **Automated logins for scripts and cron jobs:** By assigning an empty passphrase you can use ssh in a script to log in automatically. Although this is convenient, it is also dangerous, because anybody who gets to your key file can connect to any machine you can. Configuring for automatic login can also be done with a passphrase and a key agent. This is a trade-off between convenience and security, as explained below.

❑ **A two-factor authentication:** When using a passphrase-protected key for interactive logins, authentication is done using two factors (the key and the passphrase) instead of one.

Using Public Key Logins

Here's the process for setting up key-based communications between two BSD systems. In the following example, we use empty passphrases for no-password logins. If you prefer to protect your key with a passphrase, simply enter it when prompted during the first step (key pair creation).

On the client system, run the following ssh-keygen command to generate the key pair while logged in as the user who needs to initiate communications:

```
$ ssh-keygen
Generating public/private rsa key pair.
Enter file in which to save the key (/home/chris/.ssh/id_rsa): <Enter>
Enter passphrase (empty for no passphrase): <Enter>
Enter same passphrase again: <Enter>
Your identification has been saved in /home/chris/.ssh/id_rsa.
Your public key has been saved in /home/chris/.ssh/id_rsa.pub.
The key fingerprint is:
ac:db:a4:8e:3f:2a:90:4f:05:9f:b4:44:74:0e:d3:db chris@host.domain.com
```

Note that at each prompt you pressed the Enter key to create the default key file name and to enter (and verify) an empty passphrase. You now have a private key that you need to keep very safe, especially since in this procedure you didn't protect it with a passphrase.

You also now have a public key (id_rsa.pub), which was created by the previous command. This public key needs to be installed on hosts you want to connect to. The content of ~/.ssh/id_rsa.pub needs to be copied (securely) to ~/.ssh/authorized_keys for the user you want to ssh to on the remote server. The authorized_keys file can contain more than one public key, if multiple users use ssh to connect to this account.

Log in to the *remote server* system as the user that you will want to ssh as with the key. If you don't already have a ~/.ssh directory, the first step is to create it as follows:

```
$ cd
$ mkdir .ssh
$ chmod 700 .ssh
```

The next step is to copy (securely) the public key file from the client and put it in an authorized keys file on the server. This can be accomplished using scp. For example, assuming the client system named myclient and client user named chris, type the following on the server:

```
$ scp chris@myclient:/home/chris/.ssh/id_rsa.pub   Get client id_rsa.pub
$ cat id_rsa.pub >> ~/.ssh/authorized_keys          Add to your keys
$ chmod 600 ~/.ssh/authorized_keys                  Close permissions
$ rm id_rsa.pub                        Delete public key after copying its content
```

This procedure can also be accomplished by editing the ~/.ssh/authorized_keys text file on the server and copying and pasting the public key from the client. Make sure you do so securely over ssh, and make sure not to insert any line breaks in the key. The entire key should fit on one single line, even if it wraps on your screen.

Then from the client (using the client and server user accounts you just configured), you can just ssh to the server and the key will be used. If you set a passphrase, you will be asked for it as you would for a password.

Saving Private Keys to Use from a USB Flash Drive

If you'd like to store your private key somewhere safer than your hard drive, you can use a USB flash drive (sometimes called a thumbdrive or pen drive):

```
$ mv ~/.ssh/id_rsa /media/THUMBDRIVE1/myprivatekey
```

And then, when you want to use the key, insert the USB drive and type the following:

```
$ ssh -i /media/THUMBDRIVE1/myprivatekey chris@myserver
```

Using keys with passphrases is more secure than simple passwords, but also more cumbersome. To make your life easier, you can use ssh-agent to store unlocked keys for the duration of your session. When you add an unlocked key to your running ssh-agent, you can run ssh using the key without being prompted for the passphrase each time.

To see what the ssh-agent command does, run the command with no option. A three-line bash script appears when you run it, as follows:

```
$ ssh-agent
SSH_AUTH_SOCK=/tmp/ssh-SkEQZ18329/agent.18329; export SSH_AUTH_SOCK;
SSH_AGENT_PID=18330; export SSH_AGENT_PID;
echo Agent pid 18330;
```

The first two lines of the output just shown need to be executed by your shell. Copy and paste those lines into your shell now. You can avoid this extra step by starting ssh-agent and having the bash shell evaluate its output by typing the following:

```
$ eval `ssh-agent`
Agent pid 18408
```

You can now unlock keys and add them to your running agent. Assuming you have already run the ssh-keygen command to create a default key, let's add that default key using the ssh-add command:

```
$ ssh-add
Enter passphrase for /home/chris/.ssh/id_rsa: *******
Identity added: /home/chris/.ssh/id_rsa (/home/chris/.ssh/id_rsa)
```

Next you could add the key you stored on the USB thumbdrive:

```
$ ssh-add /media/THUMBDRIVE1/myprivatekey
```

Use the -1 option to ssh-add to list the keys stored in the agent:

```
$ ssh-add -l
2048 f7:b0:7a:5a:65:3c:cd:45:b5:1c:de:f8:26:ee:8d:78 /home/chris/.ssh/id_rsa
(RSA)
2048 f7:b0:7a:5a:65:3c:cd:45:b5:1c:de:f8:26:ee:8d:78
/media/THUMBDRIVE1/myprivatekey (RSA)
```

To **remove one key from the agent,** for example the one from the USB thumbdrive, run ssh-add with the -d option as follows:

```
$ ssh-add -d /media/THUMBDRIVE1/myprivatekey
```

To **remove all the keys stored in the agent,** use the -D option:

```
$ ssh-add -D
```

Using screen: A Rich Remote Shell

The ssh command gives you only one screen. If you lose that screen, you lose all you were doing on the remote computer. That can be very bad if you were in the middle of something important, such as a 12-hour compile. And if you want to do three things at once, for example vi httpd.conf, tail -f error_log, service httpd reload, you need to open three separate ssh sessions.

Essentially, screen is a terminal multiplexer. If you are a system administrator working on remote servers, screen is a great tool for managing a remote computer with only a command line interface available. Besides allowing multiple shell sessions, screen also lets you disconnect, and then reconnect to that same screen session later.

The screen software package is available with FreeBSD. To **create and install the screen package,** type the following from the FreeBSD server on which you want to use screen:

```
# cd /usr/ports/sysutils/screen
# make install
```

To **use screen,** run the ssh command from a client system to connect to the BSD server where screen is installed. Then simply type the following command:

```
$ screen
```

If you ran screen from a Terminal window, after you see the license message press Enter and you should see a regular bash prompt in the window. To control screen, press the Ctrl+A key combo, followed by another keystroke. For example, Ctrl+A followed by ? (noted as Ctrl+A, ?) displays the help screen. With screen running, here are some commands and control keys you can use to operate screen.

```
$ screen -ls                          List active screens
There is a screen on:
```

233

```
        7089.pts-2.myserver    (Attached)   Shows screen is attached
1 Socket in /var/run/screen/S-francois.
$ Ctrl+A, A                                 Change window title
Set window's title to: My Server            Type a new title
$ Ctrl+A, C                                 Create a new window
$ Ctrl+A, "                                 Show active window titles
Num Name                 Flags
  0 My Server                               Up/down arrows change windows
  1 bash
$ Ctrl+A, Ctrl+D                            Detach screen from terminal
$ screen -ls                                List active screens
There is a screen on:
        7089.pts-2.myserver    (Detached)   Shows screen is detached
1 Socket in /var/run/screen/S-francois.
```

The screen session just shown resulted in two windows (each running a bash shell) being created. You can create as many as you like and name them as you choose. Also, instead of detaching from the screen session, you could have just closed it by exiting the shell in each open window (type exit or Ctrl+D).

When the screen session is detached, you are returned to the shell that was opened when you first logged into the server. You can reconnect to that screen session as described in the following "Reconnecting to a screen Session" section.

Table 13-1 shows some other useful control key sequences available with screen.

Table 13-1: Control Keys for Using screen

Keys	Description
Ctrl+A, ?	Show help screen.
Ctrl+A, C	Create new window.
Ctrl+A, Ctrl+D	Detach screen from terminal. The screen session and its windows keep running.
Ctrl+A, "	View list of windows.
Ctrl+A, '	Prompt for number or name of window to switch to.
Ctrl+A, Ctrl+N	Go to next window, if multiple screen windows are open.
Ctrl+A, n	View next window.
Ctrl+A, P	View previous window.
Ctrl+A, A	Rename current window.
Ctrl+A, W	Show the list of window names in the title bar.

Reconnecting to a screen Session

After you detach from a screen session, you can return to that screen again later (even after you log out and disconnect from the server). To reconnect when only one screen is running, type the following:

```
$ screen -r
```

If there are several screen sessions running, screen -r won't work. For example, this shows what happens when two detached screen sessions are running:

```
$ screen -r
There are several suitable screens on:
        7089.pts-2.myserver     (Detached)
        7263.pts-2.myserver     (Detached)
Type "screen [-d] -r [pid.]tty.host" to resume one of them.
```

As the output suggests, you could identify the screen session you want by its name (which, by default, is a combination of the session's process ID, tty name, and hostname). For example:

```
$ screen -r 7089.pts-2.myserver
```

Naming screen Sessions

Instead of using the default names, you can create more descriptive names for your screen sessions when you start screen. For example:

```
$ screen -S mysession
$ screen -ls
There is a screen on:
        26523.mysession (Attached)
```

Sharing screen Sessions

The screen command also allows the sharing of screens. This feature is great for tech support, because each person connected to the session can both type into and watch the current session! Creating a named screen, as in the preceding section, makes this easier. Because you are sharing a screen, use either a temporary user account or temporary password, for security reasons. Then another person on a different computer can ssh to the server (using the same user name) and type the following:

```
$ screen -x mysession
```

Just as with screen -r, if there's only one screen running, you don't need to specify which screen you're connecting to:

```
$ screen -x
```

Using a Remote Windows Desktop

Many system administrators who become comfortable using a BSD desktop prefer to do administration of their Windows systems from BSD whenever possible. BSD systems provide tools such as rdesktop and tsclient, which enable you to connect to a Windows system running Windows Terminal Services.

NOTE *Because there are no BSD or other UNIX implementations of Microsoft's proprietary Remote Desktop Protocol (RDP), there are no methods for doing RDP-enabled Remote Windows Desktops in FreeBSD. If you are interested in encrypted remote desktop solutions, refer to projects that use SSH to encrypt remote desktops, such as NoMachine (www.nomachine.com).*

To be able to **connect to your Windows system desktop from FreeBSD**, you have to enable Remote Desktop from your Windows system. To do that from Windows XP (and others) right-click My Computer and select Properties. Then choose the Remote tab from the System Properties window and select the Allow users to connect remotely to this computer check box. Select which users you want to let connect to the Windows box and click OK.

Now, from FreeBSD, you can use either the rdesktop or tsclient (a graphical wrapper around rdesktop) to connect to the Windows system using Remote Desktop Protocol (RDP). If those applications are not already installed, type the following from your FreeBSD system:

```
# pkg_add -r rdesktop
# pkg_add -r tsclient
```

Connecting to a Windows Desktop with tsclient

If you are used to using Windows' Remote Desktop Connection (formerly known as *Terminal Services Client*) to connect from one Windows box to another, you will probably find the tsclient tool a good way to connect to a Windows desktop from a BSD system. Running tsclient opens a Terminal Server Client window that mimics the Windows remote desktop client's user interface.

When the tsclient package is installed, launch tsclient by selecting Applications ⇨ Internet ⇨ Terminal Server Client from the GNOME desktop or by typing the following from the shell:

```
$ tsclient &
```

Figure 13-2 shows the Terminal Server Client window.

Probably all you need to enter on this screen is the name or IP address of the Windows system. You will probably be prompted for user name and password, depending on how the Windows system is configured. Select different tabs to further refine your connection to the remote Windows desktop.

Figure 13-2: Terminal Server Client (tsclient) connects to Windows desktops

Note that `tsclient` can also be used as a client for VNC and XDMCP.

Connecting to a Windows Desktop with rdesktop

If you prefer not to use the `tclient` wrapper described above, you can log in to a remote Windows desktop using the `rdesktop` command. The `rdesktop` command requests a login to the Windows machine, then opens the Windows desktop for the user after you log in. Here are examples of the `rdesktop` command:

```
$ rdesktop 172.16.18.66              Login to desktop at IP address
$ rdesktop -u chris -p M6pyXX win1   Identify user/password for host win1
$ rdesktop -f win1                   Run rdesktop in full-screen mode
$ rdesktop -r sound:local win1       Direct sound from server to client
$ rdesktop -E win1                   Disable client/server encryption
```

If you disable client/server encryption, the login packet is encrypted, but everything after that is not. Although this can improve performance greatly, anyone sniffing your LAN may be able to see your clear-text communications (including any interactive logins after the initial login packet). Other `rdesktop` options that can improve performance on your Windows desktop include `-m` (don't send mouse motion events), `-D` (hide window manager's decorations), and `-K` (don't override window manager key bindings).

237

Using Remote BSD Desktop and Applications

The X Window System (X) should not be run on typical production servers for security and performance reasons. But thanks to the client-server nature of X, you can run an X-enabled program on a remote machine with its graphical output directed to your desktop. In that relationship, the application running from the remote machine is referred to as the *X client*, and your desktop is the *X server*. When running remote X applications on untrusted networks or the Internet, use SSH forwarding as described earlier. On trusted LANs, do it without SSH, as described here.

By default, your X desktop will not allow remote X applications to connect (pop-up) on your desktop. You can **allow remote apps on your desktop** using the xhost command. On your local BSD display, use the xhost command to control which remote machines can connect to X and display applications on your desktop. Here are examples of xhost:

> **NOTE**   *Listening for remote X clients is disabled in FreeBSD by default. Before you allow access to your X display, you need to start your X desktop with the* -listen_tcp *option. For example, start your desktop by typing:* startx -listen_tcp.

```
$ xhost                    List allowed hosts
access control enabled, only authorized clients can connect
$ xhost +                        Disable access control (dangerous)
access control disabled, clients can connect from any host
$ xhost -                      Re-enable access control
access control enabled, only authorized clients can connect
$ xhost remotemachine      Add an allowed host
remotemachine being added to access control list
```

Access control should be completely disabled only for troubleshooting purposes. However, with access enabled for a particular host machine (*remotemachine* in this case), you can do the following from a shell on the remote computer to have X applications from that machine appear on the local desktop (in this case called *localmachine*):

```
$ export DISPLAY=localmachine:0      Set the DISPLAY to localmachine:0
$ xterm &                            Open remote Terminal on local
$ xclock &                           Open remote clock on local
$ gtali &                            Open remote dice game on local
```

After setting the DISPLAY variable on *remotemachine* to point to *localmachine*, any application run from that shell on *remotemachine* should appear on Desktop 0 on *localmachine*. In this case, we started Terminal window, clock, and game applications.

Sharing X applications in this way between BSD and other UNIX-like hosts is pretty easy. However, it is not trivial to use across other computer platforms. If your desktop runs

Windows, you have to run an X server. A free solution is Cygwin, which includes an X server. There are also feature-rich commercial X servers but they can be very expensive. To share remote desktops across different operating system platforms, we suggest you use Virtual Network Computing (VNC).

Sharing Desktops Using VNC

Virtual Network Computing (VNC) consists of server and client software that enables you to assume remote control of a **full desktop display from one computer on another**. In FreeBSD and similar systems, you need the VNC package to access a remote desktop on your display (client) or share a desktop from your computer (server). To install those VNC client and server software components, type the following:

```
# pkg_add -r vnc
```

VNC client and server are available for, and interoperable with, many different operating systems. VNC servers are available on BSD, Linux, Windows (32-bit), Mac OS X, and UNIX systems. VNC clients are offered on those, and many other types of systems (including OS/2, PalmOS, and even as a Java application running in a web browser).

> **NOTE** *Opening access to manipulate your desktop represents a security risk. You can help minimize that risk by running the VNC server on the local host only, then having remote users connect to the machine using SSH (or Putty from Windows systems).*

Setting Up the VNC Server

Because VNC shares desktops on a per-user basis, you can start by logging in as the user whose desktop you want to share. As that user, you want to create a VNC password and launch the VNC server. Here's how:

1. Create a directory to hold the VNC settings:

```
$ mkdir $HOME/.vnc
```

2. Create a VNC password for that user:

```
$ vncpasswd
Password: *******
Verify: *******
```

3. Finally, you can start the VNC service (vncserver) either by running vncserver directly from the shell or by adding the command to a start-up file that is launched each time the system boots. For now, run the following command to start the VNC server:

```
$ vncserver
```

If you are using the firewall built into your system, make sure you open the port(s) for VNC. Each display runs on its own port. Display number N is accessed on TCP port 5900+N. For example, display 1 is accessible on port 5901. Refer to Chapter 14 for more details on firewalls.

The vncserver command will start an Xvnc process to listen on the first available display (probably :1). It will also create a basic set of X applications to start when someone connects to the server (in the $HOME/.vnc/xstartup file). You can add or change those applications as you like, including the window manager used (twm is the default). In that same directory are log files and the VNC passwd file.

A VNC client, with access to your computer and your password, can connect to your VNC service as described in the next section. If you are setting up the VNC service temporarily, after the client is done connecting to your VNC service, you can kill the VNC server as follows:

```
$ vncserver -kill :1
Killing Xvnc process ID 49901
```

Starting Up the VNC Client

With the VNC server running, you can connect to a desktop on that server from any of the client systems mentioned earlier (BSD, Windows, Linux, Mac OS X, UNIX, and so on). For example, assuming your VNC server is on a system named myserver, you could type the following command to **start that remote desktop** from another BSD system:

```
$ vncviewer myserver:1        Connect to VNC service on myserver display 1
```

You can also use tsclient to connect; for this example, you would just specify myserver:1 as the computer and VNC as the protocol. By default, once you connect via VNC, all you get is a very basic window manager (twm) and a terminal. To get the full desktop next time the user logs in, you should edit your VNC $HOME/.vnc/xstartup file on the VNC server. For example, log in as the user who started the server and type the following:

```
$ vi $HOME/.vnc/xstartup
```

When editing that file, change the following lines to include the window manager you want (replace twm) and applications you want (replace or add applications starting with the xterm line). Here is an example of the contents of that file:

```
#!/bin/sh

[ -r $HOME/.Xresources ] && xrdb $HOME/.Xresources
xsetroot -solid grey
vncconfig -iconic &
xterm -geometry 80x24+10+10 -ls -title "$VNCDESKTOP Desktop" &
twm &
```

On older version of the VNC software, the file may not exist. So create it and add the two lines above. After creating the file, set its permissions as follows:

```
# chmod 755 $HOME/.vnc/xstartup
```
Then, for the changes to take effect you need to kill and restart the VNC server.

Using VNC on Untrusted Networks with SSH

VNC is a considered to be an insecure protocol. The password is sent using fairly weak encryption and the rest of the session is not encrypted at all. For that reason, when using VNC over an untrusted network or the Internet, we recommend you tunnel it over SSH.

For a general description of how the SSH service works, refer to the "Doing Remote Login and Tunneling with SSH" section earlier in this chapter. To forward VNC display 2 (port 5902) on the computer named myserver, to the same local port, type the following:

```
$ ssh -L 5902:localhost:5902 myserver
```

In case VNC is already running on the client, you could assign the service to an arbitrary port (to avoid running into the same port number). For example:

```
$ ssh -L 55902:localhost:5902 user@myserver
$ vncviewer localhost:55902
```

> **NOTE** *If you start using VNC routinely, you may want to look at* tightvnc. *The* tightvnc *project provides another open source implementation of the VNC protocol, under active development and with newer features and optimizations. These features include built-in ssh tunneling.*

Sharing a VNC Desktop with Vino

If you're running GNOME and would like to share your existing GNOME desktop (display :0), you can do so with Vino (as root, type pkg_add -r vino). From the GNOME Desktop panel, select System ➪ Preference ➪ Remote Desktop to display the Remote Desktop Preferences window (vino-preferences command) shown in Figure 13-3.

In the Remote Desktop Preferences window, selecting the "Allow other users to view your desktop" check box enables remote VNC viewers to view your desktop; by contrast, selecting the "Allow other users to control your desktop" check box enables others to manipulate your desktop with their mouse and keyboard.

If the "Ask you for confirmation" check box is selected, a remote request to view your desktop causes a pop-up window to okay the connection before the requestor can see your desktop. Selecting the "Require the user to enter this password" check box is a good idea, to prevent those without a password from viewing your desktop. (Be sure the password is at least eight characters.)

241

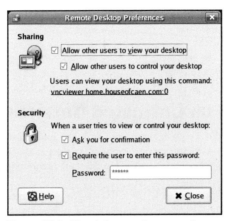

Figure 13-3: Vino lets remote users view, and possibly control, your desktop.

As the Remote Desktop Preferences window notes, you can use vncviewer from another BSD system (with the address and display number shown) to display the shared desktop to another system. However, VNC clients from many different operating systems should work as well.

Summary

If you ever find yourself in a position where you need to administer multiple BSD systems, you have a rich set of commands with BSD systems for doing remote system administration. The Secure Shell (SSH) facility offers encrypted communications between clients and servers for remote login, tunneling, and file transfer.

Virtual Network Computing (VNC) lets one BSD system share its desktop with a client system so that the remote desktop appears right on the client's desktop. With tools such as Vino, you can even share a desktop in such a way that the VNC server and client can both work from the same desktop at the same time.

14

Locking Down Security

Securing your BSD system means many things. To be secure, you need to restrict access to the user accounts and services on the system. However, after that, security means checking that no one has gotten around the defenses you have set up.

FreeBSD, NetBSD, OpenBSD, and other systems based on BSD distributions are designed in many ways to be secure by default. That means that there are no user accounts with blank passwords, that the firewall is restrictive by default, and that most network services (Web, FTP, and so on) are off by default (even if the service's software is installed).

As someone setting up a BSD system, you can go beyond the default settings to make your system even more secure. For example, by setting up services in chrooted jails you can prevent an intruder from accessing parts of the computer system that are outside the compromised service. By encrypting critical data, you can make it nearly impossible for someone to use stolen data.

IN THIS CHAPTER

Add user accounts and change user settings with adduser

Delete users with rmuser

Add and change passwords with passwd

See who's logged in with last and who

Configure firewalls with ipfw

Manage log files Syslog

Check out advanced security with tripwire and chkrootkit

Although many of the commands covered in this book can be used to check and improve the security of your BSD system, some basic BSD features are particularly geared toward security. For example, secure user accounts with good password protection, a solid firewall, and consistent logging (and log monitoring) are critical to having a secure BSD system. Commands related to those features, plus some advanced features related to protecting network services, are covered in this chapter.

> **NOTE** *Although a lot of computer security efforts focus on protecting computers from outside attackers, policies protecting data from those inside a company have become a growing issue. Procedures in this chapter should be enhanced with policies that restrict internal users from accessing data they don't need for their jobs and tracking improper access from those users.*

Working with Users and Groups

During most BSD installation procedures you are asked to assign a password to the root user (for system administration). Then you might be asked to create a user name of your choice and assign a password to that as well (for everyday computer use).

We encourage you to always log in as a regular user and only su or sudo to the root account when necessary. (In fact, by default, you are not allowed to log in remotely using ssh to a BSD system as root user.) When FreeBSD is installed, you can use commands or graphical tools to add more users, modify user accounts, and assign and change passwords.

Managing Users the GUI Way

For a GNOME desktop system with X, you can manage users and groups with the User Manager window (System ⇨ Administration ⇨ Users and Groups). When managing user accounts for servers, one option is to use web-based GUIs.

The most commonly used general-purpose tool is Webmin (www.webmin.com). Make sure you do not run Webmin on its default port (10000) for security reasons. Or, better yet, run services such as Webmin over SSH tunnels, so communication is encrypted. You can also use special-purpose web interfaces. For example, there are many web-hosting automation GUIs, such as cPanel (www.cpanel.com), Plesk (www.swsoft.com/plesk), or Ensim (www.ensim.com).

Adding User Accounts

To **add new users** you can use the adduser command. With no options, adduser steps you through the information you need to enter to add a user account. Here's an example of using adduser to **add a user interactively**:

```
# adduser                  Start an interactive session to add a user
Username: jimbo
Full name: James Bolatter
Uid (Leave empty for default):
Login group [jimbo]:
Login group is jimbo. Invite jimbo into other groups? []:
Login class [default]:
Shell (sh csh tcsh bash ksh nologin) [sh]: bash
Home directory [/home/jimbo]:
Use password-based authentication? [yes]:
Use an empty password? (yes/no) [no]:
Use a random password? (yes/no) [no]:
Enter password: *********
Enter password again: *********
Lock out the account after creation? [no]:
```

The user name must be from one to 16 characters. Most people use lowercase letters and digits, with the first character being a letter. Default user IDs (Uid) start at 1001. The default group is a new group with the same name as the user name.

Login class is something that not all UNIX-like systems have. The default class is best for regular users (more on login classes a bit later). Password-based authentication (yes) is the normal authentication. Select a good password (more on passwords later as well).

After you have answered all the questions, you have a chance to see and approve of the resulting account information.

```
Username   : jimbo
Password   : *****
Full Name  : James Bolatter
Uid        : 1005
Class      :
Groups     : jimbo
Home       : /home/jimbo
Shell      : /usr/local/bin/bash
Locked     : no
OK? (yes/no):
Add another user? (yes/no): no
Goodbye!
```

As you can see, the home directory is /home/jimbo. The bash shell was assigned, to replace sh as the default shell (some like bash for its more diverse features). Apparently this is the fifth user configured on this system (Uid 1005).

Depending on the login class of the user you just added, several things will happen. For the default user class, an entry for the user is added to the /etc/passwd file and the user's home directory is created. After that, files from the /usr/share/skel directory are added to the user's home directory and the user is added to the selected group account in the /etc/group file. A mail file in the user's name is also added to the /var/mail directory.

This is a simple example. Later examples show other features you might want to take advantage of, such as password aging or assigning different login classes. The next example, however, shows how to add a bunch of users at once.

Adding Batches of Users

If you want to add a bunch of users to your system at once, you can create an account list file and feed that to the adduser command. This can be useful if you need to add a lot of users at once or if you want the same set of users on multiple machines.

In the configuration file used by adduser, each user is represented by a 10-field, one-line, colon-separated entry. The file can be any name you like. You just have to identify it to the adduser command using the -f option. Here's an example of a file I created named users.txt:

```
wnelson:2001:2001:::::Walter Nelson:/home/wnelson:/usr/local/bin/bash:myKulPw
jbing:2002:2002:::::James Bing:/home/jbing:/bin/csh:Nmaikar
sjohnson:2003:2003:::::Sara Johnson:/home/sjohnson:/bin/sh:dwzdwN
njames:2004:2004:::::Nick James:/home/njames:/usr/local/bin/bash:MkMydaE
```

The format of the file that can be passed to the adduser command has 10 colon-separated fields. The fields are user name, user ID, group ID, login class, password aging, account expiration, full user name, home directory, default shell, and password.

As you can see, you don't need to fill in every field (just add a colon to indicate that you are stepping to the next field). I started with user ID 2001, so not to conflict with existing accounts that started at 1001. The group id (third field) was set to match the user ID in each case.

We skipped several of the fields, which we will describe later, before adding the full user name (field 7). Home directories are assigned to a subdirectory of the /home directory that is named with the user name. Several different shells are assigned (bash, csh, and sh), with the full path to each shell shown. Note that the last field contains initial passwords for each user. Plain text passwords are made to be hard to guess, but easy to remember (fashioned after phrases such as *my cool password* and *Not my car*).

> **WARNING!** *Although the passwords in the* users.txt *file we just created were plain text, they are actually stored in encrypted form in the* /etc/master.passwd *file. If you create a* users.txt *file, like the one shown, be sure to restrict permission on that file (or just delete it when you are done). Otherwise, others might be able to see the passwords assigned to your user accounts.*

Before you can add a user, the group you add that user to must exist. So before running the adduser command in this example, you would have to add the following lines (as root user) to the /etc/group file:

```
wnelson:*:2001:
jbing:*:2002:
sjohnson:*:2003:
njames:*:2004:
```

When the file is created and the groups have been added, run the adduser -f command as follows to **add the batch of accounts.**

```
# adduser -f /root/users.txt          Add all users listed in users.txt file
adduser: INFO: Successfully added (wnelson) to the user database.
adduser: INFO: Successfully added (jbing) to the user database.
adduser: INFO: Successfully added (sjohnson) to the user database.
adduser: INFO: Successfully added (njames) to the user database.
```

Setting User Account Defaults

You can create your own defaults for adduser by placing those default settings in the /etc/adduser.conf file. The best way to **create the adduser.conf file** initially is with the adduser command itself as follows (note that any additional groups you add must already exist):

```
# adduser -C              Create adduser defaults and add to /etc/adduser.conf
Uid (leave empty for default):
Login group []: sales
Enter additional groups []: acme
Login class [default]:
Shell (sh csh tcsh bash ksh nologin) [sh]: bash
Home directory [/home/]: /usr/people
Use password-based authentication? [yes]: yes
Use an empty password? (yes/no) [no]: no
Use a random password? (yes/no) [no]: no
Lock out the account after creation? [no]: no
Pass Type  : yes
Class      :
Groups     : sales acme
Home       : /usr/people
Shell      : /usr/local/bin/bash
Locked     : no
OK? (yes/no): yes
Re-edit the default configuration? (yes/no): no
Goodbye!
```

Don't feel that you have to change every setting. The defaults are fine in most cases. The result of the command just shown is an /etc/adduser.conf file that looks like the following:

```
# Configuration file for adduser(8).
# NOTE: only *some* variables are saved.
# Last Modified on Wed Feb 13 11:14:01 CST 2008.
defaultLgroup=sales
defaultclass=
defaultgroups=acme
passwdtype=yes
homeprefix=/usr/people
defaultshell=/usr/local/bin/bash
udotdir=/usr/share/skel
msgfile=/etc/adduser.msg
disableflag=
```

In most cases, the settings in /etc/adduser.conf define what is offered to use for the user account when the administrator runs adduser to add an account. You can edit the adduser.conf file manually, to change any of those setting at a later date. Type **man adduser.conf** to see descriptions of available settings for this file. Here are some **examples of settings you may want to add to adduser.conf** (these are meant to be examples so don't use any setting more than once):

```
defaultgroups="sales market acme"    # You can have multiple extra groups
passwdtype=no                        # Disable user's password, so can't login
passwdtype=none                      # No password, can login without password
passwdtype=random                    # adduser makes password and displays it
defaultshell=/bin/sh                 # Must be a shell listed in /etc/shells
upwexpire=120d                       # User password expires in 120 days
upwexpire=31-12-2008                 # Password expires on December 31, 2008
uuid=1500                            # Default userid (between 1000 and 65534)
```

Overriding these options when you use the `adduser` command can be done in a couple of ways. If you are prompted to use the default value while creating a user interactively, just type a new value if you want to not use the default. However, you can also override many of the default values by adding options to the `adduser` command line. The next section shows examples of options to `adduser`.

Using Options When Adding Users

There are command line options to `adduser` that you can use to override the default settings. For example, you can **change the default location where home directories are placed** as follows:

```
# adduser -d /usr/people        Assign /usr/people to create home directories in
```

To **use a different default shell**, use the -s option as follows:

```
# adduser -s /bin/csh           Assign /bin/csh as the default shell
```

Type `ls -a /usr/share/skel` to see the files that will be copied in each user's home directory when that user's account is created. You can add any files or directories you like to that directory that you would want to be copied to users' home directories when their account is created. To **change the location of the skel** directory, type the following:

```
# adduser -k /usr/share/myskel    Use myskel directory to hold initial user files
```

To **bypass the defaults in your /etc/adduser.conf file**, and use the system defaults instead, use the -N option as follows:

```
# adduser -N                    Don't use defaults from your adduser.conf file
```

Usually, `adduser` will try to create the home directory for the new user you are adding. If you want to explicitly **not create the new home directory**, type the following:

```
# adduser -D                    Don't create the new user's home directory
```

Instead of just using the default login class (called `default`), you can create or enable other login classes. For example, to **change the default login class** to use the dialer login class instead of default, type the following:

```
# adduser -L dialer          User a different login class (dialer)
```

Only the `default` and `root` dialer classes are enabled when you start out (actually there are a few other login class names, but they all simply point to `default`). The next section describes some ways in which you can explore the use of login classes further.

Using Login Classes

A potentially useful feature in FreeBSD that is not in other UNIX-like systems is the login class feature. When you create a normal user account, that account is assigned to the `default` login class, based on an entry in the `/etc/login.conf` file. That login class provides a lot of initial settings for the user. By creating other login classes, you can create sets of users with different attributes.

Here is how the `default` login class is defined in the `/etc/login.conf` file:

```
default:\
        :passwd_format=md5:\
        :copyright=/etc/COPYRIGHT:\
        :welcome=/etc/motd:\
        :setenv=MAIL=/var/mail/$,BLOCKSIZE=K,FTP_PASSIVE_MODE=YES:\
        :path=/sbin /bin /usr/sbin /usr/bin /usr/games /usr/local/sbin
             /usr/local/bin /usr/X11R6/bin ~/bin:\
        :nologin=/var/run/nologin:\
        :cputime=unlimited:\
        :datasize=unlimited:\
        :stacksize=unlimited:\
        :memorylocked=unlimited:\
        :memoryuse=unlimited:\
        :filesize=unlimited:\
        :coredumpsize=unlimited:\
        :openfiles=unlimited:\
        :maxproc=unlimited:\
        :sbsize=unlimited:\
        :vmemoryuse=unlimited:\
        :priority=0:\
        :ignoretime@:\
        :umask=022:
```

Seeing the default login class may answer some of your questions about where some of the initial settings each user has came from. Here are descriptions of **how features are set and how you might change them:**

❏ **passwd_format=md5:** New or changed passwords will use md5 encryption. You could also set this value to `des` or `blf` to use those encryption types.

249

❑ **copyright=/etc/COPYRIGHT:** Indicates a file containing additional copyright information. You could add your own copyright information to this file if your system contains other copyrighted code.

❑ **welcome=/etc/motd:** Assigns the message of the day to /etc/motd. Text from this file is displayed when the user first logs in.

❑ **setenv...:** Sets several shell variables (such as the location of the user's mailbox).

❑ **path...:** Sets the user's initial path. (Expect this path to be replaced by settings from other configuration files.)

❑ **nologin=/var/run/nologin:** Tells the user account that if the /var/run/nologin file exists, the user should be prevented from logging in. (A system administrator can create this file to temporarily prevent users from logging in.)

❑ **priority=0:** This is the initial nice level set for the user.

❑ **umask=022:** Sets the umask so that, by default, when the user creates a file it has 644 permission, or if it is a directory it has 755 permission. In other words, other users and groups can see and read from those files and directories, but not write to them.

The rest of the settings in this login class could be used to limit resources available to the user. However, all of them are set to unlimited. So users will not be limited in the size of files they can create, how much memory they can use, how many processes they can run, and so on. Refer to the login.conf man page for information on how to set resource limits, or for that matter, any other settings you might want to add or change in the login.conf file.

To create your own login classes you can simply uncomment some of the classes in the login.conf file or add your own to that file. If you make changes to login.conf, you need to **rebuild the login database** as follows:

```
# cap_mkdb /etc/login.conf        Create the login.conf.db database
```

The login process uses the settings in the login.conf.db file each time the user logs in to your BSD system.

Modifying User Accounts

After a user account is created, places for changing some of those initial settings are spread across multiple locations. Check the dot files (files beginning with a period) in the user's home directory for settings specific to the user's shell and applications. To change basic user account information, stored in the /etc/passwd file, you can use the vipw command as follows:

```
# vipw        Safely edit the /etc/passwd file
```

The reason for using the `vipw` file, instead of just opening the file in a regular text editor, is that `vipw` will lock the `passwd` file so that its contents can't get out of sync. Only the root user can edit this file. Here's an example of an entry in the `/etc/passwd` file:

```
mike:*:1006:1006:Mike Smith:/home/mike:/bin/csh
```

In this example, the user name is mike, with a user ID and group ID of 1006. The user's full name is Mike Smith. The home directory is `/home/mike` and his default shell is `/bin/csh`. The asterisk in the second field indicates that the user's password is stored in the `/etc/master.passwd` file.

> **WARNING!** *Be careful changing user ID and group ID numbers. Although you can do it, it will probably result in the user not being able to access files in his or her own directory.*

Deleting User Accounts

With the `rmuser` command you can **remove user accounts** from the system, as well as other files (home directories, mail spool files and so on) if you choose. Here are examples:

```
# rmuser jjones            Delete user account
Matching password entry:
jjones:*:1009:1009::0:0:John W. Jones:/home/jjones:/bin/csh

Is this the entry you wish to remove? yes
Remove user's home directory (/home/jjones)? yes
Removing user (jjones): mailspool home passwd.
```

As you can see, besides removing the entry from the `/etc/passwd` file, you also have the opportunity to remove the user's home directory. If you say *yes*, `rmuser` removes the `passwd` entry, home directory, and mail spool file (in this case, `/var/mail/jjones`).

Besides the things the `rmuser` command just told you about, it also does some other things. Those things include: removing the crontab, killing queued *at* jobs, killing all processes, removing tmp files, and removing group memberships for the user. Here are some **other options for removing user accounts**:

```
# rmuser -y jjones         Delete user account, answer yes to all questions
Removing user (jjones): mailspool home passwd.
# rmuser -v jjones         Provide much more verbose output when removing user
Matching password entry:
jjones:*:1009:1009::0:0:John W. Jones:/home/jjones:/bin/csh

Is this the entry you wish to remove? yes
Remove user's home directory (/home/jjones)? yes
Removing crontab for (jjones):.
Removing at(1) jobs owned by (jjones): 0 removed
```

```
Removing IPC mechanisms
Terminating all processes owned by (jjones): -KILL signal sent to 3 processes.
Removing files owned by (jjones) in /tmp: 28 removed
Removing files owned by (jjones) in /var/tmp: 3 removed
Removing mail spool(s) for (jjones): /var/mail/jjones
Removing user (jjones) (including home directory) from system: Done.
```

Managing Passwords

Adding or changing a password is usually done quite simply with the `passwd` command. Besides `passwd` there are commands such as `chfn` and `vipw` (described earlier) for working with user passwords.

Regular users can **change only their own passwords**, whereas the root user can change the password for any user. For example:

```
$ passwd                        Change a regular user's own password
Changing local password for chris
Old Password: ********
New Password: *********
Retype New Password: *********
# passwd joseph                 Root can change any user's password
Changing local password for joseph
New Password: *******
Retype New Password: *******
```

In the first example, a regular user (chris) changes his own password. Even while logged in, the user must type the current password before entering a new one. Unlike other UNIX-like systems, however, `passwd` doesn't prevent users from setting a password that is too short, based on a dictionary word, doesn't have enough different characters, or is otherwise easy to guess. So it is important that users choose good passwords on their own.

The root user, in the second example, can change any user password without the old password. Likewise, the root user can assign a short or easy-to-guess password, so diligence should be exercised there as well in choosing a good password.

Passwords should be at least eight characters, a combination of letters and other characters (numbers, punctuation, and so on), and not include real words. As noted earlier in this chapter, make passwords easy to remember but hard to guess.

Adding Groups

Each new user is assigned to one or more groups. You can create groups at any time and add users to those groups. The permissions that each group has to use files and directories in your BSD system depend on how the group permission bits are set on each item. Assigning users to a group enables you to attach ownership to files, directories, and applications so that those users can work together on a project or have common access to resources.

Although there are graphical tools for adding, removing, and modifying groups (such as the Users and Groups window in GNOME), most administrators just manually edit the /etc/group file to work with groups. The format of the /etc/group file is like a shortened /etc/passwd file.

Here is a shortened version of the /etc/group file to illustrate a few different groups:

```
wheel:*:0:
tty:*:4:
operator:*:5:root
mail:*:6:
bin:*:7:
www:*:80:
nogroup:*:65533:
nobody:*:65534:
cups:*:193:
sales:*:1001:curt,mike,sally
wnelson:*:2001:
jbing:*:2002:mike,sally
```

The structure of the /etc/group file is group name, password (optional), group ID, and users assigned to that group. Normally, the password field simply has an asterisk (*) in it. Users are assigned to a group in a comma-separated list.

The group conventions with FreeBSD include starting regular user accounts at 1001 and above. Accounts below 100 are administrative groups. Special groups, typically used for mapping group permissions for users across network interfaces, include nogroup (GID 65533) and nobody (GID 65534).

When you add a user with the adduser command, the default is to also create a new group and assign the user's name and ID to that group. This approach ensures that less care needs to be taken when protecting the permissions of a file the user creates. Other users can be added to a user's group if they need to work on a project together.

If you use any of the existing groups, the wheel group is the one you will most likely be interested in. Adding a user to the wheel group is a common way to provide root privilege to that user.

Keep in mind that removing a group or user doesn't remove the files, directories, devices or other items owned by that group or user. If you do a long listing (ls -l) of a file or directory assigned to a user or group that was deleted, the UID or GID of the deleted user or group is displayed, instead of a user or group name.

Checking on Users

After you have created user accounts, and let those users loose on your computer, you can use several commands to keep track of how they are using your computer.

Commands for checking on user activity on your BSD system that are covered in other chapters include the following:

❑ The find command to search the system for files anywhere on the system that are owned by selected users (see Chapter 4).

❑ The du command to see how much disk space has been used in selected users' home directories (see Chapter 7).

❑ Commands such as fuser, ps, and top to find out which processes users are running (see Chapter 9).

Aside from the commands just mentioned, there are commands for checking such things as who is logged into your system and getting general information about the users with accounts on your system. Here are examples of commands for **getting information about people logging into your system:**

```
$ last              List the most recent successful logins
greek     ttyv3               Sun Oct 5 18:05    still logged in
chris     ttyv1               Sun Oct 4 13:39    still logged in
jjones    ttyp0    thompson   Sun Oct 5 14:02    still logged in
chris     ttyp3    :0.0       Sat Oct 4 15:47    still logged in
jim       ttyp0    10.0.0.50  Fri Oct 3 13:46 - 15:40  (01:53)
francois  ttyp4                     Thu Oct 2 11:14 - 13:38 (2+02:24)
$ last -h thompson    List logins from host computer thompson
julian    ttyp0    thompson      Mon Oct  6 12:28 - 12:28  (00:00)
morris    ttyp0    thompson      Tue Sep 31 13:08 - 13:08  (00:00)
baboon    ttyp0    thompson      Sun Sep  8 09:40 - 09:40  (00:00)
francois  ttyp0    thompson      Fri Aug 22 17:23 - 17:23  (00:00)
$ who -u            List who is currently logged in (long form)
greek     ttyv3    Oct 13 18:05 17:24
jim       ttyp0    Oct 13 12:29   .
root      ttyp3    Oct 13 18:18 13:46
francois  ttyp2    Oct 13 23:05  old   (:0.0)
chris     ttyp1    Oct 13 15:47  old
$ users             List who is currently logged in (short form)
chris francois greek jim root
```

With the last command, you can see when each user logged in (or opened a new shell) and either how long they were logged in or a note that they are still logged in. The ttyv1 and ttyv3 terminal lines show users working from virtual terminals on the console. The ttyp? lines indicate a person opening a shell from a remote computer (thompson) or local X display (:0.0). The -h option to the last command lets you see who logged in most recently from a particular host computer. The who -u and users commands show information on currently logged-in users.

Here are some commands for **finding out more about individual users** on your system:

```
$ id                Your identity (UID, GID and group for current shell)
uid=1001(chris) gid=1001(chris) groups=0(wheel)
$ who am i          Your identity (user, tty, login date, location)
chris     ttyp2    Oct 3 2140 (:0.0)
```

> **NOTE** *If you were to log in as a regular user such as chris, then use* su *to get root permission, the output of* id *and* who *would show different users. That's because* id *reflects the permission you switched to (root) and* who *shows the user who logged in originally (chris).*

```
$ finger -s chris    User information (short)
Login    Name           TTy   Idle   Login Time    Office    Office Phone
chris    Chris Negus    p2      1d   Oct  4 13:39  A-111      555-1212
$ finger -l chris    User information (long)
Login: chris                           Name: Chris Negus
Directory: /home/chris                 Shell: /bin/bash
Office: A-111, 555-1212                 Home Phone: 555-2323
On since Sat Oct  4 13:39 (CDT) on tty1    2 days idle
New mail received Mon Oct  6 13:46 2008 (CDT)
     Unread since Sat Oct  4 09:32 2008 (CDT)
No Plan.
```

Besides displaying basic information about the user (login, name, home directory, shell, and so on), the finger command will also display any information stored in special files in the user's home directory. For example, the contents of the user's ~/.plan and ~/.project files, if those files exist, are displayed at the end of the finger output. With a one-line .project file and multi-line .plan file, output could appear as follows:

```
$ finger -l chris    User information (long, .project and .plan files)
     . . .
Project:
My project is to take over the world.
Plan:
My grand plan is
to take over the world
by installing BSD on every computer
```

Securing Network Services

Even a computer system with all the security features in the world won't be secure if the system administrator doesn't enable those features. Although some level of security is achieved in BSD systems by the fact that network services are not turned on or even installed by default, some of the best ways of securing network services require some extra work.

This section tells how to start various network services. Then it describes ways of configuring and securing those services.

In FreeBSD, most network services are secured by adding settings to configuration files in the /etc directory and by configuring how the network services start. Network services that start when you boot your computer do so based primarily on two features:

❑ **/etc/rc.d/ scripts:** Most network services are handled by daemon processes (such as sshd, named, and nfsd). However, those services are actually launched from

255

scripts in the /etc/rc.d directory. Those scripts can be run with simple arguments, such as start, stop, or restart in order to get the services they provide running.

❑ **rc.conf files:** When and how each of the rc.d scripts runs is determined by entries in rc.conf files. The /etc/defaults/rc.conf file contains the default setting of available services. However, it also holds tons of commented lines that can be uncommented and modified to configure and launch the service scripts in the /etc/rc.d directory. To change how services start from the default, you can create an /etc/rc.conf file, then copy and uncomment entries from the original rc.conf file.

When FreeBSD and other BSD systems boot up, the rc.conf files are read and the appropriate services (with appropriate settings) are started. The rest of this section is devoted to showing you entries you can add to your /etc/rc.conf file to start and secure a variety of network services. (Refer to Chapter 12 for some basic ways of enabling NFS and Samba network services.)

> **WARNING!** *If you make a mistake in your* /etc/rc.conf *file, it is possible for that mistake to keep your system from booting completely. Be very careful editing your* /etc/rc.conf *file (and have a rescue disk handy just in case).*

The examples below are taken from the Network Configuration Sub-Section of the /etc/defaults/rc.conf file. By adding the following settings to your own /etc/rc.conf file, you can **enable the services described**. To **start the service immediately**, run the related startup script. For example:

```
# /etc/rc.d/ftpd start          Start the FTP service after it has been enabled
```

The start-up script usually starts a service daemon (ftpd in this case). Examples in the sections below show how the resulting service daemons are run after you add different flags to the /etc/rc.conf file.

❑ **Syslog Daemon (syslogd):** Add these settings to /etc/rc.conf to configure syslogd to start at boot time:

```
syslogd_enable="YES"                 # Run syslog daemon (or NO).
syslogd_program="/usr/sbin/syslogd"  # path to syslogd,
syslogd_flags="-s"                   # Flags to syslogd (if enabled).
```

By specifying other options in quotes with syslogd_flags, you can change how the syslogd daemon operates. The following illustrates resulting syslogd command lines:

```
# /usr/sbin/syslogd -s          Default. Only log local messages (secure mode)
# /usr/sbin/syslogd -4          Log data only on IPv4 addresses
# /usr/sbin/syslogd -a 192.168.0.5/24
                                Let syslogd take datagrams from 192.168.0.5
# /usr/sbin/syslogd -b 192.168.0.1/24
                                Have syslogd bind to address 192.168.0.1
# /usr/sbin/syslogd -d          syslogd in debug mode (look if syslogd is broken)
# /usr/sbin/syslogd -m 10       Change mark message from 20 to 10 minutes
```

For more information on syslogd, see the description of system logs later in this chapter.

❑ **Internet Super Server Daemon (inetd):** Add these settings to /etc/rc.conf to configure the inetd super server. If inetd_enable="YES" is set, the inetd daemon starts at boot time to listen for requests for a variety of services (many of which are legacy UNIX services, though others can be enabled here as well). Individual services (such as rlogind, tftp, or bootpd) can be enabled by removing the comment in front of that service in the /etc/inetd.conf file):

```
inetd_enable="YES"                      # Run the network daemon dispatcher (YES/NO).
inetd_program="/usr/sbin/inetd"         # Path to inetd, if you want a different one.
inetd_flags="-wW -C 60"                 # Optional flags to inetd
```

By specifying other options in quotes with inetd_flags you can change how the inetd daemon operates. The following illustrates resulting inetd command lines:

```
# /usr/sbin/inetd -wW -C 60      Default. Use TCP wrappers for internal/external
                                 Service can be invoked only 60 times from IP addr
# /usr/sbin/inetd -wW -C 60 -R 128   Limit number of times service
                                     can be invoked in one minute to 128
# /usr/sbin/inetd -wW -a 192.168.0.1  Bind to a specific IP address
# /usr/sbin/inetd -wW -o Linux   Report system as Linux, to confuse intruders
```

❑ **Domain Name System service (named):** Add these settings to /etc/rc.conf to configure the named service, so your system can act as a DNS server. Some of the named settings shown here are on by default, but are here for your information. If named_enable="YES" is set, the named daemon starts at boot time to listen for requests for DNS service:

```
named_enable="YES"                      # Run named, the DNS server (or NO)
named_program="/usr/sbin/named"         # Path to named, if you want a different one
#named_flags=""                         # Flags for named
named_pidfile="/var/run/named/pid"      # Must set this in named.conf as well
named_uid="bind"                        # User to run named as
named_chrootdir="/var/named"            # Chroot directory (or "" not to auto-chroot)
named_chroot_autoupdate="YES"           # Automatically install/update chrooted
                                        # components of named. See /etc/rc.d/named
named_symlink_enable="YES"              # Symlink the chrooted pid file
```

DNS service is a complex and potentially dangerous (from a security standpoint) service to enable. One thing to note from a security standpoint is that named is run in a chroot environment (/var/named) by default. This makes it more secure than other services by the fact that, if the service is cracked, the intruder cannot necessarily access other services from the same location.

The service must be configured using files in the /var/named/etc/namedb directory (starting with named.conf). Whole books are written on the proper setup and maintenance of DNS service. For our purposes (commands, silly), we'll just show you a few different ways of running the named daemon which result from uncommenting and adding options to the named_flags entry:

```
# /usr/sbin/named -p 34690    Run named on alternate port (not default 53)
# /usr/sbin/named -v          Just report version of named and exit
```

```
BIND 9.3.3
# /usr/sbin/named -4        Only use IPv4 protocols
# /usr/sbin/named -6        Only use IPv6 protocols
# /usr/sbin/named -n 3      Tell named to use 3 CPUs, creating one thread each
```

❑ **Secure Shell service (sshd):** The Secure Shell service is one that is often enabled in BSD and other UNIX-like systems. There are many ways to use the SSH service (see Chapter 13 for details). However, to enable SSH you need only set the `ssh_enable="YES"` entry. Here are values associated with the SSH service that you can add to the `/etc/rc.conf` file:

```
sshd_enable="YES"                    # Enable sshd
sshd_program="/usr/sbin/sshd"        # Path to sshd, if you want a different one
sshd_flags=""                        # Additional flags for sshd.
```

To configure the `sshd` service, you need to modify files in the `/etc/ssh` directory (particularly the `sshd_config` file). By specifying other options in quotes with `sshd_flags` you can change how the `sshd` daemon operates. The following illustrates resulting `sshd` command lines:

```
# /usr/sbin/sshd -f /root/my_cfg  Specify new sshd_config file (to test)
# /usr/sbin/sshd -g 60            Change client login time from 120 to 60 secs
# /usr/sbin/sshd -p 53943         Change listening port to 53943 (for security)
```

❑ **File Transfer Protocol service (ftpd):** The FTP service is one of the oldest, and still active, services for sharing files over the Internet or other network. To enable FTP service you need only set the `ftpd_enable="YES"` entry. Here are values associated with the FTP service that you can add to the `/etc/rc.conf` file:

```
ftpd_enable="YES"                    # Enable stand-alone ftpd.
ftpd_program="/usr/libexec/ftpd"     # Path to ftpd, if you want a different one
ftpd_flags=""                        # Additional flags to stand-alone ftpd
```

Several files in the `/etc` directory control access to the FTP service: `ftpusers`, `ftpchroot`, `ftphosts`, `ftpwelcome`, and `ftpmotd`. By specifying options in quotes with `ftpd_flags` you can change how the `ftpd` daemon operates. The following illustrate resulting `ftpd` command lines:

```
# /usr/sbin/ftpd -D            Default. Run ftpd as a daemon process
# /usr/sbin/ftpd -D -A         Only allow anonymous access to FTP service
# /usr/sbin/ftpd -D -A -m      Let anonymous user write files (given file perms)
# /usr/sbin/ftpd -D -a example.com   Listen for FTP requests to example.com
```

Another service you can configure from the `/etc/rc.conf` file is your BSD firewall. Configuring firewalls, however, requires more explanation. Read on.

Configuring the Built-In Firewall

A firewall is a critical tool for keeping your computer safe from intruders over the Internet or other network. It can protect your computer by checking every packet of data that comes to your computer's network interfaces, then making a decision about what to do with that packet based on the parameters you set.

Three firewall facilities are built into FreeBSD: IPFILTER, IPFIREWALL, and PacketFilter. This section focuses on the IPFILTER firewall features. There are ports of IPFILTER available not only on FreeBSD, but also on NetBSD and OpenBSD. You can learn more about IPFILTER from the official FAQ: www.phildev.net/ipf.

When you build a firewall, there are a few things you should think about. If possible, work from the console terminal, because as you develop your firewall rules it's possible that you might lock yourself out by mistake. In your rules, be sure to handle loopback (lo and 127.0.0.0 interface) situations.

To **enable IPFILTER firewall**, add the following settings to the /etc/rc.conf file, create a rules file, and start the firewall. Here's an example of **settings to add to the /etc/rc.conf file**:

```
firewall_enable="YES"                # Set to YES to enable firewall functionality
firewall_type="/etc/ipf.rules"       # Use /etc/ipf.rules for firewall rules
firewall_logging="YES"               # Set to YES to enable events logging
firewall_script="/etc/rc.firewall"   # Which script to run to set up the firewall
firewall_quiet="NO"                  # Set to YES to suppress rule display
firewall_flags=""                    # Flags passed to ipfw when type is a file

ipfilter_enable="YES"                # Set to YES to enable ipfilter functionality
ipfilter_program="/sbin/ipf"         # Where the ipfilter program lives
ipfilter_rules="/etc/ipf.rules"      # Rules definition file for ipfilter, see
                                     # /usr/src/contrib/ipfilter/rules for example
ipfilter_flags=""                    # Additional flags for ipfilter
```

Note that firewall_enable, firewall_logging, and ipfilter_enable are all set to YES. The next important thing to notice is that the /etc/ipf.rules file is where the rules that define how your firewall behaves are stored. Here is an example of **a set of firewall rules** added to the /etc/ipf.rules file:

```
add allow all from any to any via lo0
add allow all from any to 127.0.0.0/8
add allow all from 127.0.0.0/8 to any
add check-state
add allow tcp from any to any established
add allow all from any to any out keep-state
add allow icmp from any to any
add allow tcp from any to any 22 setup keep-state
add allow tcp from any to any 25 setup keep-state
add allow tcp from any to any 53 setup keep-state
add allow udp from any to any 53 keep-state
add allow tcp from any to any 80 setup keep-state
add allow tcp from any to any 110 setup keep-state
add allow tcp from any to any 123 setup keep-state
add allow udp from any to any 123 setup keep-state
add allow tcp from any to any 143 setup keep-state
add deny log all from any to any
```

259

The first three lines above allow whatever you want to do from the local system (lo0 and 127.0.0.1). The check-state option causes packets to be checked against the dynamic ruleset. The next two lines allow packets from established connections and keep-state state. The icmp line allows other computers to ping your computer.

The rest of the lines have to do with packets that request services from your system. This machine allows connections to requests for SSH (port 22), SMTP mail (port 25), DNS service (port 53), web service (port 80), Post Office Protocol v3 (port 110), and IMAP mail v2 (143). The last line says to log services from any other ports that are denied.

To get the firewall settings in `rc.conf` working and the firewall rules in `ipf.rules`, you need to **start the ipfw firewall service**. Here's how to do that:

```
# /etc/rc.d/ipfw start          Starts the ipfw firewall service
Flushed all rules.
Starting divert daemons:Flushed all rules.
00100 allow ip from any to any via lo0
00200 allow ip from any to 127.0.0.0/8
00300 allow ip from 127.0.0.0/8 to any
00400 check-state
00500 allow tcp from any to any established
00600 allow ip from any to any out keep-state
00700 allow icmp from any to any
00800 allow tcp from any to any dst-port 22 setup keep-state
00900 allow tcp from any to any dst-port 25 setup keep-state
01000 allow tcp from any to any dst-port 53 setup keep-state
01100 allow udp from any to any dst-port 53 keep-state
01200 allow tcp from any to any dst-port 80 setup keep-state
01300 allow tcp from any to any dst-port 110 setup keep-state
01400 allow tcp from any to any dst-port 123 setup keep-state
01500 allow udp from any to any dst-port 123 setup keep-state
01600 allow tcp from any to any dst-port 143 setup keep-state
01700 deny log ip from any to any
Firewall rules loaded.
Firewall logging enabled
net.inet.ip.fw.enable: 0 -> 1
```

Once you have a working firewall, which you should at this point, you can use a variety of IPFILTER commands to work with that firewall. Keep in mind that changes you make to the firewall live will be lost at the next reboot if you don't save those changes. So, in general, it's best to make rule changes to the `ipf.rules` file and simply restart the service to test them out.

Here are some commands for **checking out the state of your firewall**:

```
# ipfw list      List the current set of firewall rules
00100 allow ip from any to any via lo0
00200 allow ip from any to 127.0.0.0/8
 ...
```

```
# ipfw show        Show statistics for each matching packet rule
# ipfw -at list    List the current rules with statistics and timestamps
# ipfw zero        Zeros the counters so you can start with fresh statistics
```

If you want to add a rule directly to the firewall (until the next reboot), you can run the `ipfw` command directly with the `add` option. You should choose a rule number that is appropriate for the type of rule.

```
# ipfw -q add 1550 allow tcp from any to 21 setup keep-state
                 Allow outside connections to FTP service (port 21)
# ipfw -q delete 1550   Delete rule number 1550
```

There are many other features in `ipfw` for setting up and working with firewall rules. Refer to the ipfw man page for details.

Working with System Logs

Most BSD systems are configured to log many of the activities that occur on those systems. Those activities are then written to log files located in the `/var/log` directory or its subdirectories. This logging is done by the Syslog facility.

FreeBSD uses the `syslogd` (system log daemon) as part of the basic installed system to manage system logging. That daemon is started automatically from the `syslogd` initialization script (`/etc/rc.d/syslogd`). Information about system activities is then directed to files in the `/var/log` directory such as `messages`, `security`, `cron`, `auth.log`, and others, based on settings in the `/etc/syslog.conf` file.

You can check any of the log files manually (using `vi` or another favorite text editor).

You can **send your own messages to the syslogd logging facility** using the `logger` command. Here are a couple of examples:

```
# logger Added new video card            Message added to messages file
# logger -p warn -t CARD -f /tmp/my.txt   Priority, tag, message file
```

In the first example, the words *Added new video card* are sent to the messages file. In the second example, priority of the message is set to info and a tag of CARD is added to each line in the message. The message text is taken from the `/tmp/my.txt` file that I created before running the command. To see these log entries in real time, use `tail -f` or `less` as described in Chapter 5.

Using Advanced Security Features

A dozen or so pages covering security-related commands are not nearly enough to address the depth of security tools available to you as a BSD system administrator.

Beyond the commands covered in this chapter, here are descriptions of some features you may want to look into to further secure your BSD system:

❏ **Central logging:** If you're managing more than a couple of BSD servers, it becomes preferable to have all your systems log to a central syslog server. When you implement your syslog server, you may want to explore using syslog-ng. (As root, type `pkg_add -r syslog-ng`).

❏ **Tripwire:** Using the tripwire package, you can take a snapshot of all the files on your system, then later use that snapshot to find if any of those files have been changed. This is particularly useful to find out if any applications have been modified that should not have been. First, you take a baseline of your system file. Then at regular intervals, you run a tripwire integrity check to see if any of your applications or configuration files have been modified.

❏ **chkrootkit:** If you suspect your system has been compromised, download and build `chkrootkit` from `www.chkrootkit.org`. To install it in FreeBSD, type `pkg_add -r chkrootkit`. This will help you detect rootkits that may have been used to take over your machine. We recommend you run chkrootkit from a LiveCD or after mounting the suspected drive on a clean system.

Summary

Although there are many tools available for securing your BSD system, the first line of security starts with securing the user accounts on your system and the services that run on your system. Commands such as `adduser`, `rmuser`, and `passwd` are standard tools for setting up user and group accounts.

Because most serious security breaches outside your organization can come from intruders accessing your systems on public networks, setting up secure firewalls is important for any system connected to the Internet. The ipfw facility is one of several facilities in FreeBSD that provides the firewall features you can configure to meet your needs.

To keep track of activities on your system, the Syslog facility logs information about nearly every aspect of the actions that take place on your system. There are also many other software packages you can add to help check the security of your system, such as chkrootkit and tripwire.

A

Using vi or Vim Editors

Although easy-to-use graphical text editors (such as gedit and kedit) are readily available with BSD systems, most power users still use vi or Emacs to edit text files. Besides the fact that vi and Emacs will work from any shell (no GUI required), they offer other advantages such as your hands never having to leave the keyboard and integration with useful utilities. And unlike GUI editors, text-based editors are usable over slow Internet connections such as dial-up or satellite.

This appendix focuses on features of the vi editor that can not only help you with basic editing, but also help you do some advanced text manipulation. We chose to cover vi rather than Emacs because vi is more universal and leaner, and also because vi keyboard shortcuts only require two arms. Because some UNIX-like systems use the Vim (Vi IMproved) editor in the place of the older vi editor, the descriptions in this appendix are extended to cover Vim as well. Some features in Vim that are not in vi include multiple undo levels, syntax highlighting, and online help.

> **NOTE** *If you have never used vi or Vim before, try out the tutor that comes with the* vim6 *package. Run the* vimtutor *command and follow the instructions to step through many of the key features of vi and Vim. To see the differences between vi and Vim, type* :help vi_diff.txt *while running the* vim *command. To install the vim6 package, type the following as root user:* pkg_add -r vim6.

Depending on how your vim6 package was built, you may or may not get all the latest vim features working at first. In many cases, the compatible option is on, which causes conflicting behaviors between vi and vim to behave like vi (see the text on undo later in this appendix). To turn on the latest vim features type :set incompatible while editing with vim or add this to your ~/.vimrc file:

```
set incompatible
```

Starting and Quitting the vi Editor

If you want to experiment with using vi, you should copy a text file to practice on. For example, type:

```
$ cp /etc/services /tmp
```

Then open that file using the vi command as follows:

```
$ vi /tmp/services
```

To benefit from all the improvements of Vim, make sure you have the FreeBSD vim6 package installed. On many systems, vi is aliased to the vim command. You may want to double-check that, using the alias command. If you want to use vim directly, type /usr/local/bin/vim. If you specifically want to use the older-style vi command, use the full path to the vi command instead:

```
/bin/vi /tmp/text.txt
```

Here are a few other ways you can **start vi**:

`$ vi +25 /tmp/services`	*Begin on line 25*
`$ vi + /tmp/services`	*Begin editing file on the last line*
`$ vi +/tty /tmp/services`	*Begin on first line with word "tty"*
`$ vi -r /tmp/services`	*Recover file from crashed edit session*
`$ view /tmp/services`	*Edit file in read-only mode*

When you are done with your vi session, you have several different ways to save and quit. To **save the file before you are ready to quit**, type **:w**. To **quit and save changes**, type either **ZZ** or **:wq**. To **quit without saving changes**, type **:q!**. If you find that you can't write to the file you are editing, it may be opened in read-only mode. If that's the case, you can try forcing a write by typing **:w!** or you can **save the contents of the file to a different name**. For example, type the following to save the contents of the current file to a file named myfile.txt:

```
:w /tmp/myfile.txt
```

> **NOTE** *It's important to understand that* :w *writes the current file out to another file. So if you continue editing, you are still editing the original file. In the example above, if you started editing the* services *file, then wrote the contents to* myfile.txt, *to continue editing* myfile.txt *you would have to change to it by typing the following:* :e /tmp/myfile.txt.

The vi editor also enables you to **line up several files at a time to edit**. For example, type:

```
$ cd /tmp
$ touch a.txt b.txt c.txt
$ vi a.txt b.txt c.txt
```

In this example, vi will open the a.txt file first. You can move to the next file by typing :n. You may want to save changes before moving to the next file (:w) or save changes as you move to the next file (:wn). To abandon changes while moving to the next file, type :n!. To go back to the previous file, type :prev.

You will probably find it easier to open multiple files using the vim feature for splitting your screen. When you're in vim and have a file open, you can split your screen multiple times either horizontally or vertically:

```
:split /etc/services
:vsplit /etc/hosts
```

Use <Tab> to complete the path to the files, just as you would in a bash shell. To navigate between split windows, press Ctrl+W, followed by the W key. To close the current window, use the usual vim exit command (:q).

Moving Around in vi

The first thing to get used to with vi is that you can't just start typing. Vi has multiple modes that enable you to perform a different set of tasks. You start a vi session in normal mode, where vi is waiting for you to type a command to get started. While you are in normal mode, you can move around the file, to position where you want to be in the file. To enter or modify text, you need to go into insert or replace modes.

Assuming vi is open with a file that contains several pages of text, Table A-1 shows some keys and combinations you can type to move around the file while in normal mode.

Table A-1: Keystroke Commands for Moving Around

Key	Result	Key	Result
PageDown or Ctrl+f	Move down one page	PageUp or Ctrl+b	Move up one page
Ctrl+d	Move down half page	Ctrl+u	Move up half page
G	Go to last line of file	:1	Go to first line of file (use any number to go to that line)
H	Move cursor to screen top	L	Move cursor to screen bottom
M	Move cursor to middle of screen	Ctrl+L	Redraw screen (if garbled)
Enter	Move cursor to beginning of the next line	-	Move cursor to beginning of the previous line

Continued

Table A-1: Keystroke Commands for Moving Around (*continued*)

Key	Result	Key	Result
End or $	Move cursor to end of line	Home or ^ or 0	Move cursor to line beginning
(	Move cursor to beginning of previous sentence	)	Move cursor to beginning of next sentence
{	Move cursor to beginning of previous paragraph	}	Move cursor to beginning of next paragraph
w	Move cursor to next word (space, new line or punctuation)	W	Move cursor to next word (space or new line)
b	Move cursor to previous word (space, new line or punctuation)	B	Move cursor to previous word (space or new line)
e	Move cursor to end of next word (space, new line or punctuation)	E	Move cursor to end of next word (space or new line)
Left arrow or Backspace or h	Move cursor left one letter	Right arrow or l	Move cursor right one letter
k or up arrow	Move cursor up one line	j or down arrow	Move cursor down one line
/*string*	Find next occurrence of *string*	?*string*	Find previous occurrence of *string*
n or /	Find same string again (forward)	N or ?	Find same string again (backwards)

Changing and Deleting Text in vi

To begin changing or adding to text with vi, you can enter insert or replace modes, as shown in Table A-2. When you enter insert or replace mode, the characters you type will appear in the text document (as opposed to being interpreted as commands).

Press the Esc key to exit to normal mode after you are done inserting or replacing text.

Table A-2: Commands for Changing Text

Key	Result	Key	Result
i	Typed text appears before current character	I	Typed text appears at the beginning of current line
a	Typed text appears after current character	A	Typed text appears at the end of current line
o	Open a new line below current line to begin typing	O	Open a new line above current line to begin typing
s	Erase current character and replace with new text	S	Erase current line and enter new text
c ?	Replace ? with l, w, $, c to change the current letter, word, end of line or line	C	Erase from cursor to end of line and enter new text.
r	Replace current character with the next one you type	R	Overwrite as you type from current character going forward

Table A-3 contains keys you type to delete or paste text.

Table A-3: Commands for Deleting and Pasting Text

Key	Result	Key	Result
x	Delete character under cursor	X	Delete character to left of cursor
d ?	Replace ? with l, w, $, d to cut the current letter, word, end of line from cursor or entire line	D	Cut from cursor to end of line
y ?	Replace ? with l, w, $ to copy (yank) the current letter, word, or end of line from cursor	Y	Yank current line
p	Pastes cut or yanked text after cursor	P	Pastes cut or yanked text before cursor

Using Miscellaneous Commands

Table A-4 shows a few miscellaneous, but important, commands you should know.

Table A-4: Miscellaneous Commands

Key	Result
u	Type **u** to undo the previous change. Multiple u commands toggles the previous undo on and off. (In vim, typing : set nocompatible will allow multi-level undos. Use Ctrl-r to undo your undos.)
.	Typing a period (.) will repeat the previous command. So, if you deleted a line, replaced a word, changed four letters, and so on, the same command will be done wherever the cursor is currently located. (Entering input mode again resets it.)
J	Join the current line with the next line.
Esc	If you didn't catch this earlier, the Esc key returns you from an input mode back to command mode. This is one of the keys you will use most often.

Modifying Commands with Numbers

Nearly every command described so far can be modified with a number. In other words, instead of deleting a word, replacing a letter or changing a line, you can delete six words, replace 12 letters and change nine lines. Table A-5 shows some examples.

Table A-5: Modifying Commands with Numbers

Command	Result
7cw	Erase the next seven words and replace them with text you type.
d5d	Cut the next five lines (including the current line).
3p	Paste the previously deleted text three times after the current cursor.
9db	Cut the nine words before the current cursor.
10j	Move the cursor down 10 lines.
y2)	Copy (yank) text from cursor to end of next two sentences.
5Ctrl+F	Move forward five pages.
6J	Join together the next six lines.

From these examples, you can see that most vi keystrokes for changing text, deleting text, or moving around in the file can be modified using numbers.

Using Ex Commands

The vi editor was originally built on an editor called Ex. Some of the vi commands you've seen so far start with a semicolon and are known as *Ex* commands. To enter Ex commands, start from normal mode and type a semicolon (:). This switches you to command line mode. In this mode, you can use the Tab key to complete your command or file name, and the arrow keys to navigate your command history, as you would in a bash shell. When you press Enter at the end of your command, you are returned to normal mode.

Table A-6 shows some examples of Ex commands.

Table A-6: Ex Command Examples

Command	Result
`:!bash`	Escape to a bash shell. When you are done, type **exit** to return to vi.
`:!date`	Run `date` (or any command you choose). Press Enter to return.
`:!!`	Rerun the command previously run.
`:20`	Go to line 20 in the file.
`:5,10w abc.txt`	Write lines 5 through 10 to the file `abc.txt`.
`:e abc.txt`	Leave the current file and begin editing the file `abc.txt`.
`:.r def.txt`	Read the contents of `def.txt` into the file below the current line.
`:s/UNIX/FreeBSD`	Substitute `FreeBSD` for the first occurrence of UNIX on the current line.
`:s/UNIX/FreeBSD/g`	Substitute `FreeBSD` for all occurrences of UNIX on the current line.
`:%s/UNIX/FreeBSD/g`	Substitute `FreeBSD` for the all occurrences of UNIX in the entire file.
`:g/FreeBSD /p`	List every line in the file that contains the string `FreeBSD`.
`:g/gaim/s//pidgin/gp`	Find every instance of `gaim` and change it to `pidgin`.

From the ex prompt you can also see and change settings related to your vi session using the set command. Table A-7 shows some examples.

Table A-7: set Commands in ex Mode

Command	Result
:set all	List all settings.
:set	List only those settings that have changed from the default.
:set number	Have line numbers appear left of each line. (Use set nonu to unset.)
:set ai	Sets autoindent, so opening a new line follows the previous indent.
:set ic	Sets ignore case, so text searches will match regardless of case.
:set list	Show $ for end of lines and ^I for tabs.
:set wm	Causes vi to add line breaks between words near the end of a line.

Working in Visual Mode

The Vim editor provides a more intuitive means of selecting text called *visual mode*. To begin visual mode, move the cursor to the first character of the text you want to select and press the v key.

At this point, you can use any of your cursor movement keys (arrow keys, Page Down, End, and so on) to move the cursor to the end of the text you want to select. As the page and cursor move, you will see text being highlighted. When all the text you want to select is highlighted, you can press keys to act on that text. For example, d deletes the text, c lets you change the selected text, :w /tmp/test.txt saves selected text to a file, and so on.

Summary

The vi command is one of the most popular text editors used for FreeBSD and UNIX systems. Using keystrokes, you go back and forth between command mode (where you can move around the file) and insert or replace modes. For a vi that is more advanced, you can use the vim command. Using ex mode, you can read and write text from files, do complex search and replace commands, and temporarily exit to a shell or other command.

B

Shell Special Characters and Variables

BSD systems offer several different shells you can use to enter commands and run scripts. Chapter 3 helps you become comfortable working in the shell. This appendix provides a reference of the numerous characters and variables that have special meaning to particular shells (such as the bash shell) or are available on most shells. Many of those elements are referenced in Table B-1 (Shell Special Characters) and Table B-2 (Shell Environment Variables).

IN THIS APPENDIX

Using special shell characters

Using shell variables

Using Special Shell Characters

You can use special characters from the shell to match multiple files, save some keystrokes, or perform special operations. Table B-1 shows some shell special characters that you may find useful.

Table B-1: Shell Special Characters

Character	Description
*	Match any string of characters.
?	Match any one character.
[...]	Match any character enclosed in the braces.
' ... '	Remove special meaning of characters between quotes. *Variables are not expanded.*
" ... "	Same as simple quotes except for the escape characters ($ ` and \) that preserve their special meaning.

Continued

Table B-1: Shell Special Characters (*continued*)

Character	Description
\	Escape character to remove the special meaning of the character that follows.
~	Refers to the $HOME directory.
~+	Value of the shell variable PWD or working directory (bash only).
~-	Refers to the previous working directory (bash only).
.	Refers to the current working directory.
. .	Refers to the directory above the current directory. Can be used repeatedly to reference several directories up.
$param	Used to expand a shell variable parameter.
cmd1 ` cmd2 ` or cmd1 $ (cmd2)	cmd2 is executed first. Then the call to cmd2 is substituted with the output of cmd2 and cmd1 is executed.
cmd1 >	Redirects standard output from command.
cmd1 <	Redirects standard input to command.
cmd1 >>	Append standard output to file from command, without erasing its current contents.
cmd1 | cmd2	Pipe the output of one command to the input of the next.
cmd &	Run the command in the background.
cmd1 && cmd2	Run first command, then, if it returns a zero exit status, run the second command.
cmd1 || cmd2	Run first command, then, if it returns a non-zero exit status, run the second command.
cmd1 ; cmd2	Run the first command and, when it completes, run the second.

Using Shell Variables

You identify a string of characters as a parameter (variable) by placing a $ in front of it (as in $HOME). Shell environment variables can hold information that is used by the shell itself, as well as by commands you run from the shell. Not all environment variables will be populated by default. Some of these variables you can change (such as the default printer in $PRINTER or your command prompt in $PS1). Others are managed by the shell (such as $OLDPWD). Table B-2 contains a list of many useful shell variables.

Table B-2: Shell Variables

Shell Variable	Description
BASH	Shows path name of the bash command (/bin/bash).
BASH_COMMAND	The command that is being executed at the moment.
BASH_VERSION	The version number of the bash command.
COLUMNS	The width of the terminal line (in characters).
DISPLAY	Identifies the X display where commands launched from the current shell will be displayed (such as :0.0). Can be a display on a remote host (such as example.com:0.0).
EUID	Effective user ID number of the current user. It is based on the user entry in /etc/passwd for the user that is logged in.
FCEDIT	Determines the text editor used by the fc command to edit history commands. The vi command is used by default.
GROUPS	Lists primary group of which current user is a member.
HISTCMD	Shows the current command's history number.
HISTFILE	Shows the location of your history file (usually located at $HOME/.bash_history).
HISTFILESIZE	Total number of history entries that will be stored (default, 1000). Older commands are discarded after this number is reached.
HOME	Location of the current user's home directory. Typing the cd command with no options returns the shell to the home directory.
HOSTNAME	The current machine's hostname.
HOSTTYPE	Contains the computer architecture on which the BSD system is running (i386, i486, i586, i686, x86_64, ppc, or ppc64).
LESSOPEN	Set to a command that converts content other than plain text (images, zip files and so on) so it can be piped through the less command.
LINES	Sets the number of lines in the current terminal.
LOGNAME	Holds the name of the current user.

Continued

273

Table B-2: Shell Variables (*continued*)

Shell Variable	Description
MACHTYPE	Displays information about the machine architecture, company and operating system (such as i686-portbld-freebsd6.2).
MAIL	Indicates the location of your mailbox file (typically the user name in the /var/mail directory).
MAILCHECK	Checks for mail in the number of seconds specified (default is 60).
OLDPWD	Directory that was the working directory before changing to the current working directory.
OSTYPE	Name identifying the current operating system (such as freebsd6.2).
PAGER	The program to use for man page display.
PATH	Colon-separated list of directories used to locate commands that you type (/bin, /usr/bin, and $HOME/bin are usually in the PATH).
PPID	Process ID of the command that started the current shell.
PRINTER	Sets the default printer, which is used by printing commands such as lpr and lpq.
PROMPT_COMMAND	Set to a command name to run that command each time before your shell prompt is displayed. (For example, PROMPT_COMMAND=ls lists commands in current directory before showing the prompt.)
PS1	Sets the shell prompt. Items in the prompt can include date, time, user name, hostname, and others. Additional prompts can be set with PS2, PS3, and so on.
PWD	The directory assigned as your current directory.
RANDOM	Accessing this variable generates a random number between 0 and 32767.
SECONDS	The number of seconds since the shell was started.
SHELL	Contains the full path to the current shell.
SHELLOPTS	Lists enabled shell options (those set to on).
SHLVL	Lists the shell levels associated with the current shell session.
TERM	Indicates the type of shell terminal window you are using. The default is xterm.

Table B-2: Shell Variables (*continued*)

Shell Variable	Description
TMOUT	Set to a number representing the number of seconds the shell can be idle without receiving input. After the number of seconds is reached, the shell exits.
UID	The user ID number assigned to the current user name. The user ID number is stored in the /etc/password file.
USER	The current user name.

C

Personal Configuration Files

In the home directory for every user account is a set of files and directories containing personal settings for that account. Because most configuration files and directories begin with a dot (.), you don't see them if you open a folder window to your home directory. Likewise, you typically need the -a option to ls to see those files when you list directory contents.

This appendix describes many of the dot files each user can work with on a BSD system. After creating configuration files you like, you can, when appropriate, do such things as save them to /usr/share/skel (so every new user gets them) or save them if the user account moves to another machine.

IN THIS APPENDIX

Shell configuration files

Browser and e-mail configuration files

Desktop configuration files

Network services configuration files

Music player configuration files

> **NOTE** *Some of the files described in this appendix won't exist until you either start the application associated with the files or create the files manually.*

Bash shell files: Home directory files for storing and changing bash settings include:

- ❑ .bash_profile: Commands added to this file are executed when you invoke bash as a login shell or use bash as your default shell.

- ❑ .bashrc: Commands added to this file are executed when you start a bash shell which is not a login shell, and your default shell is not bash. (To have .bashrc sourced on login when your default shell is set to bash, add the following line to your .bash_profile: test -f ~/.bashrc && . ~/.bashrc.)

- ❑ .bash_logout: Commands added to this file are executed when you log out from a bash shell.

- ❑ .bash_history: Stores history of commands run by the user from a bash shell.

C shell files: Besides system-wide `/etc/profile` and `/etc/csh.cshrc` files, home directory files for storing and changing C shell (`tcsh` and `csh`) settings include:

❏ `.login`: Commands added to this file are executed when you log in to a C shell shell.

❏ `.tcshrc` or `.cshrc`: Commands added to either of these files are executed when you start any C shell.

❏ `.history`: Stores history of commands run by the user from a C shell.

Bourne shell files: If you are using the Bourne (sh) shell, which is the default for regular users in FreeBSD, the `.shrc` file in your home directory is important to know about. Commands in this file are run when the sh shell starts. The file sets several aliases for you and sets your command line editor (emacs by default). This is a good place to add directories to your $PATH or to change your shell prompt. (I always change the default editor to vi from emacs.)

Elinks browser files: With the elinks text-based browser, after the system configuration file is read (`/usr/local/etc/elinks/elinks.conf`), if it exists, several other files are used for configuration settings. The following are contained in each user's .elinks directory:

❏ `elinks.conf`: Contains individual elinks configuration settings.

❏ `bookmarks`: Contains any bookmarks you set while using elinks.

❏ `cookies`: Stores cookies obtained while using elinks.

❏ `exmodehist`: Contains ex mode history.

❏ `formhist`: Contains history of information entered into forms while using elinks.

❏ `globhist`: Contains a history of web addresses visited while using elinks.

❏ `searchhist`: Contains a history of search terms entered while using elinks.

❏ `.tcshrc` or `.cshrc`: Commands added to either of these files are executed when you start any C shell.

Evolution files: Configuration files, mail boxes, calendars, contacts, and other files needed to support the Evolution groupwise suite are contained in the `.evolution` directory in each user's home directory. Files should not be edited directly in this directory structure, but rather should be modified through the Evolution client. This directory, however, is a place to check if the disk space consumed in your home directory is growing out of control.

Firefox configuration files: If you use the Firefox browser, settings for your use of the browser are stored in the `.mozilla/firefox` directory of your home directory. If you ever plan to move to another machine or a different web browser, you might want to keep your `bookmarks.html` file. That file can be exported later to a different environment.

GNOME configuration files: Users who run the GNOME desktop will have a `.gnome2` directory in their home directories. Within sub-directories are configuration files for GNOME applications you run, such as Rhythmbox music player (`rhythmbox/`), Totem video player (`totem`) and Evince document viewer (`evince/`). Many of the config files are in XML format, so you can read them (although you typically shouldn't edit them directly). Keeping this information can be useful because it can include album art, playlists, and preferences (such as colors and toolbars).

KDE configuration files: If you run the KDE desktop, the `.kde` directory will contain information relating to the KDE desktop, window manager, and related KDE applications. As with GNOME, many KDE configuration files are stored in XML format, so you can view their contents with any text editor. You can drop scripts in the `.kde/Autostart` directory to have them executed on KDE startup.

mail configuration files: Settings for the `mail` command are stored in the `.mailrc` and `.mail_aliases` files.

ncftp configuration files: If you use the `ncftp` FTP client, settings relating to your `ncftp` sessions are stored in the `.ncftp` directory in your home directory. The firewall file in that directory lets you set firewalls, including information for using `ncftp` through a proxy server. The `history` file keeps a list of commands that were previously run during FTP sessions. The log file gathers error and informational messages. The `prefs_v3` file contains ncftp preferences.

Trusted hosts files: Although regular users can't change the system-wide `hosts.allow` or `hosts.deny` files, they can add a list of trusted hosts and, optionally, users from those hosts to their own `.rhosts` file in their home directories. If services such as `rlogin` or `rcp` are enabled (`/etc/inetd.conf`), a person from the trusted host can use those commands to log in or copy files to your machine without entering a password. This is a good thing to do if all of the computers on your network are wired together, in the same room, in a cabin in the Himalayas, with no outside connections. Otherwise, you should consider using trusted hosts in this way to be very insecure.

Secure Shell configuration files: If you use the secure shell (ssh) service, the `.ssh` directory in your home directory can be used to manage security settings. Here are examples:

❑ `known_hosts`: Keeps a list of host computers you have verified as authentic.

❑ `identity`: Private authentication keys from SSH protocol version 1.

❑ `id_rsa`: Private authentication keys from SSH protocol version 2.

❑ `id_dsa`: Private authentication keys from SSH protocol version 2.

❑ `identity.pub`, `id_dsa.pub`, `id_rsa.pub`: Public keys for the three private keys just described.

❑ `authorized_keys`: File that contains public keys of remote clients.

Virtual network computing files: If you use `vncserver` utility to share your desktop with other computers on the network, settings for how `vncserver` behaves are stored in your home directory's `.vnc` directory. The `xstartup` file in that directory contains applications that run on the VNC desktop when you start it up. The `vncpasswd` file holds the passwords stored for use by `vnserver`.

For each display that is started, a file named `host:#.log` is created (where `host` is the hostname and # is the display number). There is also a `host:#.pid` file for each display containing the process ID of the Xvnc process associated with the display.

X startup files: If you start your desktop interface using the `startx` command, the `.xinitrc` file can be used to indicate which desktop environment to start. For example, add `/usr/local/bin/gnome-session` to `.xinitrc` to start the GNOME desktop environment. Add `/usr/local/bin/startkde` to `.xinitrc` to have the KDE desktop environment start.

XMMS configuration files: If you use the XMMS music player, configuration files for that player are contained in the `.xmms` directory in your home directory. Subdirectories of that directory include Plugins (which hold audio plug-ins) and Skins (which holds available skins to use with the player). The config file in that directory holds preference settings for XMMS. The `xmms.m3u` file contains paths for songs the player has played.

Index

C

F

O

P

T

U